Chaseworld

Chase

Mary Hufford

world

Foxhunting and Storytelling in New Jersey's

Pine Barrens

upp

UNIVERSITY OF PENNSYLVANIA PRESS

Philadelphia

University of Pennsylvania Press
PUBLICATIONS OF THE AMERICAN FOLKLORE
SOCIETY
NEW SERIES

Patrick Mullen, General Editor

Library of Congress Cataloging-in-Publication Data

Cover photo: Maryland hounds running a fox in Penn State Forest near Chatsworth, New Jersey. Photo by Dennis McDonald, April 1991. Copyright © 1991 by Dennis McDonald.

Figures 2.4, 3.3, 3.4, 3.7, 4.1, 5.3, 6.2, 8.1, 8.2 copyright © 1991 by Dennis McDonald.

All interviews are quoted by permission of the participants. Permission is acknowledged to reprint materials from published sources. See page following index.

932054

In memory of
JOE ALBERT, JACK DAVIS,
JOHN EARLIN, LEON HOPKINS,
DONALD POMEROY, and
RANDALL STAFFORD,
Pine Barrens foxhunters whose voices resound
in these pages.

Contents

Illustrations

Maps

Figures

Acknowledgments

AT THE OUTSET, I want to express my deep appreciation to all the Pine Barrens foxhunters and their families who took me on foxchases, told me stories, and taught me to hear their music. Their names appear throughout this book. Among them, Norman, Caroline, and Freeman Taylor deserve special thanks, both for piquing my interest in foxhunting and for their generous hospitality, making me feel welcome over the years in the woods and in their homes. Other foxhunters contributed in particular ways to this book. I especially want to thank Don Cramer, who shared with me his extensive research and writing on Maryland foxhounds, and Hubie Driscoll, Milton Collins, and Oscar Hillman, who helped me obtain needed information and who graciously issued standing invitations to go foxhunting.

Scholars, like foxhounds, rely on feedback from colleagues to keep them on course. I owe a great debt to Katharine Young, both for her work on the phenomenology of narrative, which inspired and shaped my presentation of the Chaseworld, and for an illuminating discussion in which I learned I had been barking up the wrong tree. Barbara Kirshenblatt-Gimblett and Roger Abrahams provided generous criticisms of the early draft, portions of which also benefited from the comments of Erika Brady, James Hardin, Stuart Marks, Patrick Mullen, John Sinton, and David Taylor. Herbert Halpert provided valuable leads to historical sources and permitted me to quote from his dissertation. Guidance and support from Theresa Pyott, of the University of Pennsylvania's folklore department, and Joanne van Istendal, of Medford, have been indispensable. They all deserve much credit and no blame.

Other friends and colleagues warrant special thanks. Gerald Parsons has my gratitude for sharing with me his ongoing lively and critical observations of the domains of hunting and trapping. I want to thank Alan Jabbour for encouraging me to write and for granting me the leaves of absence that made it possible to complete this work. For years of collaboration and friendship I am grateful to Marjorie Hunt and Rita Moonsammy. For assistance in documenting several foxchases I wish to acknowledge

David Cohen, Carl Fleischhauer, Dennis McDonald, Richard Monte-murro, Louis Presty, Henry Sayen, Rose Shields, Elaine Thatcher, and James Walsh.

Members of my family helped in ways that are beyond telling. My parents first alerted me to the "Hound of Heaven." My children, Christopher and Katherine, issued many necessary deadlines. My husband, Steven Oaks, critically reviewed draft after draft of the manuscript. He has truly had a shaping hand in this work, not only reacting to titles, prose style, and folkloristic notions about male camaraderie, but performing yeoman duty at kitchen sink and changing table as well. He thought the book's cover should depict him washing dishes and changing diapers. My deepest gratitude belongs to him.

Running a fox is about like telling a story, only the dogs are telling it to you.

Norman Taylor, Foxhunter

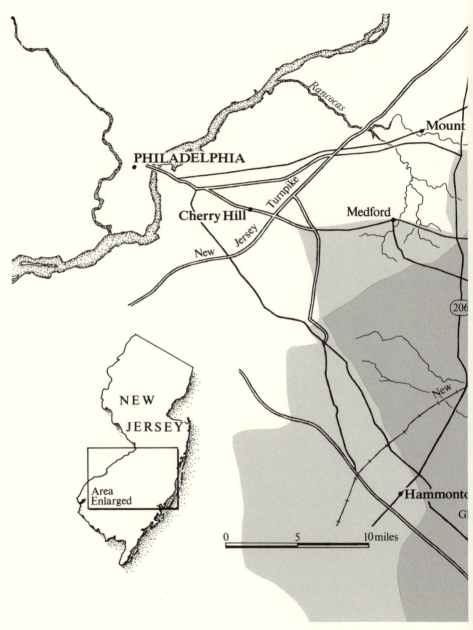

New Jersey's Central Pine Barrens and Environs. Drawing by Allen Carroll.

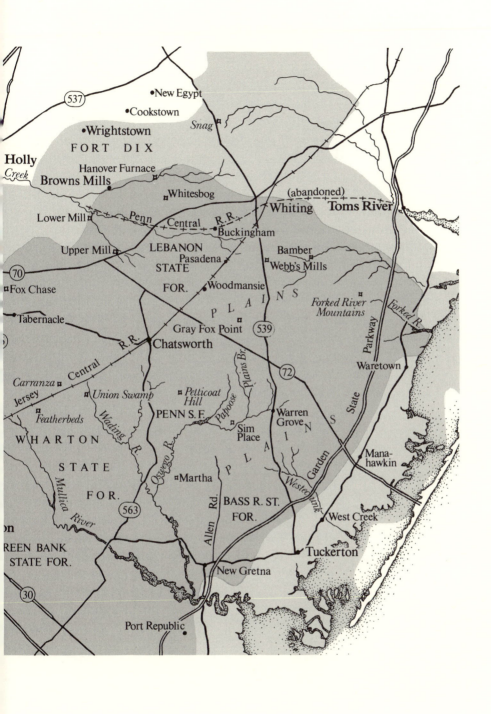

Introduction

IN THE UNITED STATES there are basically two ways to chase foxes. In the minds of many, the term *foxhunting* summons forth the image of a scarlet-coated, black-capped cavalcade, thundering over rolling hill country dotted with coverts and fences, in pursuit of full-blooded foxhounds chasing a fox. The image is associated with place names like Middleburg, Virginia and Chester County, Pennsylvania. It is for the sake of riding to hounds that red foxes were imported from England and Spain in the eighteenth century, and for the sake of the same tradition that red foxes are strictly protected in some parts of the United States to this day.

Less well known is the other kind of foxhunting, the "listening to hounds" practiced by working class men in fields, woods, and mountains from New England and the upper Midwest to the deep South. This version of the sport is known in various regions as "hilltopping," "ridge-running," "forks-of-the-creek foxhunting," and "one-gallus (that is, one suspender) foxhunting" (Van Urk 1941). Foxhunters in the state forests of southern New Jersey, where I heard my first foxchase, call it "Pine Barrens foxhunting."

Both kinds of foxhunting are organized around the same animal text: a pack of dogs in noisy pursuit of a fox. But there the resemblance ends. Pine Barrens foxhunters, dressed for comfort, ride to the hounds in pickup trucks, which they park in long rows wherever the listening is good. There they convene to interpret the canine chorus, trade "lies," and enjoy fellowship before the fox—often a gray one—takes the hounds beyond their hearing.

What the hunters are listening for is "music," uttered by hounds, each contributing its own "note" to the proceedings. In the hunters' parlance some hounds are "bass-noted," while others are "tenor-mouthed"; some hounds are soprano dogs, while others issue "horn chops," "double yells," and "bugle notes." Like aficionados of other musical traditions, hunters make audiocassette recordings of foxchases, replete with interpretive voice-overs. "Ain't that pretty music?" comments John Earlin, on a recording of his canine chorale. "You could just dance to it" (undated self-made recording).

The music is said to relate a "story," telling hunters which hounds are in the lead, how close they are to the fox, and where the canids are on the unseen landscape. "You stand there at night," said the Reverend Milton Collins, a foxhunter from Port Republic, New Jersey, "You don't see anything. That sound comes to you, and there's a beautiful *story* in it. I know that it's my dog just picked up the double and then Robly's dog took the double away my dog, and he's runnin' it, or she's runnin' it" (interview, December 18, 1980). That hounds can spin foxes' trails into hunters' tales is not deemed remarkable in the community, but seems to be something every schoolboy knows. "They run dogs back there all the time," a nine-year-old boy living near the state forest once told me. "Yeah," supplied his young compatriot, "listen to the story" (interview, September 1983).

As a folklorist, I was initially drawn to the study of foxhunting by such metaphors. I wanted to know what processes underlie the transformation of dogs into storytellers and musicians. Is storytelling merely a metaphor for chasing foxes, or are the canine performers being made to enact a social myth? How *is* a foxchase a story? How is the story constituted? Is the story about animals or human beings? If it is about human beings, why use animals? Why dogs? Why foxes?

Over the past two decades, philosophers, humanists, and social scientists of a literary bent have proposed that we look at collaboratively wrought works like cockfighting (and in this case, foxhunting) as "cultural texts"— "stories" that their human participants tell themselves about themselves (Geertz 1972:26).[1] Such texts become a means for achieving the distance necessary for self-reflection, for arriving at understandings of the forces, some of them profoundly disquieting and incomprehensible, governing the human position in society, nature, and cosmos.

Alfred Schutz writes that "meaning . . . only becomes visible to the reflective glance" (1970:63). Whether one is participating in a reflexive behavior like foxhunting or studying it from the outside, coming to an understanding of the world requires one to shift from engagement in it to reflection on it. Related to the ability, apparently peculiar to humans, to shift from absorption to abstraction is the ability to turn attention from one reality to another, thus constituting what Schutz terms "multiple realities," building on William James's notion of sub-universes of reality. Among these multiple realities Schutz identifies "finite provinces of meaning"[2]—

realms of experience that alternate with the world of everyday life, the "taken-for-granted" reality that ordinarily commands our attention (1970: 252–58).

Foxchasing shares with music and storytelling the capacity to open up such a province of meaning, which I am calling the Chaseworld. Turning their attention away from the "Ordinary" toward the Chaseworld, foxhunters enter an alternate reality replete with its own "metaphysical constants" (Schutz, in Natanson 1970:198). Reflecting upon this reality in conversation and stories, they endow it with meaning.

Curious to know how its authors go about constructing and shaping it, and how it in turn shapes them, I became an explorer in the Chaseworld, setting out to describe the elements and contours of a fictive world compelling enough to take its place beside great literature.[3] I was guided by foxhunters who oriented me to its landmarks and inhabitants, interpreting its conventions along the way. My investigation was also shaped by the pioneering work of philosophers, sociologists, folklorists, and symbolic anthropologists who have mapped out some of the salient features of alternate realities in general and offered analytical principles for approaching the complex relationship between the Chaseworld and the Ordinary.[4]

We speak of the reality we ordinarily inhabit as the "world of everyday life," "the quotidian realm," or "the real world." This reality, as we imagine it, is more like a universe than a world, in the sense that it is filled with myriad social worlds, among them worlds of work and of play. Alfred Schutz referred to it as the "Lifeworld," a reality that is far beyond the scope of the present work to describe.[5] But, like Archimedes, hunters need a place to stand when reflecting on the world of the chase, a place to move out of and back into, and that place, for the purpose of this book, is the Ordinary. The term *Ordinary* loosely denotes the reality that foxhunters do *not* experience as extraordinary; it is the world of daily routine, centered around family, work, and community. While the Ordinary must be a world experienced in common by foxhunters, or they could not collaboratively model a Chaseworld on it, it is by no means an object of such singular focus, nor as coherently rendered by hunters, as the Chaseworld.

Foxhunters have two ways of conjuring the Chaseworld. One is to be physically present, inventing it on the spot through foxchases; the other is to constitute it in stories. In other words, not only may foxhunting be viewed as a resource for storytelling—a way of generating reportable experiences (Labov 1972)—but *both* foxhunting and storytelling are resources for opening up the Chaseworld—alternative ways to enter and inhabit the same reality.[6]

Foxhunters can attend to the Chaseworld outside stories and fox-chases, for instance, through daydreams and in conversation. In order to be conjured, inhabited, and enacted, however, the Chaseworld appears to demand ritual care. Thus hunters must anchor it in the Ordinary by first setting up an *enclave*, a foxchase or story. "Enclaves," as Schutz defines them, are "regions belonging to one province of meaning enclosed by another" (Schutz 1970:256). The enclave, anchored in one space and time, opens onto a reality anchored in another space and time. The "Storyrealm" opens onto the "Taleworld" (Young 1987), the foxchase onto the "Chase-world." In foxhunting stories, the Taleworld is the Chaseworld.

The crucial distinction here is between levels of awareness and levels of discourse, between discourse that conjures and discourse about the conjuring. Continually shifting from absorption in the Chaseworld to reflection on it, foxhunters invoke, sustain, and interpret the Chaseworld. It is their attention to it that holds the Chaseworld in being. When attention to it lapses the Chaseworld vanishes (James 1890:293; Schutz 1970:252).

Conventions for setting up foxchases and Storyrealms and strategies for framing the Chaseworld within them are analogous.[7] That is, both foxchases and stories about them are bounded by formalized openings and closings, and in both enclaves the authors conceptually frame the Chase-world by orienting their audiences with respect to time, place, person, behavioral situation, and so forth, managing audience attitudes through evaluations of what transpires in a given Chaseworld.[8]

Framed paintings and theatrical performances offer examples of en-claved realms discretely bounded in space and time. Other behaviors, such as ritual and storytelling, are figuratively "framed" by metacommunicative signals (Bateson 1955), which specify that the messages within the frames are of a different order from the messages outside them, distinguishing the behavior within the frames as "not serious." Such markers "set the realm status" (Young 1987:20–21) by labeling the event as narrative, ritual, art, or work.

The Chaseworld's primary boundaries are emitted by animals. Like theater audiences turning toward the stage when the lights go down, hunters are drawn into the Chaseworld by the voices of hounds, losing awareness of themselves as listeners in the distance. As Joanne van Istendal, of Medford, who has hunted small game with hounds, characterized the experience:

> When you're hunting you sit there and you listen and you concentrate, and it's developing a whole story. When you're all done you weren't out there running through the woods, but you'll be able to come back and tell the whole story because you were there in your mind. (Interview, September 10, 1985)

Caught up in the Chaseworld through the music of hounds, hunters construct and co-inhabit a richly intersubjective world, which unfolds within its boundaries according to a unique set of "background expectancies" (Garfinkel 1973:21), relating in particular ways to the world outside.

The world within the boundaries reconstitutes in various ways the world outside it. The model may reflect, reverse, affirm, or challenge aspects of the Ordinary and other extraordinary realms as well. Here a suggestive implication of the text analogy is that, as authors, we "inscribe" certain events and behaviors with meaning, which, as readers, we then decipher and interpret (Ricoeur 1973; Geertz 1983:31). Foxhunters are both authors and readers of a text they continually inscribe onto each other and their surroundings, including hounds, foxes, and landscapes lent to the Chaseworld by the Ordinary. Inscribing hounds' voices as music and foxes as tricksters, endowing themselves with animal CB handles, hunters invent a fictive realm, governed by its own laws, that comments on realms outside itself.

Of great interest to me are the ways in which animals are made to represent human affairs, and how these animal representations help to accomplish human identity and society. The Chaseworld uniquely reconfigures nature and society, comprising a realm in which animals, many of them named for humans, perform to humans going by animal names. Anthropological theories on the subject of animal symbolism depend heavily on ethnographies of tribal and insular cultures.[9] The present study is in part an inquiry into the social construction of natural resources and the symbolic use of animals in a complex post-industrial society. The Chaseworld is only one of many such recreational realms revolving around animals, sustained by its makers at considerable expense of time and money.[10] The power of its gravitational pull is worth accounting for.

Anthropologist James Fernandez argues that animals serve as primordial metaphors, essential to the task of shaping human identity. He observes that in order to gain identity humans must first "become objects to themselves, by taking the point of view of 'the other,' before they can become subjects to themselves" (1986:35). Animals, it seems, have from time immemorial provided auspicious others. "Is it not arguable," Fernandez asks, "that primordially animals are predicates by which subjects obtain an identity and are thus objects of affinity and participation? If so, the first problem is not how animals take human shape, but how humans take animal shape and enact nature" (1986:32). The Chaseworld provides a setting not only for the taking of animal "others," but for the casting off of human constraints. Hunters, inhabiting hounds and imitating foxes, take what Ortega y Gasset terms a "vacation from the human condition" (1972:111).

My use of the term *ritual* to describe collective performances warrants some explication here.[11] Foxhunting and storytelling are not religious ceremonies and thus may not be considered true "rituals" by some scholars. In terms of form and function, however, they may be seen as "secular rituals," collective performances that "attempt to bring some particular part of life firmly and definitely into orderly control" (Moore and Myerhoff 1977:3). To call foxhunting a ritual fixes attention on the underlying serious-ness of this play form and is in keeping with the religious analogy some-times invoked by foxhunters themselves. "I don't have no trouble findin' my church," said Jack Davis, a foxhunter from Browns Mills, "cause my church is—"

"right in the woods," laughed his wife Ann.

"pine trees—" Jack continued.

"chapel in the pines," Ann elaborated.

"lot of pines," said Jack, "and got foxes and dogs."

"the choir," I suggested.

"Now didn't you enjoy that trip up to my church?" he asked (inter-view, November 21, 1980).[12]

In terms of form and function, secular rituals span a broad gamut. Foxhunting and storytelling may be seen as rites of sociality, exemplifying what Victor Turner has called the "liminoid" phenomena of complex, industrial societies (1977:43–45). Secular rituals do not invoke or render visible relationships between this world and the supernatural one, but they do conjure human society, conferring essential identities upon its members.

The Chaseworld borrows heavily from the Ordinary, but does it give anything back? What is the relationship between things inside the Chase-world boundaries and things outside them? What bearing, if any, do events in the Chaseworld have on events in other realms? It is in Storyrealms that "pivot," as Katharine Young puts it, "between Taleworld and Real," that we see the Chaseworld made consequential in everyday life. "Narrativity," writes Young, "shifts my attitude to life from my engagement in it toward my reflection on it" (1987:12). Through stories, hunters reconstitute a Chaseworld located in the past and imbue it with meaning and conse-quence, rendering it significant in the Ordinary (Young 1987:13).

As Mary Douglas points out, the boundaries between finite provinces of meaning and the world of everyday life are eminently permeable. A comparison of rules governing animal behavior in the Chaseworld and human behavior in the Ordinary reveals a number of parallels and contiguities. Such correspondences, according to Douglas, "allow meaning to leak from one context to another along the formal similarities that they show" (Douglas 1973:13).[13] The present study investigates the bearing that relationships constituted among Chaseworld characters, both human and animal, have on those present to the varied occasions of its conjuring.

The notion that storytelling is a resource for opening up the Chaseworld veers from the more conventional view that events like foxchases provide grist for storytelling. In the conventional view foxchases are seen as the reality, stories as the map of that reality, powerfully influenced by the foxchases they are about.[14] Foxchases and foxhunting stories can also be seen as complementary, *mutually* influential aspects of the same tradition. That is, foxchases have a shaping influence on stories about them, which in turn have a shaping influence on foxchases, articulating canons that shape future foxchases as well as the particular chase given shape in the story.[15] The reciprocity involved is not simply between stories and the events they are about, however, but between the Chaseworld and any occasion on which it is conjured. In conjuring the Chaseworld, foxhunters conjure society as well.

Chapter One opens the Chaseworld for the reader through narrative, introducing members of the foxhunting community and their landscapes, concerns, and themes, setting these in the context of a Pine Barrens foxchase. Chapter Two again describes the foxchase, but this time in terms of the frames and boundaries that anchor it in ordinary reality while establishing it as a world apart. Chapters Three, Four, and Five focus on the world framed within the boundaries, detailing the hunters' inscriptions of the Chaseworld onto its human and animal inhabitants and their surroundings. These three chapters examine the relationships between elements of the worlds inside and outside the boundaries. Chapters Six and Seven describe the Chaseworld as it is conjured in stories, first by a group of foxhunters collaborating in its construction, and then by a solitary hunter composing, in effect, his memoirs. Reflecting on the Chaseworld in stories and commentary, the hunters endow it with meaning.

My presentation of the hunters' stories, comments, and landscapes requires some explication here. For this translation effort I have turned to both literary and ethnopoetic models. Where my intention has been to draw the reader into the Chaseworld, I have utilized literary conventions to frame and vivify the hunters' discourse. Where my intention has been to elucidate the hunters' own framing conventions, I have presented their utterances more austerely, mapping out their discourse with signposts to guide the reader through a dense terrain of boundaries, orientations, and evaluations.[16]

The drawings of the hunters' landscapes are similarly an attempt to render one mode of experience in terms of another. These figures are not maps in the conventional sense, but represent my effort to apprehend their environmental perceptions. These graphic depictions are the result of my conversations with hunters as we pored over topographic maps to clarify for me their environmental images, vocabulary, and texts.

For the humanist and social scientist, the Chaseworld offers a rich laboratory for investigating the interrelations among ritual, self, society, and nature. But there is also a deeply humanistic investigation undertaken within the Chaseworld by its traditional authors and readers who, inscribing animals as tricksters and dupes at a safe distance from everyday life and its consequences, contemplate the contradictions and paradoxes of human society, debate ethical issues, and confront inescapable facts of existence like death, social hierarchy, and the putative nature of reality itself (Geertz 1972:27; Douglas 1968:375; Moore and Myerhoff 1977:16–17). These weighty matters are handled with much hilarity, for central to the hunters' deliberations is the fox, joker and trickster par excellence, a mysterious, paradoxical being of the sort typically found at the heart of ritual, on whose circuitous trail we shall now set forth.

Notes

1. Clifford Geertz, in his famous study of cockfighting in Bali, suggests that the cockfight is a "story [the Balinese] tell themselves about themselves" (1972:26). Here the analogy emerges in native hermeneutics, but the *dogs* are seen as the tellers. Thus foxhunters imbue their text with authority by disguising its human origins. As Mary Douglas notes, "If their man-made origins were not hidden, they would be stripped of some of their authority" (1973:15).

2. As a finite province of meaning, the Chaseworld is reminiscent of the islands that anthropologists earlier in this century set out to document exhaustively. Claude Lévi-Strauss and others have pointed to the impossibility of doing ethnography of western civilization, but we can look at how the pieces or enclaves relate to one another, constituting what folklorist John Dorst has termed "an archipelago of lifestyle islands" (Dorst 1989:2). We can attend carefully to the construction and maintenance of worlds within worlds.

3. The sport has proved a fertile resource for fantasy worlds constructed by nonfoxhunters. In western civilization at large, foxchases are conjured up and played out on a variety of musical instruments, including bagpipes, fiddles, banjos, and harmonicas (Licht 1980); children play board and chasing games entitled "Fox and Hounds"; and literary masters from the Gawain poet to Edna St. Vincent Millay and William Faulkner have used foxhunting as a backdrop against which to expose the complexities of human romance.

4. In his introduction to *Frame Analysis*, Erving Goffman traces the development of what he terms the "Schutz-James" line of inquiry and its application by ethnomethodologists, notably Howard Garfinkel (Goffman 1974). Mary Douglas provides a similar orientation for anthropologists in her introduction to *Rules and Meanings* (1973). Gregory Bateson introduced the concept of frame in his groundbreaking article "A Theory of Play and Fantasy" (1955). Peter Berger and Thomas Luckmann discuss "finite provinces of meaning" in their germinal work *The Social Construction of Reality* (1967). Folklorists have looked at how expressive behaviors like festival, ritual, and narrative relate to the business of creating and sustaining alternate realities, adapting the concepts of Schutz, Bateson, and Goffman to the analysis of folklore as performance and communication. In particular see Abrahams (1977), Babcock-Abrahams (1976), Bauman (1986), Kirshenblatt-Gimblett (1975), Stewart (1979), and Young (1987). The present study is especially indebted to Katharine Young's phenomenology of narrative.

5. In a discussion of the significance of Husserl's phenomenology for anthropologists, J. S. Lansing writes, "A complete exposition of a lifeworld as it actually exists . . . would involve analysis of the almost limitless minutiae experienced in the lifeworld, and is thus neither feasible nor interesting." Lansing goes on to propose seven simpler strategies for applying Husserl's models to anthropological materials. The present study falls under the rubric of his *"kommunikative Umwelt"*: the study of how the "communal elaboration of a surrounding world is the formation of a 'whole in which each person is a member and in which the network of exchange constitutes a surrounding world of communication [*kommunikative Umwelt*]'" (1979:78–79).

6. I am indebted to Katharine Young for this insight.

7. For example, Barbara Babcock-Abrahams relates the literary trickster cycle to the *rite de passage* (1975:171); Barbara Myerhoff relates the autobiographical impulse of the elderly to the need to undergo rites of self-definition in that stage of the life cycle (1978: 222); and Mary Douglas describes the ritual properties of jokes told at wakes (1968:374). And, of course, foxhunters themselves compare foxhunting to storytelling.

8. William Labov identifies and explores "orientations" and "evaluations" as aspects of narrative structure (1972:364–75). Katharine Young fully explicates them as strategies for framing the alternative realm (1987:47–60).

9. Anthropologists have theorized that animals are central to human rituals because they are good to eat (Radcliffe-Brown 1929), good to think (Lévi-Strauss 1972), prohibit (Tambiah 1969), and emote (Geertz 1972). The widely accepted thesis (Lévi-Strauss 1955) is that we structure the world by dividing it into binary oppositions, which we then mediate through rituals in order to resolve fundamental contradictions in the human condition. The primary contradiction has been called

the problem of man in nature: we are both animals and not-animals. The distinction between us and animals enables us to look across the gap and draw from the natural world of discrete species models for defining and contrasting the "inchoate pronouns" in human society (Fernandez 1986).

10. For a study of how hunters in Scotland County, North Carolina constitute the wildlife that is their game, apportioning it along socio-economic lines, see Marks (1991).

11. I am by no means the first to consider foxhunting as ritual. The anthropologist Edmund Leach termed English-style foxhunting "a barbarous ritual surrounded by extraordinary and fantastic taboos" (1964:52), provoking a more thorough analysis by James Howe, which he published in an article entitled "Fox Hunting as Ritual" (Howe 1981).

12. Such comparisons abound in *Hunter's Horn*, a magazine to which some Pine Barrens foxhunters subscribe and contribute. Duncan Emrich observed that *Hunter's Horn* deserves "a place, a copy or two at least, in any catholic, eclectic, Americana folklore library" (Emrich 1972:142). For example:

> You know, life is like a [fox]race, we are always running from sin and evil. God has the answer to our problems if we would just look to Him. (Sharlsono 1980:73)

> One of the reasons I have spent so much time and money looking for lost hounds is because of an inner feeling: the dog needs me as much as I need him. The same thing is true for lost men and women all over the universe. Jesus is patiently waiting at the spiritual casting grounds, ready to pick us up, heal the wounds that scar our bodies and minds as we run the race of life. (Badley 1979:58)

13. Mary Douglas argues that finite provinces of meaning are not particularly discrete, that "insulation is very difficult and unlikely" since "the very form of the rules which assign elements to categories carries the stamp of social concerns and imports these concerns into such apparently neutral areas as animal taxonomy" (1973:225).

14. For useful discussions of the problem of the relationship between stories and the events they are about, see Shuman (1986:20–22), Young (1987:186–210), and Bauman (1986:2–6).

15. Writing of practical jokes and stories about them, Richard Bauman suggests that the stories and the practical jokes are "two complementary parts of the same tradition" (Bauman 1986:35). Of the reciprocal relationship between practical jokes and stories about them, he argues that "hearing and telling stories about practical jokes [is] part of the process for these men of becoming a seasoned, skillful joker; by recounting and evaluating the jokes in narrative form, one clarifies how practical jokes work and what makes them effective" (Bauman 1986:51).

16. Katharine Young's presentation of narrative provides a model here. See Young (1987:249–56).

1. The World Of The Chase

> It's kind of funny. Foxhunters don't really hunt fox. They don't shoot
> them. They run dogs. That's the real fun for them.
> —Christian Bethmann, Superintendent, Lebanon State Forest

DAY IS BREAKING on Lebanon State Forest, breaking on the Mount Misery
Brook and its tributaries, and on the swamps, "spongs," and bogs that slope
gently away from them into pine-studded uplands laced with sand roads. It
breaks on the bluejays and rufous-sided towhees whose cries punctuate the
deep January silence, and it breaks on the cold, meandering trails of foxes
bedding down for the day.

The Pine Barrens is in its winter aspect. White sand roads, carpeted
with amber pine needles, travel past the red spikes of sweet huck, the grays
of soapbushes, and the yellow-brown hues of scrub oak. Behind and
around these the evergreen sheep laurel, cedar, and pine rise and taper off
into a fathomless blue sky. Against such a backdrop the movements of parti-
colored foxhounds, black and brown and splashed with white, leap quickly
to the hunter's eye.

Along the branches of Mount Misery Brook the silence is about to
end. On North Branch Road a pickup truck crawls slowly along surrounded by hounds busily inspecting the roadside flora. Over on the
Blacktop Road another hunter has just turned off the headlights on a
pickup full of foxhounds. And on Reeves' Bogs Road a truck door slams, a
tailgate squeaks open, and a handful of hounds bursts into the road. At this
point in a chase, hunters say, the ears of foxes perk up. On the roof of each
pickup cab is a CB antenna. The first hunter to strike a fox's line will notify
the others. Meanwhile they coordinate their reconnaissance, using CB
aliases.

Yellow Bird contacts Dogman.

"Hey Dogman, how 'boutcha Dogman, Dogman, Dogman?"

"I gotcha."

"What's your 10-4?"[1]

"I got tracks goin' out toward North Branch Road right now. I'm on
North Branch Road."

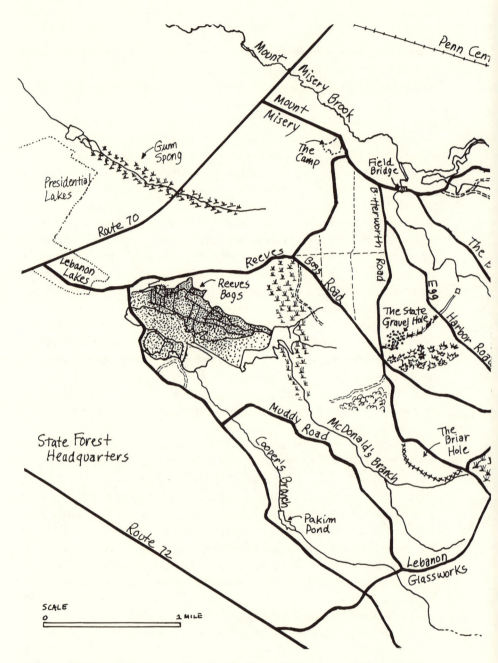

Map 1.1. Lebanon State Forest. Drawing by Donald Shomette and Kevin Hodges, based on a field sketch by the author. Courtesy of the American Folklife Center, Library of Congress.

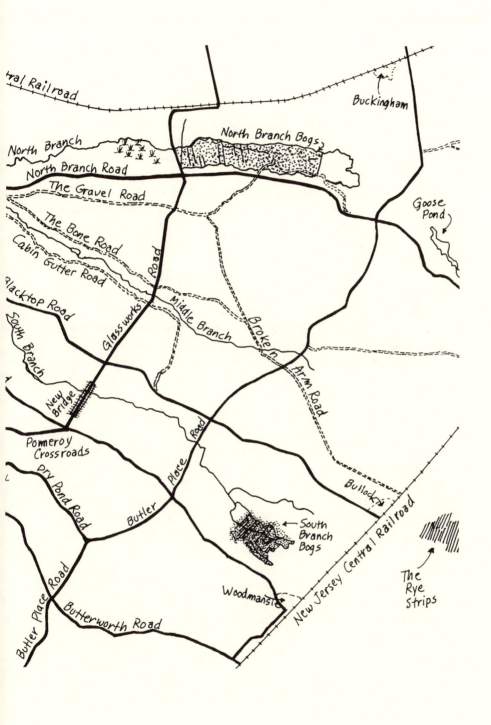

"Where'd Horsetrader go?"

"Reeves' Bogs Road."

"Okay, I'll go right up South Branch towards the head of it then."

"All right."[2]

On the back of each pickup is a large, lidded "dog box," its wooden sides attached to the truck walls. Each box contains a dozen or more hounds, their nails scrabbling on the hard metal floor of the truck bed, some of them peering out through the bars over the tailgate. These are Maryland foxhounds, born and bred to chase foxes on the Atlantic coastal plain. Their noses are constantly sniffing, evaluating and dismissing, casting about for the scent of fox. One hound, yearning to join the nascent chase at South Branch Bogs, begins to whine anxiously, a high nasal whine reminiscent of brakes needing adjustment.

"Shush! Maggie!" Norman Taylor admonishes her. He is a ruddy, pleasant-faced man, sturdily built, in his mid sixties, whose red hair is turning to white. His surname has been in the region since the early nineteenth century when his grandfather, Captain Miles Standish Taylor, quit a seafaring career to settle along the coast. Reeves ancestors, on his mother's side, were interred in local cemeteries before the Revolutionary War. Lebanon State Forest is now a patch of wilderness, preserved by the state for recreational and scientific use. To Norman, however, who grew up in and around these woods with four brothers and eight sisters, Lebanon State Forest is more like a back yard. It is dotted with remnants of family workscapes, thresholds to his past. There are swamps that he lumbered with his father, George "Topsy" Taylor, cranberry bogs that they labored in, and sawmills, some of them water powered, where they made crates for cranberries and blueberries and shingles for houses. Lebanon Lakes Estates is situated flush against the last swamp they lumbered, in the 1950s.

Topsy Taylor kept foxdogs with names like Crazy Kate, Simple Jack, and Rudolph the Red-Nosed Reindeer. Topsy told his sons about hunting with his buddy Harry Bush before the turn of the century, when they would disappear into the woods with their dogs for a week at a time. "They'd put a box in a buckboard wagon," Norman related, "they'd take a horse up in the woods, and they would stop and they would hunt here a day or two, and go further to Woodmansie and hunt there a day or two, and they caught coon, run fox, but they would kill 'em in those days for the furs of 'em" (interview, January 24, 1986). Their fraternity was rounded out by the elders of a generation ahead of Norman's own: Jack Davis's father, "Old John Davis," and John Earlin's uncles, Howard and Frank Earlin.

Figure 1.1. Norman Taylor casting his trailers on foot. Photo by Dennis McDonald, January 1989. Courtesy of the American Folklife Center, U.S. Library of Congress.

As a child, Norman lived in the house at Reeves' Bogs, which were then owned and operated by his mother's brother, Bill Reeves. His father sawed the lumber for the "Italian shanties" inhabited each summer by seasonal workers from South Philadelphia. In the 1960s Reeves sold his bogs to the state, and they are now harvested by a small cranberry company, with the assistance of Gene and Buster Emmons who live in the house. Norman marveled at their provinciality. "They was born and raised right here," he said. "Right in that house down the road. Gene was born here and Buster was born in Lower Mill. Buster and Gene Emmons. The only place they ever knew was right here" (interview, September 23, 1983).

Norman's brother Freeman recalled getting "fast" in one of their father's water-powered millwheels. The mill at Lower Mill burned down when Norman was four or five. Grapevines, pokeberries, and an old piling are the sole markers of the site. It is still indicated on the map at the shallow confluence of Greenwood Branch and Bispham's Mill Creek, flowing in from Upper Mill, which was first a sawmill, then a cranberry plantation, and is now Presidential Lakes Estates, one of dozens of lake communities in the region formed around old millponds and cranberry bogs.

In 1983, when he retired from his job of twenty-eight years as maintenance supervisor for Burlington County, Norman reached a state in life he had long anticipated. "That's what I worked for all these years," he once said. "To retire to foxhunt. I'm gonna enjoy it till I kick the bucket" (foxchase, August 12, 1982). The hood ornament on his Toyota pickup truck is a fox in flight, and a standing red fox peers out over the visor on his cap. Years ago foxhunters started calling him "Yellow Bird" after the color of his truck.

Written on the side of the pickup at Middle Branch is the name and affiliation of the hunter there: Theodore Bell, Jr., Wrightstown, New Jersey. His friends call him Junie, but foxhunters call him "Dogman" because he keeps a large pack of hounds, all females. His hat has a foxhound on it, under the word "Foxhunter," and a standing fox decal adorns his dog box. His job as custodian for the C. B. Lamb School keeps him from getting out to hunt as often as he would like, but he goes evenings and weekends, every chance he gets. Carol, his wife, sits in the cab knitting, as she usually does when accompanying him on foxchases. On weekdays she drives a school bus.

The hounds at Middle Branch are picking out a cold trail, emitting the long-drawn-out "bawl notes" that mean a fox has been through the woods. A smart hound soon learns to recognize a "backfoot"—that is, the fox's trail backwards—by the weakening scent. The hounds can tell they are headed in the right direction when the scent gets stronger, and when the scent gets stronger the voices get louder.

"Can you identify all the notes?" I ask Norman.

"Oh sure, I know all of 'em. That long high note is Sailor: 'Aiooo! Aiooo!' he says. 'Aiaaay-ay-ay-ay'—that's Becky, real quick notes like that. Smoke has got a nice—'Barooo!'—strong note. And Nip—'Arwoohr!'—is the big coarse note."

"What's Maggie's voice like?"

"Just a rolling note. It's not a real good note to tell. On her chop she sounds good, but in a big bunch of dogs she just adds noise to it, that's all."

Rarely are hounds said to bark. Rather, they yell, squall, scream, boo-hoo, babble, holler, tongue, lie, sing, and talk. A dog may be said to have a "tenor mouth," "horn chop," or "double yell," to be a "drum dog," or to be "heavy-noted," "bass-noted," "turkey-mouthed," "parrot-mouthed," or "squealy-mouthed."

"There's a crowing note," said Milton Collins, a Methodist minister from Port Republic whose avocation is foxhunting:

Just like a rooster crowing. That's an unusual one. Then there is a high shrill whistle type. That's another thrilling thing. That's what my young dog had when he was a puppy, and when that young dog would hit a fox he'd just make your hair stand on end. But the older he got, the lower the pitch became, see? Then there's a chop: "Chop-chop-chop-chop!" and then there's a screaming note. A gyp many times will have a screaming note. And there's all in between. Mike, he's got a *heavy*, heavy chop, but you can't hear him as far as the gyp that's got the shrill. (Interview, December 18, 1980)

A very few hounds possess the coveted "bugle" mouth.

Norman's Lead, a hound he had in the early 1950s, had a bugle mouth. "He had the greatest voice you ever heard in your life," Norman recalled, "They made a movie called 'The Voice of Bugle Ann,' and this dog had a better voice. Music flowed out of him."

"What was his voice like?" I asked him on several occasions.

"Just like a high roll," he replied:

Really high, and he could use it all the time. He wasn't the kind of dog that just used it here and there. It just filled the air, and that's all you could hear. . . . Sound just like a fire engine siren goin' off. And he could hold it long like that: "Aroooooo!" I've run him with as high as a hundred hounds, and you could always hear him. It just seemed like you could hear the roll over all. (Interview, November 23, 1980, and Foxchase, August 12, 1982)

But a mixture of voices is required for a symphonic effect, to make each hound's part in a chase discernible. Norman likened a pack of hounds to a band, with bass, tenor, and soprano voices. "By puttin' 'em all together," he said, "it's what makes your fox chase, and it's what makes your music good" (foxchase, January 22, 1986).

Smoke, Sailor, and Nip are among Norman's best "trailers." Hunters often "cast" their trail dogs by releasing them ahead of their pickup trucks on a road known to be in a fox's territory. In this method of casting, called "road hunting" the dogs, the truck follows the hounds slowly down the road. The hounds busily look for the sign of fox, inspecting tufts of broomsedge, pine needles, and Indian grass, pausing occasionally to void themselves, depositing their own scent on top of all the others. The air is filled with the sound of long ears flapping vigorously. The hounds' tails tick slightly in excitement as various animal scents arouse their interest, but if no scent of fox emerges, "no action," as Milton Collins put it, they remain mute, straining to isolate fox pheromones in a world crowded with aroma. Norman reflected, "A dog's nose must be something out of this world."

Figure 1.2. A well-worn snapshot of Old Lead. Courtesy of Norman Taylor.

Because you have to specifically smell the difference between a fox, a rabbit, a deer—and yet, they get to the point where I've seen hounds that would run red fox and wouldn't run gray, and vice versa. Now their nose is that keen that they can tell the difference between a red fox and a gray fox.

Without seeing it, foxhunters can tell a fox's running pattern by the way the hounds sound, and a fox tells them by the way it runs whether it is red or gray. Red and gray foxes offer radically different chases.

The red fox, model for Reynard, the indomitable trickster of the medieval animal world, is the flashier creature. Far fleeter of foot than either gray foxes or dogs, it prefers open running and will lead the dogs for miles down fire lanes and railroad tracks, across open fields and busy highways. It also gives off a stronger scent than a gray fox, enabling the hounds to run faster, harder, and louder in its wake. Foxhunters and some naturalists contend that the red fox was introduced by English colonists in the eighteenth century for the sake of the sport (Fox 1975; Hufford 1987:165–69).

Norman remembers that red foxes first appeared in Lebanon State Forest in the 1940s, an era considered by old-timers to be the heyday of foxhunting in the region. One of the earliest and most memorable was a fox they named "Fireball." "He would let you run him," Norman recalled. "He was a nice fox. He liked to be run" (interview, November 23, 1980).

While red foxes run straight through open areas for miles, gray foxes circle, clinging to the brush and briars. "The gray fox," said Norman, "he keeps you in heavy cover all the time." Because the hunting area is becoming more congested with traffic, and because of competing noises from air traffic, chain saws, recreational vehicles, and military testing, Pine Barrens foxhunters sometimes prefer the gray foxes that circle, keeping the dogs within hearing range, away from the hazards of major highways.

The gray fox signals that "it has had enough" when it begins "doubling back" continuously. Then the hunters will "break" the dogs, driving their trucks to a point where the fox is apt to cross. Killing the fox is not their aim, for within their lifetimes the fox has gone from being despised as vermin to being prized as a conductor of canine symphonies. Most foxhunters have abandoned the practice of shooting foxes after running them for hours because the destruction of fox habitat has depleted fox populations in the region. Because the dogs would kill the fox if they caught it, hunters call them off the chase at the first signs of fox fatigue. "There's no sense of catchin' him," Norman said, "because once he's caught, you're done with that fox forever" (interview, January 22, 1986).

Until the dogs find a track they can "move," they are guided by the truck, a surrogate alpha hound with its own distinctive rallying cry. It is not the sound of the classic brass hunter's horn, curved and tassled, but the horn beneath the hood of a given truck that these foxhounds respond to. Norman has a special horn installed for this purpose. It gives out a high "Hwah!" of a honk, in contrast to the more restrained tenor toot that comes from Horsetrader's Chevrolet pickup. Leon Hopkins, known to foxhunters as "Horsetrader," has had that horn on three different trucks.

Sometimes the hunter guides the hounds on foot away from the road, down a deer path toward the swamp, encouraging them. "Hark up!" says Norman. "Hark on it, Smoke!" "Go on 'im, Nip!" "Spring to 'im, Sailor!"

This morning the action is brewing over by Reeves' Bogs, where Horsetrader has found a hot track.

The CB radio sputters and Horsetrader says, "You got a copy of me, Dogman? How 'boutcha Yellow Bird, you got a copy of me?"

Yellow Bird grabs the mike and says, "Yeah, I got a copy of you."

"My dogs are running, I'm crossin' the blacktop here and goin' to the Muddy Road," Horsetrader informs him.

"Alrighty," says Yellow Bird. "We'll pick some dogs up and come over."

Leon Hopkins has foxhunted for nearly seven decades. He traded hounds with Norman's father, in the days when they would load their dogs into a horse-drawn buckboard wagon and repair to the woods for days on end. His hat, a gift from his son-in-law, has a reclining fox on it, hand-painted by a neighbor. Leon's handle, "Horsetrader," alludes to the forty horses he boards on his farm in Cookstown near McGuire Air Force Base, and the dozens more he is usually buying, selling, and trading. Because of his emphysema he depends on an inhalator, and his wife Betty often joins him on foxchases to help him load and unload his dogs.

While Horsetrader keeps his ear on the action, Dogman and Yellow Bird summon their dogs from the cold trails. Norman pushes his way into the swamp, about fifty yards from the road, and calls to his dogs, using a coarse "Heeyah!" and a "Whoop!" Hunters have an assortment of vocal calls for collecting their dogs, ranging from the more guttural "Eeyah! Eeyah! Hah! Hah! Hah! Hah!" to a shrill "Whoo!" that sometimes sounds like a gusty sneeze. But each dog knows the voice of its master, just as it knows the horn of the master's truck.

When he has loaded his six trailers, adding them to the eight in his truck, Norman starts the engine and sets off at a terrific speed for his destination, the fox's projected crossing place about a mile and a half away.

In contrast to the hounds, foxhunters follow the chase prospectively, predicting where a given fox will lead the hounds so they can watch them cross the roads. For this task it is the pickup truck, not the horse, that is the perfect vehicle for riding to hounds in the Pine Barrens, for circumnavigating foxchases on narrow sand roads overhung with pine boughs. They take the CB antennae into the cab for these forays, during which one is all but deafened by the sound of pine branches slapping and scraping against the sides of the truck.

Figure 1.3. Theodore "Junie" Bell, his wife Carol, and Leon
Hopkins, in Cookstown. Photo by the author, October 1986.

There are only a few paved roads through the forest, referred to by
foxhunters as "blacktops," and only local people can travel with assurance
the unpaved labyrinth from Chatsworth to Browns Mills on routes that
were established well before highways 70 and 72 became major routes to the
Jersey shore. The passable roads circumscribe "pieces of woods" inlaid with
miles and miles of one-lane sand roads, crossways, and dams, traces of the
waves of enterprise that overswept the region in earlier centuries. In the
eighteenth century, the woods boomed as glass and iron industries melted
sand and smelted bog iron. They hummed with sawmills slicing cedar into

boat boards and house shingles. And they smoldered as hundreds of thousands of pitch pines were rendered into charcoal.

Around the iron plantations of Hanover Furnace and Mary Ann Forge, the water, turf, and sand were sculpted into dams, dikes, canals, and reservoirs to power the mills and transport the products. The discovery of anthracite coal changed the fortunes of these plantations, shifting the nation's industrial base to the cities, but intrepid nineteenth-century entrepreneurs recycled the landscapes, turning them into cranberry plantations. The dams and millponds were readily converted into dikes, canals, irrigation ditches and reservoirs for cranberry cultivation. The biggest plantation was at Whitesbog, which Josiah J. White's descendants, the Darlingtons, still operate through a lease agreement with the state. Red foxes are said to lose the dogs by running down the airstrip there.

In contrast to most of the forest's urban visitors, foxhunters know the landscapes as only people who worked them can know them. Though for most of their lives they have worked at jobs outside of the forest, Norman Taylor, Junie Bell, and Leon Hopkins think of themselves first as woodsmen. Within their lifetimes, however, the woods have changed from private to public ownership. The swamps in the forest have gone from workplaces to recreational and scientific landscapes. Roads made by charcoalers are substrata for dirt bikers; the crossways and dams are access roads for "birders" (birdwatchers), "herpers" (reptile collectors), and "bogtrotters" (botanizers); and Lebanon Glassworks is the humble backdrop for a campsite. Where once farmers welcomed the canine chorus, newcomers complain about it. Foxes have gone from being "outlaws," as Leon Hopkins put it, to being valued beasts of the chase, and the woods, once exhausted of deer, are now full of them. Norman's father unintentionally ran his first deer with dogs in the second decade of this century, when the state reintroduced them to Lebanon State Forest (Forman 1979:29);

> He often told me about the first deer that his dogs ever run and that was up at Raceground Hill. And they didn't know what they was runnin'. He said it was a long time before they figured out what they was runnin'. That's one of the first deer they ever knew to be around here and I think they were probably turned out—or he seemed to think they were, yeah. From then on they just multiplied and multiplied. (Interview, January 24, 1986)[3]

To foxhunters, deer are a nuisance, the worst of the trash quarry.

And the improved roads have exacerbated another blight. In foxhunters' road parlance, unpaved but improved roads include "tar roads," "gravel roads," and "dirt roads." "When they put those gravel roads in, they ruined

Lebanon State Forest," complained Norman. "They do to all forests, because that lets everybody in. Everybody with a car can ride up and down them good roads."

But not everyone with a car can enter the Chaseworld. John Earlin, who foxhunted for nearly seven decades before his death in 1986, made this point in a story he told when I first met him. "A man pulled up here in a pink Cadillac one night," he began,

> About two o'clock in the morning, and wanted to know what I was doin' out here at that hour. "Well," I said, "you roll down your window, mister, and you'll hear some of the prettiest music you ever heard in your life." So the guy rolled down his window and listened. After a bit he said, "How can you hear any music when those dogs are making all that racket?" (Foxchase, November 15, 1980)[4]

Norman pulls up to the blacktop where Leon's pickup is parked. Leon's dogs have crossed and are making a racket. Norman stops, and his hounds, some of them younger and still learning "what their noses are for," hear Leon's dogs from the box and grow frantic with desire to join the chase. Norman lets his more experienced dogs out first, the ones that can "locate."

Once Sailor, a methodical hound, has found and verified the track, Norman opens the box and the others pour forth, a stream of brown, black, and white, of scrambled ears, noses, legs, tails, and ribs, issuing forth in a single canine rush, each hound siphoning out the one behind it. Crying out eagerly to the dogs ahead of them, they disappear into the brush. "That's all they know is gettin' in there," says Norman. Having started the fox, hounds on the "hot track" begin to "chop," flooding the air with staccato notes. They are no longer trailing but running. Another foxchase—a dynamic fusion of landscape, animals, and hunters—has materialized.

The single roar produced by all the hounds running in a pack together helps make a group of the hunters at the edge, who are united by the sound and their shared understanding of it. Members of the human collective playfully named for animals listen to storytellers in an animal pack whose members are named for people.[5] It's a story of epic proportions, told over and over by Maggie, Becky, Lil, Sailor, Maude, Jake, Mike, Dave, Smiley, and Kate to an appreciative audience comprised of Yellow Bird, Dogman, Piggy, Green Fox, Blowfish, Mustang, Horsetrader, Redbone, Blue Tick, Gray Fox, and others in the community. This is a community defined by the capacity of its members to hear hounds' voices as music. The aliases of its members catch up the landscape's animals and hues.

Figure 1.4. Norman Taylor harking his hounds into a chase. Photos by Dennis McDonald, January 1989. Courtesy of the American Folklife Center, Library of Congress.

As we listen, the voices dwindle, bobbing away in the distance. Horse-trader and Dogman have strategically placed themselves where the chase might emerge on the far side of the "piece of woods." Others have joined us here, lengthening the caravan of parked pickups and swelling the group of listeners. Not all are foxhunters, but many are related to the hunters and are accustomed to checking in on foxchases. Donald Taylor is here with his son, Greg, and his father, Harry, who is Norman's older brother. Norman's cousin Hank Stevenson is here, and so is Norman's wife Caroline. Her CB handle is "Cranberry Lady," because she works in the office at the J. J. White cranberry bogs near Baffin's Meadows where a red fox will sometimes lead the dogs. She comes bearing Fig Newtons and hot water for tea and coffee.

"If it's not a gray fox, I would be surprised, really," says Norman.

"If he was a red, he'da been over North Branch by this time," Hank Stevenson agrees.

"He'll be back here," Norman predicts.

A burst of static from the CB and a voice says, "Tally-ho!"

"Who said 'Tally-ho'?" I ask.

"Junie, because he seen the fox," says Norman. "'Tally-ho!' means you see him."

It was a gray fox, as Norman predicted.

At the edge of the soundscape emanating from their dogs, the hunters try to hear the fox's trail as the hounds take possession of it. The hounds must follow the trail on the ground, not the scent on the wind. The narrowness of the trail forces the hounds to "bunch up" or "pack together." They should "bunch up" so tightly that, as Norman's brother Freeman put it, "you could throw a blanket over them" (foxchase, March 1979).

The hound in the lead may be said to "own the line." This line is a raw material that hounds transform into an expressive medium. Each hound has its own style of expressing the trail, and something of a hound's character is revealed in its style of running. Comparing the process to a craft, Norman distinguishes his hounds according to whether they run "neat" or "clean"; whether they "swing," "cut," "hunt 'em wide," or tend to "boo-hoo."

"There's the kind of hound that boo-hoos," Norman explained. "They just get a track and they can't move it" (interview, January 22, 1986).

Norman recalled how his favorite hound, Lead, made the trail come alive. "When the smellin' got right that he could run fast," said Norman, "he was fast, and when it was bad, you could see him—like a snake, he'd wiggle it (interview, January 24, 1986).

Hunters fashion foxchases in part around the fox's ability to fabricate, that is, to concoct a scheme that leads to "a falsification of some part of the world" (Goffman 1974:83). The part of the world the fox falsifies is its own trail. The fox can lead dogs to think that it has crossed the road when it has in fact come to the road and doubled back on its trail, or that it has doubled back, following a previous pattern, when in fact it has gone up a tree.

On this occasion the fox has already tricked the dogs several times, emerging at the blacktop and running over its surface in order to "outfox the dogs," as Hank Stevenson put it. Thus it buys time for itself as the dogs scatter to sniff frantically for its point of entry back into the brush. The hound that finds the line again is a bit of a hero. "When they almost missed that fox there," said Norman, replaying one scene,

> Sailor threw out just wide enough to get on it where no dogs had been on it. And I said, "Boy, they better hark if they're gonna get with him," and sure enough, they all harked, and that was it. Soon as he hollered, I knew he was right, 'cause he never hollers unless he's right. Nope. He's a hunter.

When it cannot mystify, the fox ensnares, eking out more lead for itself by taking the hounds through treacherous briars or "lap"-strewn swamps. "They're briarin' in there," says Norman, listening. "If you had a bird's-eye view, he's crawlin' right underneath the briars—that's why you don't get no noise outa the dogs. He's right underneath them briars. He's skinnier'n a rabbit dog."

The hunters, listening to the canine nucleus galloping over the many surfaces of the forest, listening until their ears become their eyes, strive to achieve consensus over the exact location of the chase. They bring the implied narrative to completion in human terms, giving form in language to the images of chase and landscape that condense out of the sound before their minds' eyes.

"Now they're gettin' out in the open stuff," observes Norman, listening.

Underlying the Pine Barrens is an enormous aquifer, the Cohansey sands, which is two thousand feet thick. It contains 17 trillion gallons of water widely acclaimed for its purity. This water, entirely replenished by precipitation, submerges the wetlands, and in uplands it is never more than twenty feet below the surface.[6] Thus Pine Barrens landscapes modulate rapidly from sandy, dry uplands to spongy, low wetlands. The State Forest is a sampler of all of them: treeless marshes—spongs, savannahs, and ponds—where groundwater is present throughout the year; poorly drained lowlands—bogs, cedar and hardwood swamps, and pitch-pine lowlands—that may dry up during certain seasons; and the well-drained uplands, where pitch pines, blackjack and scrub oaks, ferns, and a variety of huckleberries and briars resprout abundantly within one season of a fire.

We stand in the road, facing a solid wall of pine trees, a filter for canine voices. Beyond them we can see the tops of cedars. The voices grow louder.

"They're right in the cedar swamp," says Norman, translating hound voices into vision. "Lot of water. Yeah, and if it was frozen up in there in the ice, you couldn't run that fox in there, could you?"

"No," says Leon.

"Nope," Norman continues. "Right where they're at now, beavers have made a dam in there. It goes right around and if it was froze up, you wouldn't hear no music at all, yeah."

"With that much water on top of the ice, that has trouble too," Leon elaborates. "They *walk* through it, you know. The fox does, and the dogs."

"Leaves no scent," adds Norman, "where he goes through on top of the ice, and there's water on top of it, yeah."

But cedar swamps, while difficult for dogs to negotiate because they are full of "laps" and "hassocks," are acoustically magnificent. "It's a sound that carries the foxhounds," said Norman once in conversation with Junie and Leon. "I love to hear 'em run in the cedar. Don't you?"

"Butterworth Crossway is a good spot," affirmed Junie. "When they're comin' through that swamp there, that's just a roar."

"There to the crossway," Leon reiterated. "Boy, they roar in there" (interview, October 18, 1986).

According to Christian Bethmann, superintendent of Lebanon State Forest, the Pine Barrens have the second highest incidence of forest fires in the country. The Pine Barrens is known among naturalists as a fire-climax forest, wherein the cycle of ecological succession culminates in fire, preventing the oak and pine uplands from evolving into a mixed-deciduous forest. The stunted morphology of the Plains, a celebrated tract of volatile pine trees, scrub oaks (locally called "ground oak bushes"), and huckleberry brush, is the result of thousands of years of fires, many of them caused by lightning. Vegetation in the "pygmy forest," as botanizers call the Plains, has incorporated fire into its cycle. Pine cones on the Plains will only open

and reseed the forest when heated to 150 degrees. The vegetation has become increasingly volatile, rapidly spreading the fires on which it now depends. On warm sunny days the Plains is an oven, its sands gathering and ra-
diating heat, its giant resinous oak leaves refracting the glare. While no one
lives on the Plains, firefighting is a way of life in surrounding communities.

Fires have made aspects of the landscape ephemeral by constantly
erasing the kinds of artifacts that elsewhere preserve communal memories:
old homesteads, historic mills, and hunting cabins, like one that hunters
used to frequent at Webb's Mill.

The name Webb's Mill now denotes a small bog on Route 539 where
naturalists can observe a variety of rare and endemic plant species, including
the rare and minute curly grass fern (*Schizea pusilla*), from a boardwalk
constructed for that purpose. The stop is de rigueur for all botanical tours
of the Pine Barrens. But half a century ago it was the stomping ground for a
rollicking group of local hunters who based themselves in Will Earlin's
cabin there. "You know," said Norman,

> years ago we used to have a cabin down to Webb's Mill, and that's before 539
> went through. And I think it's the most joyous time of my life, I know, because
> I was still going to school and whatnot. And that was the time between—we'd
> go down the day after Christmas and stay till New Year's. (Interview, January
> 24, 1986)

Such cabins are known as places to gather and trade hunting stories, bases
away from the dwellings of everyday life, which are often less than ten miles
away. This distance is now less significant than it was in the 1930s, when
Earlin and his friends used a Model A Ford to travel the narrow sand road
that eventually became 539, going down early in deer week to kill the deer
that would sustain them during a solid week of chasing foxes.

In between chases they ate "like kings," as Norman put it, played
pranks on one another, substituted pinochle for sleep, and maintained a
communal diary on the walls of the cabin. "I remember," said Norman,

> . . . on the walls it was just sheetrock, and everybody wrote their messages on
> the walls. So you could go there and see from year to year what it was. I
> remember one time Apie put "100 hounds runnin' deer today." Apie kept the
> history of every day. You could go down every year. . . . Year after year you'd go
> around every year and read the diary was kept on the walls. (Interview, January
> 24, 1986)

In the late 1930s the diary was destroyed in a forest fire.

The woodlands are dotted with such cabins, wherein hunters continue to render their stories and histories. From the 1940s until he died in 1988, Joe Albert recorded foxhunters' exploits in the journal he kept at his "Homeplace" in the Forked River Mountains. Of a chase they held on Friday, April 8, 1955, he wrote:

> Left Mabel and Full go at the camp. They hit a track at the mouth of our camp road. And he went straight to the Parkway but did not cross. And we did have a hunt. We left them run about five hours and caught all the dogs off because George was coming down Saturday to hear a hunt. They had the fox pretty tired. All the dogs done fine. There was Mabel, Full, Empty. If you ask how they run you would only be talking silly. There was Jr. and Tilley who did very good. Track and King the two new dogs done very good. Harry had Bell in too, he said she was in the front all the time. We had a good gang. Harry, Homer, Russell, Joe.

The journal, which also served as a guest registry, contains entries written by hunters who stayed at the Homeplace over the years.

Unassisted by journals, hounds prompt involuntary memories through their voices, thresholds to the past that are in some ways less destructible than cabins and journals.[7] The languages of hounds and foxes do not vary over time or space as radically as do the languages of humans.[8] Hounds' voices animate landscape features saturated with personal memories and meanings. Foxes and hounds career over the landscapes, roaring out their images, lighting up scenes that were long ago emblazoned in the mind. The foxchase loosens nuggets of memory that, like cranberries dislodged from vines by mechanical wet harvesters, pop to the surface.

Hank is reminded of something that happened not far from where the dogs are running. "Remember about thirty years ago when you had that fox treed right there on the upper end of that reservoir?"

Norman does not, exactly.

Hank persists. "You don't remember that? You and I and Herb Anderson was in there."

Norman helps him paint the picture. "One time I had a couple good tree dogs, and if the gray fox run up a tree, they stayed right there and barked, yeah. Those two dogs had every dog barkin', yeah. But now if you tree a fox you'll probably—it's just the end of your chase."

"Never know it," avers Hank.

"It's just a matter of havin' a good tree dog, yeah," says Norman, bragging a little. "I've treed a lot of foxes when my dogs was runnin' 'em, yeah."

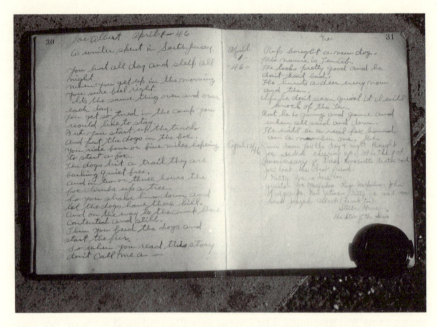

Figure 1.5. Pages in Joe Albert's foxhunting journal. Photo by the author, August 1982.

"When we got in there that day, the fox was in the tree," Hank reiterates.

"Up the tree, yeah," Norman picks up. "I had Jacky then, probably. A dog called Jacky. A blue dog, and man, he was the best tree dog I ever saw in my life. He could tree a fox. Sat right there and had all the dogs around treein'."

Hank starts the reprise. "Well, you and I and Herb Anderson went in there that day."

"Yeah, how about that," Norman muses.

"That's been a while ago," says Hank. "Yeah, a few moons's went by."

Norman brings them back to the present, reorienting them. "I can just [i.e., barely] hear 'em," he says, "They went off that way."

Though hounds' voices are powerful tools for unearthing such memories, in conversation and stories hunters also inhabit the world of the Chase unassisted by hounds. When visiting places like the Homeplace, Three Bridges Shanty, and Foxchase Farm, one expects to be caught up in the world of the chase through stories told while the hounds are resting. Finding himself in the absence of both hunters and hounds one evening in

Figure 1.6. Foxhounds tree-barking a fox, ca. 1935. From the family album of Randall Stafford.

his cabin at Foxchase Farm, John Earlin conjured both Chaseworld and audience, creating a record of it on an audiocassette tape. "I got some tales that you probably would like to record," he told me the first time I met him. 'I sit down one night and from nothin' at all I started tellin' stories. And I sit there for forty minutes and told stories about foxhuntin'" (foxchase, November 15, 1980). Afterward he compensated for his momentary lack of an audience by inviting people to come to the cabin and listen to the tape, which has become well known among foxhunters and has been circulating in the community since he died of cancer in 1986.

In a sense, hunters keep their deceased colleagues alive through foxhunting stories, conjuring them as Chaseworld characters. At the final rite of passage and afterward, through ceremonial behaviors and self-definitional rites, hunters inscribe themselves as players in the world of the chase, a world that opens up to them over thresholds they etch onto physical and cognitive terrains, a world made visible to others through careful design.

At a heavily used intersection officially known as Five Corners there stands a handsome stone marker bearing the name "Pomeroy Crossroads." Engraved on the marker commissioned by the New Jersey Sporting Dogs Association is a hound pursuing a fox. "Believe it or not," said Norman

Taylor, "by puttin' the sign there, people will see it, and they'll start usin' that name. Pomeroy Crossroads yeah, and that's how it'll get established, yeah."

Donald Pomeroy was killed in late 1985 when his pickup truck went out of control and crashed into a pine tree, the day before deer season opened. The truck was green, and for that reason his name on the air was "Green Fox." Hunters always heard Green Fox before they saw him, entering the Chaseworld voice first. "You could hear him every morning comin' in," said Norman. "You could tell how far away he was. You could tell when he was gettin' closer:

> "Hey, who's up there who's up there? Who's in the woods? Piggy, Piggy, Piggy, where are you? Dogman, Dogman, I can't hear you." He'd like sing all the way down to you. Then he'd say, "Yell-llow Bi-ird!" Like he was singing to you! Yeah, he was funny. (Interview, January 24, 1986)

Pomeroy's funeral service was held in Lebanon State Forest during deer week. According to those who attended, a funeral caravan of thirty-two vehicles processed slowly along the Blacktop Road toward Pasadena. First came the funeral limousine, followed by Pomeroy's wife, Patsy, and their son, Donald. Junie Bell and Jeff Powell drove the pickup truck that came next, carrying Pomeroy's foxhounds. Behind them Norman Taylor and Leon Hopkins led the procession of cars. Deerhunters for whom Pomeroy had served as a guide emerged from their gun club and stood in a row. One man on each end held a gun. "No guns in the middle," Norman emphasized.

"They all lined up along the road," he said, "and they was just at attention when we went by. Beautiful."

"And when the hearse went by," added Caroline, "they all took their hats off and crossed their hearts with 'em and stood at attention, till the whole procession got by" (interview, January 24, 1986).

The service was conducted at the Rye Strips, a feeding ground for deer. The casket was decorated with a floral reproduction of a fox. The hounds are said to have watched in silence as the minister read the Twenty-Third Psalm and delivered the eulogy. The ceremony's conclusion was punctuated by an unscheduled two-gun salute (Grekoski 1986:48), and the rich opportunity to glean meaning from such a turn of events was not squandered.

"Two shots went off just about the time the minister finished with the verse," said Norman. "Just like it was timed."

"Back off in the woods someplace," Caroline elaborated. "We don't know if it was a deer."

Figure 1.7. Monument to Donald Pomeroy, at Pomeroy's Crossroads in Lebanon State Forest. Photo by Dennis McDonald, January 1989. Courtesy of the American Folklife Center, U.S. Library of Congress.

"Oh, no doubt they shot a deer," said Norman. "It was 'Bang!' 'Bang!' Yeah."

"It wasn't anything that was planned," said Caroline. "It was spontaneous. And what made it so perfect is that it was just at the right time. . . . Patsy and her son was standin' there, and they both looked at each other and smiled."

"Grinned, yeah," said Norman (interview, January 24, 1986).

After the funeral Patsy distributed Pomeroy's hounds among his fox-hunting buddies: four to Yellow Bird, four to Dogman, three to Piggy.

The gray fox has circled now for six hours, crossing Reeves' Bogs and the State Gravel Hole a number of times on its trek from Muddy Road to South Branch and back. He has run in the blueberries, the swamps, and the spongs, around the cranberry bogs, and through the briars. He has "shown himself" to hunters a half-dozen times or more. His circles are tightening, a sign to foxhunters that it is time to break the dogs.

The trucks are lined up on Egg Harbor Road. The hunters are poised; several have long leather bullwhips which they grip more firmly when the fox emerges from the woods and races down the road for about fifteen yards before the woods on the other side close behind him. The onrushing dogs, a minute behind him, are getting louder. As those in the lead explode out of the brush, hunters begin tooting horns, whooping, and cracking whips against the road, as if to sever the impalpable line of scent and concentration that binds hounds to the fox. The world of the chase is shattered, and the dogs begin to mill around, climbing into the nearest dog boxes.

"Get in that truck!" shouts Norman, fiercely. "Get up in there! Smoke! You know better than to go by me! Get up, Sailor! Get up, Smoke! Watch that dog, Junie! Jimmy, get in that truck! Get in that truck, Punch!"

Sometimes, the hunters say, if a fox is tired enough they can catch it first and put it in the cab long enough for it to catch its wind. Wilted and musky, such a fox feels just like a wet dishrag, Norman once observed (interview, November 23, 1980). The dogs are broken but not sorted. The hunters pull their trucks together in a clearing and raise the hinged lids of the dog boxes. Junie has Norman's Becky, and Norman has several of Junie's. "Junie, don't let her go," says Norman. "That's Becky. If I lose Becky I'd cry. . . . Man, they're wet! They've been in the water." His voice is gentle now, not harsh, as it is when controlling dogs out of the box or kennel. "Doggy! Hello there Maggie! Here Maggie, here Maggie. There's one of yours, Junie. Another one of yours, Junie. Another one of yours, Junie."

The mighty instrument that made the soundscapes has been dismantled, its components restored to their boxes. Their hounds gathered in, the hunters begin taking leave of each other and Lebanon State Forest, repairing to the kennels and homes of everyday life.

This last separation occurs gradually. The hounds are silent now, but the air is alive with the voices of hunters. It is midnight, an old midnight several years ago. Yellow Bird, Green Fox, Blowfish, and Dogman have loaded the dogs and are parting company, each in his own truck. Their voices are the last things touching.

"You got all your dogs?" says Blowfish.

"Yeah, got all mine," returns Yellow Bird.

"About time to go the hell home then," declares Blowfish.

Figure 1.8. Norman Taylor breaking his hounds from the fox's trail (above) and loading them into his pickup (below). Photos by Dennis McDonald, January 1989. Courtesy of the American Folklife Center, U.S. Library of Congress.

"Everybody got all our dogs," says Yellow Bird. "You on the tar road goin' home? Got a 10-4 on that. Good night, I'm gonna sign off, I'm gonna shut the CB off."

"You ain't even gonna talk to me on the way home?" protests Blowfish. "I don't know about you. I don't know about you, Yellow Bird. Come on back there, ya Yellow Bird."

"How about that, Blowfish, Blowfish?" chimes in Green Fox.

"Aw, come on back," says Blowfish, still working on Yellow Bird.

"Did you hear Green Fox?" says Green Fox, again. "You still got a Green Fox there Blowfish? Come back, ya Blowfish, Blowfish."

"Caughtcha there, Green Green Green Fox. Ya gotcher ears on?"

"10-4," says Green Fox. "I got 'em there, Buddy, Buddy. Where you at?"

"I'm headed for the camp," says Blowfish.

Dogman comes in. "What about you there Blowfish, do you read me?"

"I gotcha there, Dogman, Dogman," says Blowfish. "I hear you!"

But they are beginning to fade.

"10-4," says the indefatigable Blowfish, "10-4 and out" (foxchase, October 20, 1982).

Notes

1. This is a deviation from the standard CB scale, where "10-4" means "Roger" or "affirmative." Here it means location, i.e., a hunter's position on the landscape.

2. Unless otherwise indicated, all quotations in this chapter are from the foxchase of January 25, 1986.

3. The Pine Barrens deer population, seriously depleted in the latter half of the nineteenth century, increased dramatically in the first decades of this century as a result of a concerted management program launched by the state of New Jersey. See Forman (1979:28–29).

4. I am grateful to Herbert Halpert for directing me to W. Carew Hazlitt's *Shakespeare's Jest Books* for two Elizabethan versions of this anecdote. The following is the twenty-seventh jest in "Taylors Wit and Mirth," in volume 3: "Another Mayor that was on hunting, (by chance) one asked him how hee liked the Cry. A p** take the Dogs! saith hee, they make such a bawling, that I cannot heare the Cry."

5. Interestingly, canine ethologists define a "pack" as "a social group which hunts together" (Fox 1975:445).

6. To protect the Pine Barrens and the system of wetlands on which its rare and endemic species depend, Congress created the Pinelands National Reserve in 1978. Under the provisions of the enabling legislation, people may continue to own property and reside within the region, but their land use must conform to the

policies set forth by the Pinelands Commission—the Reserve's managing body constituted by the same legislation—in its Comprehensive Management Plan. The creation of the National Reserve has had an enormous impact on patterns of development and land use in the region. For discussions of the controversies surrounding the Pinelands Commission's procedures and policies, and of the cultural implications of these policies, see Hufford 1987 and Berger and Sinton 1985.

7. In 1940 Charles Grant of New Egypt told a tall tale to Herbert Halpert that in a sense addresses the triumph of hounds' voices over ephemerality. In his fabrication the voices literally become an artifact hovering over the landscape:

> [Ed Leek] went down there fox huntin'. Said he stood up there on the Hundred Dollar Bridge Hill we called it, and, uh, he heared his dogs runnin' a fox, comin' right towards him. An' he said he stood there an hour and they didn't get no closer, and they were only half a mile from him when he heard them an' they didn't get no closer. He said he started to go in there where they was, and see what was the matter—he got excited about it. An' he found their tracks on an old sand road where they'd scratched and gone by, and they'd gone by 'fore he got there. It was so cold it froze their voice up in the air, and they stayed right there. The voice stayed there and didn't leave. There was the string of their voice for a mile long, an' that stayed there after the dogs gone by. Their yells stayed there; kept right on yellin'. The cold ketched it up in the air and never let it go—till it thawed out next spring some time, when it got warm. (Halpert 1947:343)

8. W. Keith Perceval points out that this was seen as a distinguishing feature of animal communication by the eighteenth-century Jesuit priest Guillaume-Hyacinthe Bougeant, who also observed that animals "always tell the truth and never deceive" (1982:63–64).

2. Ritual Moorings

> Each world whilst it is attended to is real after its own fashion; only the reality lapses with the attention.
> —William James, "The Perception of Reality" (1890:293)

Constructing the Enclave

FOXHUNTERS CONJURE THE CHASEWORLD by first constructing an enclave in the Ordinary—the foxchase or the story—through which they enter and inhabit the Chaseworld. Both foxchases and stories are enclaves (Schutz 1970:256), structures set apart from the world of everyday life by means of "boundaries," which serve, like the frame around a picture, to mark the Chaseworld's physical or literal limits (Bateson 1955:46; Goffman 1974: 252).[1] Like curtains opening and closing on a stage, a foxchase's opening and closing sequences help to locate the Chaseworld in a time and space that is different from Ordinary time and space. Unfolding across a particular portion of Lebanon State Forest and progressing through a ritualized sequence of events, the Chaseworld is set apart from the world of everyday life. Within these boundaries, Chaseworld places and inhabitants assume an ontological status different from the ones they possess outside the Chaseworld.

Turning their attention toward foxes and hounds, and toward each other as Chaseworld inhabitants, hunters establish and maintain the Chaseworld's conceptual parameters through frames that operate at a higher level of abstraction than the Chaseworld and its physical boundaries. Continually orienting themselves to Chaseworld time and space, hunters frame their world, distinguishing what is going on inside the Chaseworld from what goes on in the Ordinary, endowing Chaseworld events with meaning. Through orientations and evaluations hunters also bridge the gap they have opened between two realities, attaching the Chaseworld to the occasions of its conjuring, making its relevance and meanings clear to varied audiences (Goffman 1974; Young 1987; Labov 1972).[2]

Whether invoked through foxchases or stories, the Chaseworld is sustained wholly by the attention of its authors. Attending at some times to the Chaseworld, at others to its frames and boundaries, the hunters may shift continuously from absorption to abstraction and back again (Young 1987:18). When attention strays beyond the Chaseworld and its horizons, the Chaseworld vanishes entirely until reinstated by the hunters' renewed attention (Schutz 1970:252).

Ritual Phases and Chaseworld Boundaries

A foxchase unfolds in time and space according to a clearly bounded sequence of events. (See Figure 2.1.) Outside the foxchase, hunters and their hounds are separately quartered. Deep within it their identities converge. No one would say of hounds in a kennel, as John Earlin says of hounds in the Chaseworld, "along there came a pack of dogs . . . and that was Norman Taylor." The sequence in a foxchase provides a ritualized way of getting into and out of this state, in which hunters merge not only with their own hounds, but with each other, viewing the world together through their hounds, united as a pack on the trail of a fox.

In terms of its sequence, the foxchase emulates the tripartite structure of the rite de passage: (1) an opening sequence (the separation phase) during which hunters and their hounds cross the divide between the world of the Ordinary and the world of the Chase; (2) running the fox (the liminal phase) during which hunters inhabit the Chaseworld through their hounds; and (3) a closing sequence (the reaggregation phase) during which hunters exit the Chaseworld and reenter the Ordinary, wherein hunters and their hounds resume separate quarters and identities.

A word of clarification regarding the depiction of foxchases as ritual, replete with liminal process, is in order here. Although a foxchase is clearly a secular ritual, not a rite of passage, it does contain a liminal, antistructural phase. (Figure 2.1). Entering this phase, the participants clearly move, as Victor Turner puts it, "from the indicative quotidian social structure into the subjunctive antistructure of the liminal process" (1980: 159). They then return "transformed by liminal experiences, through rites of reaggregation to social structural participation in the indicative mood" (1980:159). The "transformation" here does not entail the passage from one clearly defined state in life to another; rather, it involves the subtle, ongoing development and maintenance of human social identity.[3]

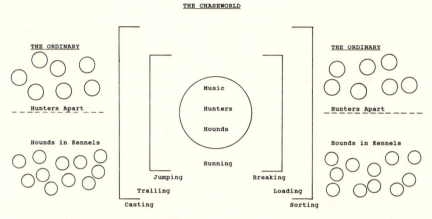

Figure 2.1. Chaseworld boundaries.

Phase 1. The Opening Sequence

A hunter begins to open the Chaseworld from the Ordinary when he backs his pickup to the kennel and opens the gate to "load" his hounds. The truck at this point undergoes a shift in status. In everyday life the truck may be used for transportation and for work, but because the dog box is a permanent fixture on the back of the truck it always alludes to the Chaseworld (as do icons like fox hood ornaments and fox decals posted in rear windows and on bumpers). Foxhunting accessories permanently installed in the truck include CB radios and separate horns for calling the dogs. When the Chaseworld is established the truck orbits the soundscape, pausing frequently to become a conversational leaning post, its hood a picnic table for laying out food and beverages. Bob Hayes, a foxhunter from Port Elizabeth, claims to keep his dinner of baked beans hot by attaching a can of them to the tailpipe, thus rendering his truck a portable campfire (foxchase, April 7, 1991).

Pressed into the service of the Chaseworld, the truck becomes a traveling kennel. Enfolding hunter and hounds in a single unit, the truck materializes the emerging conflation of hunter/hound identities. Within the Chaseworld the truck will continue as an extension of the hunter, a tool for casting the hounds on a fox track, its horn a means of summoning them home. Hunters often speak of how many trucks were present in accounting for numbers of packs and hunters, and CB handles such as Green Fox, Yellow Bird, and Brown Jug allude to the colors of pickup trucks.

The organization of hounds in the dog box anticipates the Chaseworld. A "tailgate" or "t-bar" in the dog box, used en route to the foxchase, divides the hounds according to Chaseworld functions: trail or "starter" dogs on one side and younger, less experienced dogs for volume and endurance on the other. This organization is dropped when reentering the Ordinary, where dogs in kennels are sorted according to disposition ("ornery" dogs live alone) and gender (females in heat are quartered separately).

As the hunters approach the state forest they activate CB handles expressly devised for use in foxhunting, over a channel referred to locally as the "foxhunters' channel." These handles that give men animal identities also serve to sharpen the discontinuity between the Chaseworld and everyday life. Though the use of animal names for CB handles is in fact widespread in the tradition of CB communication, names like Dogman, Yellow Bird, Horsetrader, Mustang, Red Fox, Gray Fox, Green Fox, Redbone, Blue Tick, Flea Patch, Piggy, and Blowfish are Chaseworld identities that help to invoke the alternate world, emphasizing the extraordinary relationship between humans and animals obtaining within it. The ordinary names that also are used within the Chaseworld in face-to-face situations—Norman, Junie, Leon, and so forth—pivot between the hunters' Chaseworld identities and those of everyday life. Hounds, whose ontological status never changes, bear the same names inside and out.

Hunters cast their dogs simultaneously in different places, looking for tracks along the roadside, Chaseworld ports of entry. Until they find a track, the hounds are still bound to the truck and the hunter. If the hunter turns a corner, he toots his horn to summon any hounds that turned the other way. When guiding the hounds on foot—down a deer trail or plowed lane, or into a swamp—hunters use stylized commands, reserved solely for conjuring the Chaseworld: "Hark to 'em, Sailor!" "Spring to 'em, Kate!" "Find it, Susie!"

The Chaseworld opens up when hounds orient away from the hunters toward another realm in which the fox is centered. "They stay with you," said Norman Taylor, "until such time as they find a fox, and then naturally they go where the fox goes" (foxchase, January 25, 1986). The chase has two parts: "trailing" and "running." The "cold trail" is an old track, which the hounds follow until they get close enough to the fox to "jump" it. The cold trail is signaled by long-drawn-out notes whereby the hounds "give voice to the line." At this point a separation occurs between what Goffman calls the "inner activity" and the "outer spectacle" (1974), and hunters and hounds reverse roles. This vocal shift is so important to Pine Barrens hunters that

Figure 2.2. Jack Davis and Jake Meredith casting their hounds with a pickup truck in Penn State Forest. Photo by the author, November 1980.

they devised hounds who would articulate it cleanly, remaining with the hunter until the hot track materializes. Said Norman:

> Lotta times you take hounds, you can take 'em up there in the woods and turn 'em loose, and you just don't see 'em no more until dark, and we didn't want that kind of a dog. We wanted a dog that would hunt with you until he found somethin' to run. If you went down the road, if you walked or you could holler, he'd be around you like a beagle would. And when they found track they started givin' you tongue and you followed 'em in. And up until that time they followed you, yeah. And that's what the name of the game is. They stayed with you until they found fox. (Interview, January 24, 1986)

Once the hounds find a fox, hunters no longer control them with their voices; rather the hunters become absorbed in the voices of the hounds. Then, interpreting the voices in the manner of sportscasters, the hunters conjure the Chaseworld.

An abrupt change in the voice of a foxhound marks the transition from cold trail to hot track. On hearing the shift from a long, legato "bawl" to a

Figure 2.3. Norman Taylor and hounds, waiting for his trailers to sound the hot track in Lebanon State Forest. Photo by Dennis McDonald, January 1989. Courtesy of the American Folklife Center, U.S. Library of Congress.

staccato "chop," hunters say that the hounds have "started" or "jumped" the fox. Having "hit the hot track," the hounds are no longer trailing but "running." The intensification of hound voices enhances the distinction between the Chaseworld and the world of the Ordinary. Hunters now begin calculating where the fox will go, rather than where it has been, initially in order to merge their hounds, subsequently to "stay in hearing of them," and finally to break them from the fox's trail.

DELINEATING THE SPATIO-TEMPORAL MATRIX
Time and space in the Chaseworld are defined by the voices of hounds, hovering over particular pieces of geography, bracketing particular moments in the formal sequence of the chase. The actual space of a foxchase is aromatically and acoustically delineated. Its center and point of origin is the trail of the fox. This trail does not circumscribe the space occupied by the Chaseworld; rather it traces the Chaseworld's peripatetic heart: ground zero. The outer boundary of the Chaseworld is acoustic, uttered by hounds claiming the fox's line. Beyond the pale of hounds' voices the Chaseworld tapers off into silence, defining an outer space.

Inscribed as "music," the voices help to cancel ordinary time and space. Yi Fu Tuan observes:

> Music can negate a person's awareness of directional time and space. Rhythmic sound that synchronizes with body movement cancels one's sense of purposeful action, of moving through historical space and time toward a goal. . . . The idea of a precisely located goal loses relevance. (1977:128)

(In foxchases, of course, the goal is imprecisely located—the fox keeps shifting the center.) Hunters engrossed in the Chaseworld must reorient to Ordinary time by checking their watches. When describing chases, hunters commonly note the exact time that the hounds jumped the fox and the time the chase ended; these are, in short, the precise moments of departure from and reentry into quotidian time and space.

LH: They jumped the fox at five minutes to nine. (Foxchase, January 22, 1986)

NT: I picked her up at 5:19, still runnin' the fox. (Foxchase, January 25, 1986)

JE: We put the fox in his hole at two o'clock this morning. (Undated self-made recording)

But within the Chaseworld, time is internally plotted. The structured sequence of events, indicated by hounds' voices, helps to distinguish Chaseworld time from Ordinary time. Chaseworld time is reckoned in part according to the recurrent sequence of casting, trailing, jumping, running, and breaking. These points of activity, which do not correlate in any way with clock time, are used to organize events:

FT: As soon as they jump him, he'll go on that burnt ground. (Foxchase, March 17, 1979)

DT: When they get him warmed up he'll show himself. (Foxchase, January 25, 1986)

Through the music of hounds, the Chaseworld emerges as a world apart from the Ordinary, whose spaces it claims for itself. Like pheromones, acoustic communication establishes territory, dominating spheres by flooding them with sound. And through their hounds, hunters become the proprietors of this acoustic space, "maintaining authority by insistent, high profile sound" (Schafer 1985:90). The fox's line is materialized as real property, "owned" by the hound in the lead or "stolen" away by unscrupulous canine interlopers from behind. The voice of the hound in the lead is packed with aggrandizement: "I got it! I got it! I got it!" as Norman Taylor translated it.

Articulating the trail in time and in space, the hounds' voices are made to isolate events within the Chaseworld. Hunters claim that certain hounds vocally distinguish the "backtrack" (or "backfoot") from a track they can "move," the cold trail from the hot track, or the "miss" from the "hit" or "strike." Thus, for instance, Robly Champion's Fancy let him know when other men's hounds had the backtrack:

> On a backtrack the track gets weaker and the dog learns. I've had dogs that was bad on a backfoot and they got so they wouldn't take a backfoot. I had one by the name of Fancy, and nine times out of ten she'd take a backfoot, and after I run her for a couple years she'd never take a backfoot. If other dogs was there I used her. I'd turn her in there, and if she left these long howls out of her I'd know they had a backfoot. (Interview, April 1979)

As the canine players move around the forest, hunters anticipate and follow them, developing scenes that open and close with formal and dramatic devices.[4] These scenes are conjured or enacted both over the CB radio and in face-to-face interactions. When determining the course of the Chaseworld on the CB, the hunters open with statements like "Dogman, what's your 10-4?" and "Do you read me, Yellow Bird?" and respond with "I gotcha, Horsetrader," and so forth. The closings of these sequences are less formulaic, serving as stage directions, notification of where the hunter is going:

> NT: I'll go around to the Muddy Road then.
> JB: Alright. (Foxchase, January 25, 1986)

The truck is like a movable backstage from which hunters enter and into which they exit, the opening and closing of doors neatly bounding each scene. Hunters generally exit into their trucks with a comment about where they are going, a stage direction for the next scene. When approaching a group gathered together with their trucks, hunters and other witnesses may be dramatically welcomed onto the stage. Thus, when his

Figure 2.4. Bob Hayes, Alvin Stafford, Leonard Duffy, and Bud Anderson at the Sporting Dogs of New Jersey annual foxchase in Penn State Forest. Photo by Dennis McDonald, April 1991.

brother Freeman approaches the group, Norman announces loudly, "We got Freeman here now!" and on seeing his brother Harry, Norman declares "I gotta say hi to Harry here!" Or a hunter makes some sort of narrative comment about the proceedings. Thus Junie gets out of his truck and greets Leon with, "So you're runnin' the legs off of him, huh?" to which Leon responds, "They're runnin' good, Junie" (foxchase, January 22, 1986). And Milton Collins consistently addressed the group as "Ladies and Gentlemen," even when I was the only female present (foxchase, November 18, 1983). Of course, during their conversations hunters slip in and out of the present Chaseworld, attending to its past and future. Conversations often stray into such Ordinary affairs as the fall harvest, the winter hog butchering, deer season, the NFL playoffs, local and national politics, and the weather. When this happens, hunters reorient themselves to the present Chaseworld, their attention drawn back to it by shifts in hound voices.

PHASE 2. INHABITING THE CHASEWORLD
Having opened up the Chaseworld, the hunters begin to inhabit and enact it. Becoming absorbed in the animal activity, they adopt the perspectives of

the canine players and perform these to their audiences and to each other. Encircling the inner activity in their trucks and communicating by radio, they issue the Chaseworld in many voices.

As Chaseworld inhabitants, hunters become socially redefined, sharing in what Alfred Schutz terms a "cognitive style" distinctive to each finite province of meaning. According to Schutz, the cognitive style of the paramount reality of work includes the following features:

1. A specific tension of consciousness, namely wide-awakeness, originating in full attention to life.
2. A specific *époche*, namely suspension of doubt.
3. A prevalent form of spontaneity, namely working (a meaningful spontaneity based upon a project and characterized by the intention to bring about the projected state of affairs by bodily movements gearing into the outer world).
4. A specific form of experiencing one's self (the working self as the total self).
5. A specific form of sociality (the common intersubjective world of communication and social action).
6. A specific time-perspective (the standard time originating in an intersection between *durée* and cosmic time as the universal temporal structure of the intersubjective world). (1970:253–54)

As Chaseworld inhabitants, hounds direct their full attention toward the trail of the fox, hunters toward the music of the hounds (1). All inhabitants are engaged in making a foxchase and keeping it going, gearing their bodily movements into the outer world with that intention (3). Hunters subscribe fully to the laws of the Chaseworld, within which, for example, animals are cast as musicians, and hounds, governed by the same laws, eschew all quarry except fox (2). Within the Chaseworld the self of the hunter is an expanded self that incorporates his hounds. Taking on his Chaseworld persona, a hunter projects himself into a foxchase via his hounds (4). The Chaseworld exists in an alternate space and time, described by hounds' voices and experienced by hunters sharing the same flow of experience in inner time (6). Chaseworld inhabitants are caught up in the pursuit of fellowship, which hunters craft from the turn-taking of hounds and their own sociable talk (5). A weakening of or removal of any of these features causes a breach in the Chaseworld or engenders its total collapse.

Listening to the music of hounds, the hunters live through a vivid present together, immersed in the same flux of events in inner time. In some

Figure 2.5. Freeman Taylor, Bobby Emmons, and Donald Pomeroy listening to a chase in Lebanon State Forest. Photo by the author, March 1979.

respects, the hunters' inscription of hounds' voices as music is not metaphoric. There is no difference between the *durée* experienced by hunters listening to hounds and the *durée* experienced by those listening to a string quartet. Schutz observes that in the performance of a musical composition the inner times of composer, performer, and listener merge. Extending this model to apply to all communication, he writes:

> It appears that all possible communication presupposes a mutual tuning-in relationship between the communicator and the addressee of the communication. This relationship is established by the reciprocal sharing of the other's flux of experiences in inner time, by living through a vivid present together, by experiencing this togetherness as a "We." (Schutz 1970:216)

This is true in the case of foxhunting, wherein hunters both compose and listen to the performing hounds, through whom they share the same inner or felt time. What music accomplishes for musicians, hounds accomplish for foxhunters.

The music of hounds not only cancels quotidian time and space, it evokes and epitomizes an alternative to the structured hierarchies of every-day life. This unstructured model, typically produced in rituals, is termed "communitas" by Victor Turner, who describes it as a "communion of equal individuals who submit together to the general authority of the ritual elders" (Turner 1969:96). In the Chaseworld, of course, the position of ritual elder shifts. The ritual elders are the hounds in the lead and, by extension, their owners, who keep them there by keeping them in shape.

In foxhunting, where the alternative model for society is enacted by hounds, hunters "take the (animal) other" not only at the level of the individual, but at the level of the (pack) society. And "pack" is a term applied to humans as well as canids: "Junie's the leader this year," said Donald Pomeroy, emerging from his truck to join his colleagues at a Chaseworld juncture. "Junie's the leader of the pack. Junie's been runnin' ten times more than I have this year. I missed a whole month" (foxchase October 22, 1983).

The music of the hounds dissolves the boundary between the selves of its human listeners and the selves of others, both animal and human.[5] In the Chaseworld, the minimum psychological unit is a hunter plus his hounds. The communal pack of hounds carries the community of hunters, epito-mizing their unity in the single sound it produces. Listening, the hunters dramatize their immersion in the same flow of experience, jointly construct-ing the animal scenario:

> DT: He come out, hit the blacktop road, and run up the road a ways to try to
> HS: outfox the dogs.
> DT: Yeah, that's what he's tryin' to do, yeah. (Foxchase, January 25, 1986)

The ability of foxhunters to adumbrate and complete each other's utter-ances without missing a beat is a hallmark of the shared understandings that distinguish them as a community, co-inhabiting a unique time and space:

> JB: Now, what he's done before, he goes in and fools around in there, and then he'll come back. And where he's gonna come out is
> DT: anybody's guess.
> JB: Yep. (Foxchase, January 25, 1986)

As Chaseworld inhabitants, the hunters anchor themselves in the sensibilities of hounds and foxes, losing awareness of themselves as makers of hounds and as listeners and interactants in the outer spectacle. A hunter's capacity for absorption in the animal activity hinges on his intimate knowledge of the hounds. "I don't get no kick out of it unless I know the dogs," said Freeman Taylor (foxchase, March 17, 1979).

"You have to raise 'em from a puppy," said Donald Pomeroy. "Get to know each one's personality" (foxchase, November 15, 1980).[6]

Inhabiting both foxes and hounds, hunters report on the interior states of the canine players, translating the hounds' messages with authority and implanting thoughts and intentions in the minds of foxes as well. "Old Blue says 'Look out now, he's goin' back,'" said Jack Davis, listening from his truck (foxchase, January 5, 1981). And John Earlin, speaking of a fox under pressure says, "He has to do something. He has to do something very desperate" (foxchase, November 15, 1980).

Hunters also identify with the mental states of hounds and foxes in speaking to or about them: "Them briars'll dump ya," said Norman to Maggie, picking her up when she got "thrown out" of the chase (foxchase, January 25, 1986).

"He's listenin' the other way for the dogs," observed Freeman Taylor of a disoriented hound. "That's what happens when you get old," replied Donald Pomeroy (foxchase, March 17, 1979).

"Whoop! C'mon! The dogs must think I'm crazy," said Norman, during a cast. "See if I can't find a track down in here. Whoop! Go on Till!" (foxchase, January 22, 1986).

"What do you smell Mary?" inquired Leon Hopkins of a hound (foxchase, January 22, 1986).

"Hot damn, fox!" exclaimed Norman on another occasion, in surprise at a vulpine maneuver reported by the hounds (foxchase, October 22, 1983).

Hunters also animate the canine players through voice throwing, through the use of what Goffman calls "say fors" (1974:534–35) whereby they narrate the Chaseworld from the hounds' perspective. Thus Milton Collins, speaking for his dog, said, "We don't like that old track. That fox traveled four o'clock this afternoon" (foxchase, November 18, 1983).

Since in the Chaseworld the self of a hunter includes his hounds, hunters conflate human/hound identities within a single pronoun: "I hit a hot-track," "I was runnin'," "Junie dumped out with me," "We . . . listened to Norman," "My dogs and Ben got in." Here the pronouns and proper nouns pivot between selves and worlds (Young 1987:231), providing hunters with yet another way to perform within the animal activity.

Similarly, hunters align audience perspectives with those of Chase-world characters by stacking them together in pronouns. Thus Norman invites his audience to share his perspective through the use of an omnibus "you":

> after you're around 'em enough, and hearin' 'em and whatnot you can tell just about every dog that's runnin' if you just happen to hear 'im yell by himself at a certain time, yeah. (Foxchase, January 25, 1986)

Hunters also make the Chaseworld available from the dog's point of view. Thus Norman helps his audience to achieve a canine perspective through second person pronouns that pivot between human self and animal other:

> he's [the dog] gotta get up underneath him and get him runnin' hard, and then you gotta outwind him. You gotta outrun, you gotta have more wind than the fox has. (Foxchase, August 11, 1982)

Similarly, in describing the reputations of dogs among dogs, Leon Hopkins briefly enters the society of dogs, taking his listeners with him:

> The dogs all know—they know each other, if you're kiddin' or not, you know. Some of 'em's anxious and they bark anyway so they don't pay any attention to that one, till they know for sure that one of 'em barks that they can depend on. (Foxchase, January 22, 1986)

The "you" in "if you're kiddin' or not" enfolds audience, hunter, and hounds. The "you" in "you know" returns the audience to itself. Through this device Leon expresses the shared understandings of the group and invites his audience to partake of some of them.

As musicians playing at a dance may shift from center stage to background in the awareness of the dancers, so do the dogs in the hunters' awareness. Once the hounds are running, the hunters drift into small islands of jocularity, and the singular focus required to lauch the Chaseworld dissolves into a melee of kidding around and "dogtalk" (a form of discourse to be considered in Chapter Four). Hunters so engaged do not entirely lose awareness of the dogs, any more than dancers lose awareness of the music coordinating their movements. Rather, they endeavor to keep the human spectacle loosely stitched to the current foxchase through narrative remarks about the dogs or the fox. When the dogs move out of hearing or change their notes in any way, the hunters' attention fuses again, reverting to the foxchase at hand.[7]

PHASE 3. THE CLOSING SEQUENCE

Chaseworld closure is indicated either when the hounds lose the fox or the fox shows signs of fatigue. In the latter instance, hunters break the hounds from the trail in order to save the fox. In summoning hounds out of the Chaseworld the hunters use nonlexical commands, reestablishing the hounds' subordinacy, cracking whips against the road and harshly hollering: "Hyeah! Hyeah! Whoop! Whoop! Cah! Cah! Cah!" and the like. In the same harsh tones, hunters may also address their hounds in English at this point, ordering them to "Get in the truck!" and so forth.

Hounds have been moved from the freedom of the trail to the confines of the trucks, but the order of everyday life has yet to be fully recovered. Shreds of the communion of hunters and packs established by the chase remain to be tidied; hounds must be sorted, farewells taken. Once the hunters are rejoined with their own individual packs they begin to exit the Chaseworld. The "10-4" of CB parlance closes out the post-foxchase fellowship. Having shed his CB identity but still traveling together with his dogs, each hunter drives homeward, where he backs his pickup to the kennel gate and ushers the dogs out of the trucks into their pens to be fed and watered. Now the dogs, considerably enervated since morning, drop from the truck, landing limply on legs that offer reluctant support. For a day or two they will rest, replenishing themselves for another chase. Closing off the Chaseworld from the Ordinary as he shuts the gate to the pen, the hunter invokes the final separation between residents of kennels and residents of houses, reinstating all components of the Chaseworld to their proper positions in everyday life.

Chaseworld Frames

The Chaseworld is illuminated from both inside and outside through shifts in perspective. Hunters hop briskly from one point of view to another, traversing levels of abstraction, moving backward and forward in time; now considering the Chaseworld from the point of view of dog, fox, or hunter, now from the perspective of the audience; now identifying the edges of the soundscape, now translating a message from within; now intent on conjuring, now attending to the means of conjuring. When

Figure 2.6. Sorting the hounds. Above, from left: Norman Taylor, Nick Harker, Jim Giglio, and Harvey Baker, Jr. Below, Jim Giglio transfers a hound to his truck from Norman Taylor's. Photos by Dennis McDonald, January 1989. Courtesy of the American Folklife Center, U.S. Library of Congress.

necessary, they shift from absorption to abstraction in order to orient each other and their audiences to the proceedings. Through orientations they supply whatever information is necessary to impart a full understanding of the players and events. Through evaluations they endow events with meaning, coaching their audiences on how to respond properly to what is transpiring.

Hunters can exit and reenter the Chaseworld at any point during a foxchase, and these passages have nothing to do with their ability to hear the dogs. They can attend to the Chaseworld while not hearing, or disattend it while hearing. Of course, when attention to the Chaseworld lapses, the realm vanishes (Schutz 1973:252) until, through orientations, hunters reinstate it.

Here I would like to orient the reader to some of the transcription devices used in this and following chapters. To illustrate the hunters' orchestration of the Chaseworld through their talk, I have marked the appropriate frames and boundaries of the Chaseworld and indicated other aspects of conversational talk with these symbols:

Initials plus : = abbreviation of speaker's name
Capital letters = start of utterance
[= simultaneous utterances
— = interruption

Often the speakers' utterances run together in their jointly constructed commentaries, with one speaker furnishing a quick comment in the space of another speaker's pause. In such cases, in an effort to preserve some sense of the hunters' conversational rhythms, I have omitted punctuation at the end of one speaker's remark and have not capitalized the beginning of the next speaker's remark.

ORIENTATIONS

The hunters draw attention to the Chaseworld by narrating it, largely through brief statements like "Junie's left dogs out"; "They've got him straightened out now"; and "That fox's been here last night sometime and they smell it goin' up the road." These narrative clauses are deeply situated in an elaborate framework of orientations and evaluations whereby the hunters stitch the Chaseworld to its immediate setting, making it relevant to its audience, whose interest and attention they continually monitor and manage.

Orientations highlight and bridge the gap between the Chaseworld and the Ordinary. Whether employed in foxchases or in stories, orientations connect Chaseworlds to particular occasions, making the Chaseworld accessible to the audience. Through orientations, hunters heighten the audience's appreciation for the Chaseworld while continuing to enhance, test, and verify their own shared understandings.

Orientations supply information about time, place, person, and situation, at just those junctures when authors deem such information necessary (Labov 1972:364; Young 1987:174). Hunters use orientations to map the Chaseworld onto the world of the Ordinary, as when, for example, Norman Taylor alerts an audience consisting of myself and Caroline, his wife, to the implications of weather conditions for the Chaseworld:

[Ordinary]
> NT: You know, it mighta rained up here the other night but it's still dry in the woods.
> CT: Oh yeah, I can see the dust.

[Orientation to Chaseworld]
> NT: And that makes it hard runnin'. That's why I say you're better off goin' out in the morning when you get a little moisture on the ground. (Foxchase, August 12, 1982)

On another occasion Norman pulls Donald Taylor and Hank Stevenson back into the Chaseworld when they stray into a discussion of the weather by apprising them of its potential impact on the Chaseworld outcome:

[Ordinary]
> DT: It wasn't s'posed to rain 'til afternoon.
> HS: Weatherman's wrong again.
> NT: Yep. It's spittin' rain now.

[Orientation]
> But you know, that ain't gonna help that fox any if they get up underneath him. He'll get wet and it's not gonna help him a bit.

[Ontological orientation]
> What they do—they'll tire him right out by steady runnin' him and if it gets too wet, and he gets too tired, and his coat gets wet and gets heavy, they're apt to catch that darn fox right in here. (Foxchase, January 25, 1986)

Attaching the Chaseworld to the occasions of its conjuring, foxhunters orient each other and their audiences to Chaseworld person, time, and place, and to their own "background expectancies" (Garfinkel 1973:21) through orientations that are ontological, spatial, temporal, and personal (Young 1987:49).

Ontological Orientations
Ontological orientations present the Chaseworld as a realm governed by its own laws. They deliver information about Chaseworld reality, revealing truths and behaviors endemic to the Chaseworld, disclosing the natural facts of life that Chaseworld inhabitants take for granted.

> FT: I think them dogs are in here.
> MH: When you hear them it makes you want to see the fox.
> [Ontological orientation]
> FT: When they get a fox tired out playin', when they get to runnin' him real hard, you can see him a lot of times twenty or thirty times right quick—they run back and forth. (Foxchase, March 17, 1979)

Anyone can request an orientation, which is something I routinely did as an ethnographer:

> MH: What kind of wind is it today?
> NT: I think it's
> HS: East
> NT: an east wind, yeah.
> [Ontological orientation)
> That old saying "When the wind's in the east the dogs run least"—did you ever hear that?
> MH: (shakes head)
> NT: "when it's west they'll run the best."
> HS: I always heard that.
> [Chaseworld]
> NT: Junie's let dogs out. (Foxchase, January 25, 1986)

Given my interest in discovering the Chaseworld's background expectancies, I requested a great many ontological orientations, in contrast to hunters, who do not need to articulate such shared understandings. Intent on building a "community of space and a community of time" (Schutz

1970:184), the hunters regale each other with orientations that are spatial, temporal, and personal.

Ontological orientations also reveal and reinforce shared understandings about the way dogs are supposed to behave, tying the behavior of dogs on a particular occasion to the normative Chaseworld in the minds of the hunters. On one occasion when the dogs began running, Norman said to the bystanders, "You can see now how these foxhounds operate. As soon as one of 'em makes a yell they all get bunched together, and that's the way they should run together, and then they should stay together" (foxchase, January 25, 1986).

Hunters also orient witnesses to distinctions between red and gray foxes, distinctions that emerge only in the Chaseworld:

[Chaseworld]
　　NT: This is a gray fox.
[Evaluation]
　　Typical.
[Ontological orientation]
　　If they was on a red fox, Mary, they would go three times as fast and they would—you could never stay with 'em runnin' a red fox today. (Foxchase, January 25, 1986)

And a red fox may be distinguished in terms of its age and behavior:

　　NT: Yeah this fox went out to 70 just about. He went out to the airport. Went right down the edge of the airport I imagine. He's a worthless fox.
　　MH: Wonder what makes foxes so different?
　　NT: It depends on—
[Personal orientation]
　　This is probably a real old fox's been here for a long while, Mary.
[Ontological orientation]
　　A young fox wouldn't do that to you.
[Personal orientation]
　　This is probably a real old fox been here a long while and he knows every inch of the ground, and every trick in the book. That's what he's runnin' those roads for. (Foxchase, January 22, 1986)

Ontological orientations make explicit the taken-for-granted aspects of Chaseworld reality, rendering visible its "seen but unnoticed backgrounds"

(Garfinkel 1977:22). As we will see shortly, evaluations of events as extraordinary provide another vantage point from which to view these backgrounds.

Spatial Orientations

Spatial orientations map the Chaseworld onto the state forest, plot the locations of its inhabitants, characterize the terrain, and develop an identity for Chaseworld places. Attempting to keep in earshot of their hounds, the hunters build an image of the foxchase in space.

Thus Yellow Bird, Dogman, and Horsetrader, who cannot see each other, position themselves around the canine soundscape, determine its location and direction, and devise a plan to keep themselves "in hearing." Spatial orientations set the scene, providing answers to the questions "Where is the scene unfolding?" and "Where will the next act occur?"

> NT: I'm gonna call Junie and tell him right where I'm at. Hey Dogman, you got a readin' on me?
> JB: I gotcha.
> NT: They're a long ways from here—right toward the blueberry patches. I can just about hear 'em.
> JB: Yeah. Well I'm headin' for Muddy Road. I'll see if I can get in hearin' of 'em
> LH: Yellow Bird they're gettin' close to the Blacktop, but I'm not sure.
> . . .
> NT: All right I'll come around to the Blacktop then. (Foxchase, January 25, 1986)

Hunters must orient spatially to each other as well as to the hounds, and in so doing they overlay the canine soundscape with a human soundscape emanating from trucks, CB parlance, and talk, centered around the pursuit of fellowship. Accordingly, hunters plot the perimeters of these soundscapes, those within the soundscapes conveying information to those on the outside trying to get in. Spatial orientations over the radio codify a hunter's location as 10-4:

[Spatial orientation]
> NT: Hey Dogman! What's your 10-4?
> JB: I'm at Middle Branch here, on the dirt road.
> NT: You're on the Bone Road?
> JB: Yeah. (Foxchase, January 25, 1986)

The shared environmental image that hunters carry in their minds, which they build collaboratively and to which they refer as though it were charted on paper before them, is a mentifact, which planner Kevin Lynch likened to "a body of belief or a set of social customs: it is an organizer of facts and possiblities" (Lynch 1960:6). The ability to orient in space is an admired skill, the hallmark of a good woodsman, according to Jack Davis:

> You know what I call a good woodsman? Johnny Earlin. Good woodsman. I'll tell you why. He can be on a gravel road, foxhuntin', and if he knew there was another gravel road—now this was at night—he'd say "I'll meet you over on the other road." I'll drive the truck and get over there and here come Johnny walkin' out. When you can get through them places in the night, then's when you're a good woodsman. (Interview, December 1980)

Such intimacy with the topography enables hunters to glean information about the chase from the voices of hounds. The shape of the terrain is conveyed in the volume and intensity of the sound. Said Norman:

> You can almost tell by the way they're runnin'. In the laps and whatnot it's hard gettin' through, and the noise will ease up. Or if they're runnin' in the cricks your noise, as soon as they get in good where all the dogs can bunch right back up again, then you get a good volume. (Interview, November 23, 1980)

Spatial orientations also relate Chaseworld places to the Ordinary, making those places more accessible to the audience. In advising his nephew, Donald Taylor, that a cranberry bog in the soundscape is owned by a mutual acquaintance, Norman Taylor fits the Chaseworld into the social and genealogical system of everyday life, fleshing out the landscape vocalized by hounds:

[Chaseworld]
    NT: They're goin' up to the South Branch bogs—
[Spatial orientation]
    there are cranberry bogs up there you know, right along the railroad
[Personal orientation]
    where Harold Haines used to have his. Old Bill Ridgway bought it and now Billy Poinsett owns it. (Foxchase, January 25, 1986)[8]

Spatial orientations can also make the Chaseworld more appreciable to its audience by tying it to other finite provinces of meaning. Thus Norman engages his nephew, who is not a foxhunter, in a brief discourse about the difficulty of running in briars.

Figure 2.7. Cranberry bogs and surrounding woodlands. Photo by Joseph Czar-necki, October 1983. Courtesy of the American Folklife Center, U.S. Library of Congress.

[Spatial orientation]
> NT: Did you ever rabbit hunt in there, Don?
> DT: I haven't this year.
> NT: There's some briars in there isn't there?
> DT: I run in there a couple years ago. Didn't get much.

[Ontological orientation]
> NT: You won't in them briars. They can crawl right around under-neath 'em.

[Chaseworld]
> There's Sailor right there. Now he'll bunch 'em up again.
> (Dog voice)

[Spatial orientation]
> DT: There?
> NT: Nope—see that dog's hit behind where he [Sailor] did.

[Setup]
> He'll [the fox] stay in there longer this time. (Foxchase, January 25, 1986)

Through spatial orientations, hunters resolve the problem posed by the differential distribution of information among themselves, matching their understandings of the terrain, disclosing and bridging the gaps among geographies of the Chaseworld, other provinces of meaning, and the world of everyday life.

Temporal Orientations

Hounds' voices are the timepiece of the Chaseworld. Hunters orient each other to a Chaseworld time uniquely structured in terms of its own sequences, frequencies, durations, and locations. Temporal orientations answer the questions "when?" "how often?" "how long?" and "how far behind?" and locate the Chaseworld in the present, past, or future. Hunters constitute changes in the frequency and duration of hound utterances as transitions between trailing and running, running and missing, and missing and striking again. Foxes begin to "show themselves" frequently when "warmed up," and a sense of the duration of time between showings helps hunters coordinate their movements around the state forest. These measurements of Chaseworld time do not calibrate with the Ordinary time from which hunters escape when they enter the Chaseworld. Though the outside listener may become easily disoriented in time, hunters effortlessly coordinate their experience of the Chaseworld, once inside it, without recourse to calendar or cosmos.

The reckoning of time in the Chaseworld coordinates relations among the Chaseworld's human and animal inhabitants. Thus hunters may plot time internally in terms of the Chaseworld sequence, as when one asks another, "Are they runnin'?" and the other responds, "No, just trailin'," or when hunters determine it is time to break the dogs because the fox is getting fatigued.

Hunters who are growing old together do not need to measure the passage of Chaseworld time in minutes or in decades. When Jack Davis alluded to "the twenty-one-fox time" hunters knew he was talking about a remarkable season four decades ago when they started twenty-three foxes and caught twenty-one of them. Hunters commonly locate Chaseworld events in time internally, as when Norman says, "I had a dog named Jackie then, a blue dog," or "That was before Johnny had his cabin, so you know that was a long time ago," or when he jogs Caroline's memory by telling her which dogs were involved in a certain episode:

NT: Don't you remember cows chasin' us out of the field that one night?
CT: (shakes head)
NT: We got laughed at about it, Elwood and I.

[Internal temporal location]
>   That's when I had King and Speck and Spotty. Remember I hung two
>   of 'em the first night down there? (Foxchase, August 12, 1982)

Temporal orientations may fit the Chaseworld to Ordinary time, as
when a hunter checks his watch to see what time the hounds started the fox
or how long they have been running. Hunters can use orientations to pivot
between Chaseworld and Ordinary time, pointing out, for example, that a
fox "showed itself" ten times in the space of an hour. Thus Freeman Taylor
locates a remembered Chaseworld in Ordinary time:

[Spatio-temporal orientation—memory]
>   FT: One time you could come up here
[External temporal location]
>   about ten years ago
[Chaseworld]
>   there'd be packs of dogs runnin', twenty packs of dogs runnin, wouldn't
>   it? Right here. And every one had a different fox. The dogs wouldn't
>   shift to another one, they stayed right together on 'im. (Foxchase,
>   March 1979)

Orientations to the past add time depth to the Chaseworld, bestowing a
history on its places and characters and building up identities for inhabitants and places out of disjunct moments in history.

[Chaseworld]
>   NT: Yeah, they're windin'.
[Spatio-temporal orientation—the past]
>   I've seen a time right through here, I've seen six different bunch of
>   dogs runnin'—
[Chaseworld]
>   CT: I hear a dog—
(Pause)
[Spatio-temporal orientation]
>   NT: six different bunch of dogs runnin' foxes in here. We had all kinds
>   of foxes in here.
[Internal temporal location]
>   That's the year they killed so many of 'em deer season. (Foxchase,
>   August 12, 1982)

Temporal orientations convey a sense that the Chaseworld has had its eras, eras in which certain kinds of things occurred, and that they no longer happen: "These foxes don't tree like they used to," said John Earlin (fox-chase, November 15, 1980). Shared understandings about the past endow each generation of foxhunters with a distinctive history, associated with Chaseworld patterns, characters, and places no longer in existence:

[Temporal orientation—frequency]
    NT: We hunted almost every day then, yeah
[Location in Ordinary time]
      about '45, '46.
    HS: You're talkin' about forty years ago though, boy!
    NT: You're talkin' about the good days then, yeah.
[Spatial orientation]
    You could run any place down there. Paul used to like to go over to Union Swamp there, yeah. Union Swamp was his great place he wanted to go, yeah.
[Temporal orientation—present]
    HS: That's all in cranberries and blueberries now.
    NT: Yeah, how 'bout that, yeah. Martha [place name] got all tore up, Jake Spong.
    HS: Yeah.
    NT: No more Jake Spong?
    HS: That's all in cranberries and blueberries now.
    NT: How 'bout that.
[Temporal Orientation—memory]
    Well that's where we used to run. Everything was gray fox there, yeah.
    (Foxchase, January 25, 1986)

Steeped in the same flow of experience, hunters share an inner time of remembrance and expectation, enabling them to anticipate and complete each other's thoughts:

    DP: I think they killed all our male foxes during deer season.
    FT: Huh.
[Temporal orientation—memory]
    There used to be a big black one
[Duration]
    he'd run all day right here

[Frequency]
>   back and forth across this road
> DP: with a white spot on his side. Nicest runnin' fox you ever seen.
> (Foxchase, March 17, 1979)

Temporal orientations also direct attention to the Chaseworld's near future. During foxchases hunters engage the audience's interest in the outcome through predictions about what the fox will do next, where it will cross and which dogs will be in the lead.

> FT: Soon as they jump he'll go on that burnt ground, burnt black as the ace of spades. (Foxchase, March 17, 1979)

> NT: Now watch. You're apt to see the fox here anytime go across. (Foxchase, January 25, 1986)

> NT: I don't look for him to leave here. He's gonna run right in this heavy stuff right now, cause he's probably a little tired and he's gonna stay in here and run, yeah. (Foxchase, January 25, 1986)

Participating in the Chaseworld *durée*, hunters collaborate in their predictions:

> FT: We oughta see this—see him when he crosses back here.
> DP: He'll either cross here or down where that water is down around the corner. (Foxchase, March 17, 1979)

Such predictions arouse in audiences the sort of expectations that hunters can fulfill,[9] hinting at what is yet unrevealed, nurturing in spectators a vital curiosity about the ending (Goffman 1974:506). Like storytellers, hunters must generate suspense. Unlike storytellers, however, hunters staging foxchases have to solve the problem of generating suspense without really knowing what the ending will be themselves.[10]

Personal Orientations

Hunters further consolidate the Chaseworld through personal orientations that tie together its inhabitants—the hunters, hounds, fox, and spectators. Personal orientations can be used to develop the character of a Chaseworld inhabitant, a character uniquely revealed through Chaseworld relationships. Thus, as we saw above, Jack Davis uses John Earlin's behavior in the

Chaseworld to illustrate his point that John Earlin was a good woodsman, and Norman Taylor illuminates the generous nature of a park ranger in terms of the ranger's solicitude for lost hounds:

[Personal orientation]

> NT: If he could, he would spend half a day up here, if you had to go home, and look for your dogs for you. He's gotta be here anyhow. He's just some nice fella. You don't have to worry if he's got your dog. You know that it's gonna be taken care of. It's gonna be taken over there, and if he's got his lunch, he'll wanna give it his lunch! It's the truth! That's the type of guy he is. (Foxchase, January 25, 1986)

Through personal orientations, hunters characterize hounds and foxes as well, inscribing each with an inimitable Chaseworld identity. "He was a real good dog, but he was a dog that would kind of slide along rather than jump," said John Earlin of a dog named Blockhead. And Leon Hopkins extolled his favorite hound, Maeve, who revealed her personality in the way she jumped a fox:

[Personal orientation]

> LH: She's one of the last ones I usually pick up. Independent a little bit. She's got a funny way: when she hits a trail she rares up on her back legs and barks right up in the air when she first hits. Yeah it's comical to watch her. If she struck out here in the road she'd rear right up in the air and bark and then put her nose back down again and go. (Foxchase, January 22, 1986)

Through personal orientations to the hounds, hunters disclose the ties to the animal players that entitle hunters to be authors. On one occasion, attending a chase in which his hounds did not participate, Norman heightened its relevance for his wife Caroline and myself through personal orientations to other hunters' hounds, revealing something of the genealogy of the collective pack:

> NT: You see that ringnecked dog there, Caroline?

[Personal orientation]

> His brother's that pure white one I got, the one I call Whitey—
> CT: Mhm.

[Personal orientation]

> NT: the one that barks all the time: "Bdu! Bdu! Bdu!" (Foxchase, August 12, 1982)

Personal orientations can also be used to deepen connections between the Chaseworld and its audience. Thus Norman cross-references an audience member to a feature highlighted in soundscapes, identifying him to another foxhunter through a connection to the Chaseworld landscape:

[Personal orientation]
    NT: (To Junie) You know Billy Poinsett? He's the guy owns the bogs up 'ere—South Branch. Billy Poinsett.
[Chaseworld]
    They're comin'. You can't hear today, can you? (Foxchase, October 22, 1983)

Personal orientations may bridge the gap between the Chaseworld and the Ordinary by identifying Chaseworld inhabitants as familiars from the world of everyday life, giving the audience to understand something about the social locations of foxhunters and what kind of people they are, that it, that they are local, related by blood or marriage, hard working, of modest means or well-to-do. Linking his relatives—his nephew, Donald, and his brother, Harry, who is Donald's father—to the everyday world outside of the forest as well as to himself, Norman Taylor moves outward from their genealogical locations within the Chaseworld to their social locations in the Ordinary:

    MH: Lotta red hair in the Taylor family
    NT: That's the Scandinavian in us I guess, yeah.
[Personal orientations]
    And Donald, he's head plumber at the State School. My brother he's retired from the Browns Mills Supply Company. He went to work there when he was eighteen years old until—I guess he was close to 70. That's how long he stayed with them. Only job he ever had in his life. (Foxchase, January 25, 1986)

And later on the same occasion Norman apprised his nephew Donald of another hunter's connection to a familiar place in the quotidian:

[Personal orientation]
    NT: (to DT) You know Charlie Jameson?
    DT: I saw him last Monday with you, that's the first I've ever seen of him.

NT: He lives right there over the Browns Mills Feed Store.

DT: Oh does he? I didn't know that.

NT: In that little white place there, yeah. (Foxchase, January 25, 1986)

Hunters may also orient occasional witnesses (like myself) to familiar spectators who aren't foxhunters, but who nonetheless belong there. Thus Bob Hayes draws my attention to the presence of a man from Chatsworth known as Possum Sooy, saying, "That guy is the grandfather of all Pineys. His name is Poss Sooy. He don't say much, but he was born and raised up here" (Foxchase, April 7, 1991). Others may be connected to the proceedings as relatives of the hunters. At another point Norman welcomes his brother Harry onto the stage: "I gotta say hi to Harry here!" and shortly thereafter when we are driving to the next scene he provides me with an orientation:

[Personal orientation]

NT: Harry's my brother and—you have no trouble tellin' he's my brother.

MH: He's your older brother, right?

NT: Yeah, he's older. Yeah Harry's retired. He's about 72 I'd say Harry is. And the other boy is his son—the big one's drivin' this truck—and the other one would be Donny's son. So Harry would be his grandfather.

[Evaluation]

So you can see it's stayin' right in the family, right on down. (Foxchase, January 25, 1986)

Knowing of my interest in tradition, Norman directs my attention to the intergenerational aspect of the sport, disclosing through an evaluation the point behind this genealogical digression, even as he returns our attention to the Chaseworld.

EVALUATIONS

Evaluation is a large part of the job of the Chaseworld inhabitant. Hounds are made to evaluate fox trails, while hunters evaluate hound utterances and Chaseworld conditions. Evaluations "disclose perspectives on, attitudes toward, or feelings about" conditions, events, and players in the inner event and outer spectacle (Young 1987:53). They assign greater or lesser importance to some Chaseworld aspects or events over others, establishing relationships among elements. Evaluations manage audience attitudes, telling audiences how they should feel and what to think about events that transpire in the Chaseworld. Through evaluations, hunters argue that the Chaseworld is worth witnessing and direct its audiences to understand events within it as comical, amazing, sad, embarrassing, exciting, and so forth.

Evaluations render the point of the Chaseworld explicit, making it clear that foxchasing is not about catching foxes (and in some sense never was) but about good dogmanship and fellowship. Evaluations draw attention to what is especially noteworthy in a given foxchase.[11] In recent decades the restructured ending has altered the point of the sport, which was to prove the worth of the dogs by catching foxes. Now that foxes are routinely spared, however, the worth of the dogs still may be proven in other ways. Hunters seize opportunities to demonstrate, for example, that the hounds are "dead game" and "straight fox," that is, that they don't run trash quarry; that they are easy to handle; that they "pack together" and don't "lounge" out of place.

Any of these aspects can be singled out in evaluations. Thus Norman Taylor observes that we're doing what we came here to do: to listen to hounds chase a fox, and chase it well.

[Chaseworld]
    NT: Well, they've all made 'em then.
[Evaluation]
    This is what it's all about [heh heh heh].
[Temporal orientation (duration)]
    This goes on all til the end of April.
[Ontological orientation]
    That's all they know is to run fox. That's their life. (Foxchase, October 22, 1983)

[Chaseworld]
    NT: Now if we'da been watchin' we'da seen that fox, he'da went across there. Probably he was a little ahead of 'em
[Evaluation]
    but that's what it's all about, huh Hank? Just stay here till they run the rest of the day or they lose him. (Foxchase, January 25, 1986)

Here Norman makes it plain that the point of foxchasing is more to listen to dogs chase foxes properly than to catch foxes. On another occasion he reveals the point of foxchasing as the pursuit of action, drawing attention to how that point was made in this particular chase and contrasting foxhunting favorably with another traditional activity in which he knew I was interested:

> NT: This is not like boatbuilding—this is *action*.
> MH: This is action?
> NT: Yeah—you've seen that the dogs don't run deer and they all run together. (Foxchase, January 25, 1986)

Hunters also use evaluations of uneventful foxchases to disclose the idealized realm. As Ortega y Gasset points out:

> Once understood in its exemplary form, the reality is also elucidated in its obscure, confused, and deficient forms. A person who has never seen a good bullfight cannot understand what the mediocre and awful ones are. This is because bad bullfights, which are almost all of them, exist only at the expense of the good ones, which are very unusual. (1972:87)

Similarly, foxhunters present the uneventful foxchase as a necessary feature of a system in which the good foxchases make the bad ones worthwhile. Milton Collins, observing that the hounds may be trailing backwards, offers a reflection on the importance of foxless chases:

> [Chaseworld]
> MC: It could be backwards too.
> [Evaluation]
> See, this is the sport of foxhunting. If you come out every time and started a fox, why I guess you'd get used to it. This way, why it's the fascination of tryin' to find out where that fox went. (Foxchase, November 18, 1983)

Thus he informs his audience that, while this chase is not a good one, it still merits our attention and theirs for the sake of the good chases.

Hunters evaluate other hunters' performances in terms of dogmanship and fellowship. Through evaluations, hunters direct attention to their abilities as dogmakers who keep their packs in shape or who can interpret hound signals correctly:

OO: Trouble is with him, he'll get one'll run halfway decent and then sell it to somebody.

OO: To tell the truth, X don't know whether he runs or not.

Hunters may also evaluate each other as good or poor sports in the circle of fellowship:

[Evaluation]
OO: He thinks he's the only guy that's got any dogs worth anything. If you got a dog that's runnin' 'im hard he'll complain, but he can have one that'll run the devil outa you, and that's all well and good. He thinks that's funny. But if *you* got one that'll run him hard he starts complainin' to you.

Hunters insert evaluative frames wherever they are deemed necessary for clarification:

[Evaluation]
LH: I've got a good young bitch home that she run deer with me. Junie beat her. I don't know whether she'll run another one or not, but I'm not takin' her. I told Jake I wanted another good one. I said I'll pay the difference.
[Personal orientation]
She's one of the young bitches, a pretty little bitch. She run deer after they come out of the Beaver Dams the other day.
[Chaseworld]
NT: They're right in the hearin' of us.
[Spatial orientation]
I'd say they're right where the water's at.
LH: Yeah.
[Evaluation]
NT: Now there ain't no simpleness into 'em. When we want 'em to holler—
[Chaseworld]
now he's on it.
[Temporal orientation (future)]
LH: He might double around and come back here yet.
NT: Yeah.

LH: He hadn't gone out this way.
[Spatial orientation]
    NT: Where'd he cross? Right by the bridge?
    LH: Just on the other side.
    NT: Just on the other side?
    LH: Yeah.
    NT: Between there and the old road.
    LH: Yeah.
    NT: Yeah. (foxchase, January 25, 1986)

In evaluating their dogs, hunters endeavor to show that their hounds are worthy of running with the pack, and moreover that they are not only law-abiding members but leaders who help to set the standards and who deserve to succeed. Deer dogs and babblers are not likely to succeed, and "cheaters" don't deserve to. By extension, hound characterizations justify the hunter's continued position as a Chaseworld character himself.

Foxes are also evaluated, and fox evaluations reveal a margin of disorder within which foxes are expected to perform. In challenging the Chaseworld order, foxes are expected to show intelligence, gameness, and endurance:

[Evaluation]
    NT: Well that fox was worthless, but we got about an hour out of him I guess. (Foxchase, August 12, 1982)

[Evaluation]
    NT: This is a crazy fox.
    MH: A crazy fox?
    NT: Yeah, that runs like this.
    MH: Does he have a name?
    NT: If I called him a name it'd be a bad name. It's not a good fox to run. (Foxchase, January 22, 1986)

[Evaluation]
    NT: It's a wild fox anyhow, yeah. He's a wild one, he don't like to stay in one spot. (Foxchase, October 22, 1983)

    NT: It's been a good fox to run. He showed himself a lot of times, and he's tired. (Foxchase, January 25, 1986)

Chaseworld evaluations elucidate what is being enacted, whether by hounds, foxes, or humans, imbuing the realm with meaning. The pack with "no simpleness" enacts intelligence; the hound that keeps dogs together enacts leadership. The hunter who complains when his dogs are bested enacts poor sportsmanship. The fox that is too disorderly enacts insanity. Through evaluations hunters summon forth and contemplate a full range of positive qualities embodied in human and hound behaviors: technical skill, team spirit, generosity, honesty, good judgment, discipline, sanity, and so forth. The corresponding negative qualities are also played out: lack of skill, poor sportsmanship, stinginess, dishonesty, stupidity, laziness, and so on.

Hunters continually monitor the presence and quality of fellowship. "It's a sport where you have fellowship," as Norman put it, speaking as omniscient author. "And everybody gets along and they enjoy it. You could have some old grump here and not enjoy it and it wouldn't be fun no more" (foxchase, January 25, 1986). Hunters may be given good marks in fellowship, poor marks in dogmanship. Because the two are inextricably linked, low marks in either can disqualify a participant. Thus the hunters evaluate the cast of characters, determining who's in, who's out, and why. Norman Taylor commented to Leon Hopkins, "It's a shame old Piggy wasn't here today" (Foxchase, January 25, 1986). And on another occasion one hunter remarked of another, "It's a shame he keeps the kind of hounds he does, because he's a lot of fun."

Shifting their attention away from the Chaseworld, hunters become aware of themselves as social interactants in the outer spectacle engaged in fellowship, whose abilities to sustain the reality are subject to evaluation. In the following exchange, Hank Stevenson confesses to having missed seeing the fox, a lapse in attention that makes him a prime target for teasing:

[Spatio-temporal orientation]
    NT: How far was the dogs—when they come through there, how far was the dogs behind him?
    DT: They wasn't a minute behind him. No they was close.
    HS: I'm not sure. They said they seen the fox. I didn't see it.
    NT: You haven't seen it yet?
    HS: No!
[Evaluation]
    NT: You better get those glasses changed, Hank!
    HS: Haven't seen the fox yet.
    NT: Change those glasses! Mary, let's ride back there.

[Temporal orientation (future)]

I'm gonna get in hearin' of 'em.

[Spatial orientation]

DT: Where you goin'?

NT: Right to the other side of Leon, over in the woods. (in truck)

[Evaluation]

NT: Yeah, foxhuntin's—this is what it's all about—good fellowship, where you can kid and nobody gets mad at each other. (Foxchase, January 25, 1986)

Framing the Chaseworld from the edge, and reporting on it from the center, hunters orchestrate their reality. Through such shifts in their awareness they erect and sustain the Chaseworld, now enacting it from within, now constructing it from without, fussing with matters of form, bouncing from one perspective to another and back and forth across realms.

Notes

1. Gregory Bateson writes that "the analogy of the picture frame is excessively concrete. The psychological concept which we are trying to define is neither physical nor logical. Rather, the actual physical frame is, we believe, added by human beings to physical pictures because these human beings operate more easily in a universe in which some of their psychological characteristics are externalized" (1955:47).

2. Erving Goffman writes that the markers, which he terms "brackets," separating collectively organized activity from surrounding events serve to differentiate the activity in time and space. He points out that, like picture frames, these brackets are actually between realities, paradoxically belonging to neither world yet to both (1974:251–52). Goffman's brackets are the equivalent of what Katharine Young calls "boundaries," and which she distinguishes from "frames": "Boundaries locate the literal or physical borders between realms. Frames locate their conceptual limits. Events are bounded; realms are framed. Or, more precisely, events are framed as to their realm status" (1987:22). Young's view clarifies the nature of "orientations" and "evaluations," which William Labov identifies as elements of narrative structure. Young's elaboration brings the structural elements more sharply into focus as framing behaviors.

3. Victor Turner distinguishes "true ritual," which "transforms" its initiands, from "secular ritual," which he says "indicates" and celebrates the status quo. The liminal process, he argues, is an "antisecular" one, though as he points out, he has "found it fruitful to extend the notion of liminality as metaphor beyond ritual to other domains of expressive cultural action" (1980:157).

4. These are akin to what Goffman terms "internal brackets"—a way of

distinguishing "time-in" from "time-out" (1974:260). However, time spent in traveling from one site to another is not time-out as much as it is time apart.

5. Mihaly Csikszentmihalyi refers to this experiential state, common in various forms of play, as "flow," a condition experienced as "a unified flowing from one moment to the next, in which we feel in control of our actions, and in which there is little distinction between self and environment; between stimulus and response; or between past, present, and future." The condition "is made possible by a centering of attention on a limited stimulus field" (1975:43, 47). He points out that the autotelism of the flow process raises it "to a central position in the hierarchy of human behaviors" (1975:55). Csikszentmihalyi's psychological study is based on descriptions of the flow experience offered by interviewees. The present ethnomethodological study documents the hunters' actual shifts into and out of the flow state that they are trying to sustain.

6. Hounds are shaped by human intentionality, by what Csikszentmihalyi and Rochberg-Halton call "the investment of psychic energy of their interpreter" (1981:14). In this view, hounds are not mere expressions of self, since as Csikszentmihalyi and Rochberg-Halton further observe, "the things one uses are in fact, part of one's self; not in any mystical or metaphorical sense, but in cold, concrete actuality" (1981:15).

7. This centering of spectacle around the animal enactment is characteristic of ritual, which Turner describes as "a synchronization of many performative genres . . . often ordered by a *dramatic* structure, a plot, frequently involving an act of sacrifice or self-sacrifice, which energizes and gives emotional coloring to the interdependent communicative codes which express in manifold ways the meanings inherent in the dramatic leitmotiv" (1980:157–58).

8. For an insightful study of the fit between landscape and genealogy and the discourse that constitutes this fit, see Allen 1990.

9. As Roger Abrahams notes, citing Kenneth Burke: "enactment involves an 'arousing and fulfillment of desires,' desires occasioned by the anticipation built into the intensive form and experience itself, desires conditioned by the promise of fulfillment in which the audience is 'gratified by the sequence'" (Burke 1968:143, cited in Abrahams 1977:97).

10. Chaseworlds conjured up in stories have endings known to the storyteller, who can excite curiosity and sustain attention through foreshadowings. Goffman points out that in everyday life the possibilities for prefabrications, setups, and "playing the world backwards" are limited, something that distinguishes the world of everyday life from fictive realms lodged within it (1974:506–7). It is partly because foxchases are "more narrowly organized" than the world of everyday life that the Chaseworld can unfold as a drama structured from the beginning in terms of its outcome. For while foxchases rely to a degree on uncertainty, this uncertainty remains only partial. As Seymour Chatman observes of uncertainty in drama, "At best it must be a partial uncertainty: the end is certain, all that is uncertain is the means. (A parallel with bullfighting: the bull must finally die, but how he dies is the question)" (1978:59).

11. William Labov writes that evaluation functions in narrative as "the means used by the narrator to indicate the point of the narrative, its raison d'etre: why it was told and what the narrator was getting at" (1972:366).

3. Inscribing the Stage and Its Players

> No "forest" exists as an objectively prescribed environment. There exists only forester-, hunter-, botanist-, walker-, nature enthusiast-, woodgatherer-, berry picker- and a fairytale-forest in which Hansel and Gretel lose their way.
> —Werner Sombart, cited in von Uexküll (1980:29)

PHYSICAL NATURE IS attached to myriad socially constructed realities through inscriptions. The variety and nature of these inscriptions bear careful investigation in public settings where realities like the Chaseworld are hidden, wedged in among countless others. Anchored in the same physical spaces of the state forest, the Chaseworld jockeys for position with the worlds of deerhunters, dog-sledders, trappers, dirt bikers, all-terrain vehicle users, hikers, campers, scientists, and growers who, under a lease agreement with the state, cultivate the cranberry bogs and blueberry fields.[1]

The very boundedness of the state forest helps to heighten the distinction between the many realities to which it must be receptive and the world of everyday life. The state forest, the point of departure for multiple provinces of meaning, is itself an environmental enclave, a "point of separation from the rest of the world," as Maurice Natanson explains, writing of parks in general:

> in it we are reduced from the business world, the academic world, the realm of other worries. We go to the park for greenery and release, for a soothing contemplation, and for love. . . . The brackets of the park make possible what is akin to artistic awareness: a reflexive consciousness that momentarily isolates the park from the huge givenness of reality and permits the artist to achieve a fresh mode of cognition. (1962:83)

"When I'm up in the woods," said Ann Davis, speaking from her home in Browns Mills, "I forget about this place here" (interview, November 14, 1980). As a point of separation, the state forest provides a place, like the one requested by Archimedes, where hunters may stand in order not so much to move the world as to invent and inhabit a new one, enabling them to reflect upon the world they are temporarily vacating. Within the state forest, alternate realities like the Chaseworld open the forest's fixed quantity of land out into a limitless frontier. The forest becomes, in Einstein's terms, "bounded but infinite."

This chapter takes a closer look at how foxhunters inscribe the Chaseworld onto the Ordinary, shaping it through inscriptions that are physical as well as mental and that distinguish and pivot between the fictive realm they are producing and the world of everyday life they are suspending. Onto the landscapes of childhood and family, the settings of work and home, and the blank spaces of the designated wilderness, foxhunters map the Chaseworld. Shaping the landscape to accommodate trucks, foxes, and hounds, they mark its spaces with signs, assigning its flora and fauna to classes and "holding them there by rules" (Douglas 1973).

Within boundaries that are spatial, temporal, and social, the Chaseworld unfolds as a world governed by its own laws, a world in which alternative social and natural hierarchies are invented and played out. Endowing the ordinary terrain and its populace with a distinctive ontological status, hunters recast landscape, humans, and animals alike in Chaseworld terms. Through names and categories that subdivide things united in the Ordinary, and that lump together things ordinarily held apart, hunters consolidate the Chaseworld.[2] These distinctions and groupings are crystallized in the foxhunters' vocabulary, whereby separations and connections between things are invented and rigorously maintained.

Chaseworld props exist as enclaves within the Ordinary landscapes of home and forest, managed there as separate orders of event: hounds lodged within their kennels; trucks imprinted with images of the fox and outfitted with dog boxes and horns for summoning hounds; foxes sustained by feeding piles, which they surround with tracks that become portals to Chaseworlds. Woods, homes, and yards are rife with Chaseworld thresholds:[3] places engendered by Chaseworld incidents, some of them marked with signs; brush roads carved out to facilitate access to the soundscape; fox dens, some of them man-made; burial places of foxhounds; and hunting cabins, which serve as backstages for foxchasing and, as we will see in Chapter 6, stages for storytelling.

Chaseworld Topography and Toponymy

The state forest provides the space that Yi Fu Tuan says humans need in order to escape the confines of known worlds. "Open space," he writes,

Figure 3.1. Hound graves decorated with lilies. Photo by the author, October 1983. Courtesy of the American Folklife Center, U.S. Library of Congress.

"has no trodden paths and signposts. It has no fixed pattern of established human meaning; it is like a blank sheet on which meaning may be imposed" (1977:54). Transforming the forest into a stage for their enactment, fox-hunters endow it with a Chaseworld perspective.

Hunters inscribe various landscape features—burnt ground, tar roads, plowed lanes—from the perspectives of the animal players. "Pushcover," for example, is a kind of vegetation that slows dogs down in their pursuit of fox. "He's runnin' in the swamp now," said Norman Taylor, listening from the Blacktop Road. "It's real heavy huckleberry and ganderbrush swamp, yeah."

"What other kinds of swamp are there?" I asked.

"There's open swamps like your gum swamps and whatnot, but this is all heavy pushcover, yeah. Where dogs have to just push through it" (foxchase, January 25, 1986).

"Ganderbrush" is the local term for wet areas covered with leatherleaf. "Ganderbrush ponds, we call 'em," said Jack Davis. "Hassocks all through 'em," qualified his wife, Ann.

"You sink right down in that right up to your hips," said Jack. "Foxes generally know where there's a deer path through 'em" (interview, November 14, 1980).

Figure 3.2. The pawprint of Hector, a favorite hound of Joe
Albert's, imprinted on the front stoop of his "Homeplace."
Photo by the author, August 1982.

Hunters recast Pine Barrens landscapes in terms of what the fox can do
with them. The landscape features available within a given piece of the
forest are like a hand of cards dealt to the fox, who, according to hunters,
frequents settings that diminish its scent and enhance its lead, manipulating
landscapes to foil the dogs. "He won't go out in these oaks," said Norman,
"He doesn't have enough lead to go out in these oaks" (foxchase, January
25, 1986).

A briar patch is the gray fox's trump card. "That's the thing your gray fox does," said Jack Davis. "He likes to take you in the briars" (interview, November 21, 1980). Foxes can debilitate dogs in warm weather, say fox-hunters, by running up on the Plains where there is no water. Controlled burning, done by the state in early spring to eliminate brush that lets fires get out of control, leaves a charred landscape that overpowers scent. "If they get one [a fox]," said Freeman Taylor, "he'll go on that burnt ground so they can't run him" (foxchase, March 17, 1979). In winter the bogs, ponds, and swamps may turn to ice that foxes scamper across but that dogs negotiate with difficulty. "A gray fox," said Norman Taylor, "he'll take to these swamps and, if there's ice, which is in the swamps today, he can give 'em—he gives 'em fits, yeah, because the smelling's not that good in the ice, and they have a harder job runnin' 'im, yeah" (interview, January 22, 1986).

The landscape is not simply a static backdrop, but a dynamic player conspiring with or against the Chaseworld, and foxchases, combined with passing seasons, generate an array of landscape behaviors uniquely wit-nessed by hunters. "Every day it's different," said Norman Taylor. Land-scape features are viewed in terms of how they affect the soundscape. "The bad thing about plowed lanes," said John Earlin, "is that the dogs have to go single file—spread out so that the dogs in the back lose the scent and you lose the music" (interview, November 22, 1980). Cedar swamps, coupled with the right air conditions, enhance the music. "some days in the cedar swamps," said Norman,

> it's just a ring. . . . Like at night you go down and you holler "Yo!" and you hear it ring right down through the swamp. Well, that's the way with them dogs. Every now and then you get runnin' those right kinda nights and man, you'd be surprised. It just sounds like the whole swamp is ringin'. (Interview, January 24, 1986)

The places defined by the silences and soundings of hounds are not always verifiable. Yet listening hunters inscribe and inhabit them, witness-ing dogs and foxes in a stock comic routine anchored in putative land-scapes. "We stand on the road," said Milton Collins, "and there's a certain direction. Every time they hit that particular spot, he loses them. Now we think there's a big pond in there. He goes overboard, and swims across. About five minutes one dog will find his way around that pond, lookin' for this track, and hit it and go."

"Have you ever seen this happen?" I ask.

"No, haven't seen the pond. Too thick" (interview, December 12, 1980).

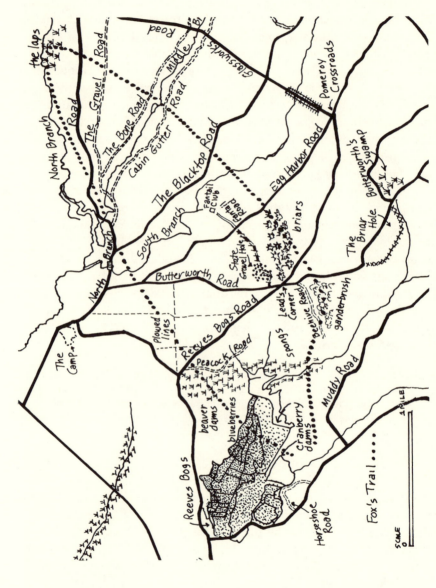

Map 3.1. The gray fox's trajectory through Chaseworld landscapes. Drawing by Donald Shomette and Kevin Hodges, based on a field sketch by the author. Courtesy of the American Folklife Center, Library of Congress.

Figure 3.3. Watching for the gray fox to cross Butterworth Road, Junie Bell and Norman Taylor stand poised to break the dogs from its trail. Photo by Dennis McDonald, January 1989. Courtesy of the American Folklife Center, U.S. Library of Congress.

Figure 3.4. Oscar Hillman and Jake Meredith casting their hounds along a plowed lane. Photo by Dennis McDonald, April 1991.

The forest is full of places articulated by hounds' voices, and named by hunters, who have over the years developed a distinctive Chaseworld toponymy. Names for places to cast hounds include "Chicken Line," "Feeding Pile," and "Bone Road," where hunters put out food to attract foxes. Such places are respected and interpreted by knowledgeable non-foxhunters as Chaseworld thresholds. "This is one of the sure signs that there were foxhunters around," said Christian Bethmann, superintendent of Lebanon State Forest, pointing to a pile of bones near the Goose Pond, "the bones from cattle or horses or whatever they can get their hands on."

Figure 3.5. Bob Hayes casting his hounds in Papoose swamp, where cedar "knees" and sphagnum moss sometimes combine to form "hassocks." Photo by Dennis McDonald, April 1991.

"What do they do with them?" I asked.

"Well, they'll dump piles of bones like that, with meat still on 'em," he explained:

> That will attract the fox, and that'll give them someplace to start their dogs from, because they'll know that the fox'll be there after dark, gnawin' away on those bones. They'll release their dogs around this area and let them scare the fox up and they're off and running. Sometimes you'll find just piles and piles and piles of bones. (Interview, September 16, 1983)

Names for places where foxes routinely lose dogs include "the Bad Place," "the Briar Hole," and "the Featherbeds," a quaking bog near Chatsworth. And a place called "Underwear" came into being because of the capture of a fox, according to Joe Albert:

> There was a place over in Warren Grove, and I went over there one time to hear guys' dogs, you know, and I said, "Damn if I ain't comin' over here some night." And I went over, and the first night I went there, they caught the fox, and I pulled a bush down on the cranberry bogs, and I hung a note. And there was a pair of winter underwear hangin' on this road where I caught it, you know. The guy musta got warm, and he took 'em off and hung 'em up. And I

put, "Caught fox by underwear," you know. And the guys laughed. They told me that so many times. They caught fox by Underwear. (Interview, August 12, 1982)

Such spaces, once distinguished, become important reference points in conversation.

"So you call that area "Underwear" now?" I asked.

"Yeah," said Joe Albert. "After that they'd tell ya, they'd say, "We was right where the Underwear was. We was runnin' one,' you know" (interview, August 12, 1982).

Burial places for particular hounds also serve as reference points. Milton Collins buried his favorite dog, Spike, in what is now known as "Spike's Field," an excellent place to start foxes. "He's buried," said Milton Collins, "where a fox crosses his grave" (interview, December 1980). Lead, the best fox dog that Norman Taylor ever owned, is buried in Lebanon State Forest, "where he run his first fox," at the edge of Butterworth Crossway in a place now referred to as "Lead's Corner."

"And any foxhunter that goes by knows where it's at," said Norman Taylor, "and they always say, 'Old Lead's buried there.' That's what we call it—'Lead's Corner'" (interview, January 22, 1986).

Explorers in a largely uncharted realm, foxhunters try to broadcast their discoveries and have them take hold in common parlance. Their territorial triumph is to have others recognize their places and make use of the names in everyday life—to make their reality so real that it transpierces the paramount reality of the forest.

The Chaseworld is also riddled with places that for many exist only in books and on old maps. The names of "forgotten towns" (Beck 1963) along the old Pennsylvania-Tuckerton Railroad—Buckingham, Pasadena, Woodmansie, Mount Misery, Martha, Mary Ann Forge and Webb's Mills—are actively used by foxhunters whose family memories reach back to an era when these towns were bustling. Though little remains in any of these locations to suggest that they were ever populous, in the conversation of foxhunters they are alive and pulsing with Chaseworld activity, touchstones to a regional history not shared by newcomers.

Insiders and Outsiders

The Chaseworld stage teems with a large assortment of creatures, some of which support the text and some of which are adversaries. Foxhunters recast and manage the forest's human and animal denizens according to whether they are key players, support players, trash animals, or threats to the Chaseworld.

For foxhunters, the forest is centered around foxes. In the past, some hunters were known to plant foxes. Rescuing them from farmers intent on destroying vulpine pests, hunters would inoculate fox pups against rabies and distemper. They would then place the pups in the care of feline wet nurses (called "putting them on a cat") and, when the pups were old enough, move them into woodland shelters, feeding them dog food until they could fend for themselves.

Hunters still provide for foxes in every way they can think of in order to persuade restless foxes to remain in the hunting territory. The men forage for fox food as opportunistically as wild parent foxes, placing within a fox's feeding range everything from road-killed animals to surplus jelly donuts. If foxes appear mangy, hunters spread "slop" oil around, claiming that foxes are smart enough to find it and treat themselves. Hunters note with approval indications that foxes have a goodly supply of small game to draw upon. Jack Davis once planned to support a tentative fox population by transplanting some rabbits that were bothering a neighbor's garden.

"It's in the law that you can't do that now," his wife Ann reminded him.

"Aw to hell with 'em!" Jack expostulated. "If you lived according to the law you'd die!" (interview, November 14, 1980).

Anything that is not fox, but might attract the interest of hounds is considered "trash": a threat to the Chaseworld's boundaries. Thus disparate animals in everyday life are lumped together and connected within this realm by virtue of their shared negative impact on it. Trash quarry include deer, rabbit, raccoon, and possum. A hound that pursues any of these is said to be trashing. Interestingly, English-style hunters call this behavior "rioting." Like the concept of dirt in Mary Douglas's formulation, terms like "trash" and "riot" imply two conditions, "a set of ordered relations and a contravention of that order. Dirt, then, is never a unique isolated event. Where there is dirt there is system" (Douglas 1966:48). Rabbits and deer fit into other realms within the state forest: rabbits are quarry for beagles; deer are the central figures in another important social ritual. The impact of deer on the Chaseworld is minimized by structuring them out of the foxhound's legitimate domain through training. Hounds that cannot be "deerproofed" are culled from the pack and given away to nonfoxhunters or sold to deerhunters who use hounds in parts of the country where the practice is legal.

In the Chaseworld, a special problem is posed by the ambiguity of "woods cats"—domestic cats gone feral. Not only do such cats compete with foxes for food, but a cat track, easily confused with the track of a gray fox, leads to travesty in the Chaseworld. Jack Davis reported:

> You go up there in the woods when there's snow on the ground, and you gotta be careful that you don't try to run the wrong thing. They look an awful lot alike, gray fox track and a cat track, an awful lot alike. I've seen a man get mad and cuss the dog cause it wouldn't go on, and here the goddam thing would turn out to be a damn cat!
>
> We had 'em up here one time, a woods cat way down by the Briar Hole. The guy run him up a tree, and I asked him, I said, "Well, did you kill him?" He said, "No." I said, "Why the hell didn't you?" Well, I'm going down through there one day, and I seen him cross the road, stood there lookin' at me, but he didn't go no further. I killed him right there. You know they gotta be livin' on games and birds—that cat was just as nice and shiny as anything you ever saw. (Interview, November 21, 1980)

While feral cats fly in the face of the Chaseworld order, they are not life threatening as are traps set for foxes, which can injure hounds, nor can they destroy the Chaseworld entirely, as could anti-fox or anti-foxhunting legislation. Such onslaughts from competing realities require a vigilant and ongoing defense.

Defending the Stage

Foxhunters must defend the Chaseworld stage and its animal players against competing realities that impinge upon it. Dirt bikers tear up the roads, making them impassible for foxhunters' trucks. Chain saws of woodcutters and the noises of air traffic muffle the music of hounds. Trappers intent on catching foxes snare hounds as well. Environmentalists and animal rights activists, Chaseworld enemies whom foxhunters ironically and derisively call "do-gooders," misread and destroy Chaseworld properties like man-made fox dens.

"Have you ever made a fox den?" I asked Jack Davis.

"I haven't, but *he* has," he answered, speaking of another hunter.

"They had one over in here," said Ann Davis, "and when they were puttin' through this conservation and stuff, they went and dug it out, and throwed it out. Now why would they do a thing like that?"

"The idea is that the fox can go down where they [the hounds] can't dig in to him," said Jack. "But then some of these guys find 'em, they take a shovel and dig right on back."

"Just to be ornery," said Ann.

"Break it up, throw it on top of the ground," said Jack.

"They think you're doin' it to catch fox," said Ann. "And you're doin' it to preserve 'em" (interview, November 14, 1980).[4]

Donald Pomeroy, battling a negative public perception of hunting, reported in outrage, "I seen a write-up in the paper where the do-gooders said, 'The hunters set the woods on fire so they can stand there with their guns and shoot the deer.' Did you ever hear anything like that?" (foxchase, March 17, 1979). Galvanized by the passage of a law permitting deerhunters to shoot fox during bow and arrow season, foxhunters formally organized the Sporting Dogs Association in 1986 in order to influence policies of the State Fish and Game Commission. Said Norman:

> They're tryin' to take more of our season away. They're allowin' another season for bow and arrow for fox. Now who the devil would want to kill a fox with a bow and arrow, for God's sakes? . . . That's the reason we got together. And it's not to be called any foxhunting, because you get the do-gooders against you then. The Sporting Dogs of New Jersey. (Interview, October 17, 1986)

The title "Sporting Dogs" contrasts with the "South Jersey Foxhunters' Association" of thirty years ago, in drawing attention to the sport's emphasis on hounds rather than on killing the fox, and reflects the rising tide of anti-hunting sentiment over the past several decades.

Before steel leg-hold traps were banned throughout the state of New Jersey in 1986, irresponsible trappers were also seen as Chaseworld enemies. Not only were trappers endangering hounds with steel leg-hold traps and snares, but they were harvesting foxes in which hunters had a proprietary stake. "I had baby foxes put out over there, and the damn trappers got 'em all," expostulated one hunter. "I'm scared to go out now because the traps—you can find traps there in the middle of the summertime!"

Foxhunters have become vigilant defenders of laws banning the use of steel leghold traps, first in Burlington County, and then in the entire state of New Jersey. A hunter reported to his colleagues during a chase:

> One dog got caught in a steel trap—a guy musta been just settin' the steel traps there. I went around and pulled 'em right up, throwed 'em in the truck. Great big old traps just like that. I heard the dog holler and I ran in there, it had him right around the foot. Right opposite Warren Grove. They got traps all over in

there. If he got one of my dogs I'd wrap it around his neck. (Foxchase, November 15, 1980)

Keeping the Chaseworld tidy and intact, hunters defend its order on multiple fronts.

Audiences

Foxhunting is not a spectator sport in the conventional sense. There are no bleachers or balconies, no roadsides or tall buildings from which onlookers may catch a glimpse of the proceedings. Yet foxhunting, as a staged enactment or ritualized performance of communal values, requires an audience, a reflecting surface that affirms those values (Myerhoff 1978:222). Foxhunters serve as audiences for each other, of course, but they also perform to those who, wittingly or unwittingly, happen to pass through the Chaseworld. Again the landscape serves as a resource, furnishing foxhunters with spectators.

Some spectators are members of the local community, who know that by tuning in to "the foxhunters' channel" on the CB they can find a foxchase. "A lot of guys that come in the woods know Norman and Freeman," said Donald Taylor. "You just hang around for a half hour listening to the dogs, and then you move on about your own business. Most of the people around here just like to hear the dogs run" (foxchase, January 25, 1986). But members of the audience are just as apt to be strangers who appear serendipitously, passing through on their way somewhere else, at work or at play, attending to other realms in the forest.

Sometimes the spectators are men at work. Joe Albert recalled opportunities afforded by the Civilian Conservation Corps, "native guys—diggin' the stumps outa the side of the road, makin' backwoods roads" while he and his buddies were foxhunting. "Them guys was trimmin' the rows all this while, see, and they're only about maybe a quarter mile from where the dogs was. . . . I'd show off a little, too. I'd go by them guys, you know" (interview, August 12, 1982). Such an audience provides hunters with yet another angle from which to imagine and evaluate the Chaseworld. "I bet they're wonderin' how we ever get all these dogs back," said Norman of one pair of onlookers. Accidental onlookers often reappear in stories as witnesses suitably impressed by the foxhunters' exploits, as skeptics whose conversion in the story is designed to disarm skepticism in listeners to the story.

The voices of hounds whereby hunters establish dominance over the landscape also serve as perceptual barriers that define the Chaseworld as a region from which outsiders may be barred. The inability of strangers to perceive hounds' voices as music is the topic of a popular anecdote often told to novice spectators. "I think I told you that one about the people from Pennsylvania," said Jack Davis, in my second interview with him:

> We stopped 'em, the dogs was runnin' close to a fox, goin' to catch it, goin' across 70. And we had to stop these people. And I was standin' there and I said "Boy ain't that music for your ears?" And this one guy said "I'd like to know how in the hell anybody could hear music with this goddam bunch of dogs yattlin' away!" (Interview, November 14, 1980)

The telling of such a traditional anecdote, well known to foxhunters and their regular audiences, requires an outsider audience, whose presence affords an opportunity for hunters to perform this joke to each other (Toelken 1979:112; Bauman 1986:18).

Other foxhunters, of course, provide the most cultivated and critical audience of all, for no one else can better appreciate what the hounds are doing. In stories, foxhunters commonly transform onlookers into witnesses who evaluate the proceedings. Casting another foxhunter as a witness adds authority to the account.

"See," said Norman to his wife Caroline and I during a foxchase, "I got a different horn for my dogs so I can call 'em with my horn. I got a mouth horn, and then I got one under here [the steering column] that's different."

"Leon's dogs wouldn't come to it?" I asked.

"Nope. Jakie—we was runnin' down on the Plains last year, and somethin' happened to the fox, so they lost it. And they was pickin' up dogs. And I was four miles from Jakie, and he had Lil and Becky. He couldn't catch either of 'em, you know, the scary pair?"

"Mhm," said Caroline.

"And they would stay around his truck, and somehow or other I blew my horn, and he said they cocked their ears up, and the second time I blew that, it was just like somebody shot them. They left him.

"And when I went around he says, 'What dogs!' I said, 'I got the two, Becky and Lil!' He said, 'Well them son-of-a-guns was with *me* here five minutes ago.' He couldn't get over how quick they got to me. But they knew my horn. That's what they was listenin' for" (foxchase, August 12, 1982).

The account, rendered to a pair of nonfoxhunters, depicts one hunter performing successfully to another, who can properly evaluate the performance. William Labov points out that this tactic of embedding evaluations deeply within the narrative is typical of "older, highly skilled narrators from traditional working-class backgrounds" (1972:373). The embedded evaluation, a hallmark of the deft raconteur, serves among other things to deflect charges of bragging and stretching the truth.

Social Identity in the Chaseworld

The Chaseworld's central players—hunters, hounds, and foxes—are diligently inscribed as Chaseworld characters, mutually defined, contrasted, and cross-referenced. Hunters liberally label themselves and their surroundings with images of their quarry. "My father's a fox man," said John Earlin's daughter, Ramona. Presenting themselves as fox men, hunters wear hats and belt buckles on which foxes are printed or engraved; paste fox decals on truck windshields, license plates, and mailboxes; sport fox figurines as hood ornaments and birdbath centerpieces; and display paintings, photographs, and figures of foxes in their living rooms, on letterhead, and on welcome mats.[5] And at the funerals of John Earlin and Donald Pomeroy, the floral arrangements on the caskets took the form of red foxes.

Hunters also inscribe each other with Chaseworld identities, embodied in nicknames and CB handles. The Chaseworld emerges as the locus of distinctive social identities. "Every name implies a nomenclature," write Berger and Luckmann, "which in turn implies a designated social location. To be given an identity involves being assigned a specific place in the world" (1967:132).

Most hunters possess nicknames that pivot between Chaseworld and Ordinary identities. These are often diminutive versions of their given names: "Webby" for Clarence Webb; "Johnny" for John Earlin; "Jakie" for Jake Meredith, Jr.; "Josie" for Joseph Anderson; "Junie" for Theodore Bell, Jr.; "Haysie" for Robert Hayes; and "Hubie" for Hubert Driscoll. These compressed names are indicative of the close social bonds existing among those who hunt together, bonds that frequently are underscored by familial ties.

Norman Taylor inherited his nickname of "Topsy." Norman's father, who was a champion top spinner, earned this nickname in his youth. It passed first to his son Harry in high school and eventually onto Norman, where it has settled to this day, despite Norman's professed inability to

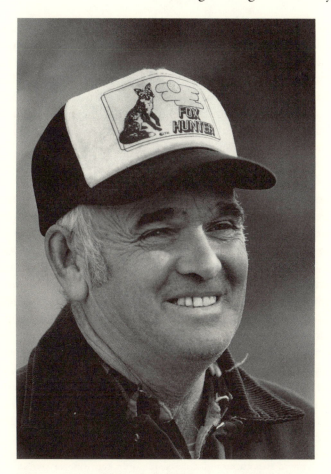

Figure 3.6. Theodore "Junie" Bell, Jr. of Wrightstown. Photo by Dennis McDonald, January 1989. Courtesy of the American Folklife Center, U.S. Library of Congress.

throw a top. Those who use the name "Topsy" are most apt to be locals whose biographies overlap for several generations, who are deeply rooted in and familiar with this Pine Barrens community. Locals who hunt together are often related by blood or by marriage, and their diminutives are borrowed from the Ordinary. Others may be given new diminutives. For example, impressed with James Fisher's habit of dipping snuff, Norman bestowed on him the Chaseworld identity of "Snuffy." "I gave him that name," Norman pointed out (interview, January 24, 1986).

In addition to nicknames, there are, as we have seen, CB handles that specifically relate to the Chaseworld. Through their handles, men graft animal identities onto their ordinary ones. Junie Bell, who keeps a large number of puppies is "Dogman," Wayne Giberson is "Blue Tick," and Gary Croshaw is "Redbone." George D'Andrade's great concern about canine cardiac parasites earned him the handle of "Heartworm." Still others are named for animal aspects of their quotidian lives: Leon Hopkins, who bought, sold, and boarded race horses, was called "Horsetrader." Jeff Powell, who raises hogs, is "Piggy." Jimmy Taylor, who did not own hounds but regularly attended, and who liked to talk, was "Blowfish." Some handles also conflate the identities of hunters with their pickup trucks. Thus Norman, who drove a Yellow Toyota when Donald Pomeroy named him, became "Yellow Bird." Donald Pomeroy, who drove a green Chevrolet pickup, was "Green Fox." Harry LaBell, who drives a gray pickup, is "Gray Fox." Donald Pomeroy dubbed Ted Goff "Brown Jug," for the brown pickup that Ted drives. Other names are plays on the person's given name and appearance. Nick Harker, whose abundant white beard resembles that of Saint Nick, is "Santa Claus," while Milton Collins, a Methodist preacher with a compelling stage presence, is known as "MC."

The hunters' behaviors within the Chaseworld furnish them with grist for inscribing each other as Chaseworld characters. The Chaseworld becomes a lens through which the personalities of its players are magnified. Thus Norman Taylor illustrates the extraordinary determination of a fox-hunting compatriot:

> He was a guy that if he wanted a dog, if you asked him two thousand dollars, he'd give you two thousand dollars. He only kept one or two dogs, and he wanted the best, and money didn't mean nothin' to him. If you had a dog and he wanted it, he'd get it. If you had a dog and he wanted it, he would just overpower you. (Interview, January 24, 1986)

And Herb Anderson, a foxhunter from Chatsworth, was described as a great guy who loved hounds so much that he would never sell one. "Had all his dogs buried right around his house," said Norman Taylor (interview, February 2, 1991).

It is this love of hounds that distinguishes hunters from nonhunters and particularly from women. Even though women regularly attend fox-chases, the Chaseworld is constituted as a male domain, to which women may relate in very proscribed ways. If women actually hunt they may be reinscribed as masculine.

"Why don't women foxhunt?" I asked Joe Albert.

"Oh, they don't like that," he replied. "Only that Society [i.e., English-style] races, that's all."

"They foxhunt with the horses," elaborated a friend of Joe Albert's, visiting with him on the screened-in porch at "The Homeplace," as Albert's cabin in the Forked River Mountains was called. "But that's all class, you know. Up on Haskells in Middletown Township."

"Don't they like to listen to the dogs?" I persisted.

"Oh, you'll find one or two of 'em," answered the friend. "There used to be a woman used to ride with her husband—"

"Brownie's mother, she used to gun through the woods just like a man," Joe agreed.

"I seen women deer hunt, quail hunt," said the friend.

"They gotta like to hear the sound of the dogs," said Joe. "To a man it's like music to his ears to hear that dog chasing. But to a woman it's different. Unless she really loves the dogs."

"But to a man it's music to 'im," said the friend, "and he knows what that dog's gonna do, and how long he's gonna run, and—I've sat up there and listened to them run for hours and hours on the back porch."

"So a woman doesn't get so involved with the dogs?" I asked.

Joe replied, "I've never seen a woman have dogs. Her husband would have dogs and she'd help him out, but I've never actually seen a woman with fox dogs" (interview, August 12, 1982).

The solidarity constructed in the sport is a distinctly male solidarity.[6] In the Chaseworld, women are by definition people who do not love dogs, to whom the hounds' voices are not really music. All the women I met on foxchases were related to foxhunters as girlfriends, wives, daughters, or granddaughters. The women referred to the hounds as "our dogs" and helped, when needed, to put them in the trucks. But they did not personally own or train hounds, and they did not partake of the competition and communitas that absorb the men in hounds. Their understanding of the proceedings was mediated by foxhunters.

The issue of gender, of course, raises the question of whether my own gender posed an obstacle to my interest in foxhunting. It merits noting that other women were often present, sometimes intentionally furnished out of consideration for me, during foxchases and interviews. It seemed to me that I was readily accepted as an occasional member of the audience, though an unusual one, given that I have no relatives who foxhunt in the Pine Barrens or anywhere else. The foxhunters knew of my general interest in the region's traditional culture, and of my affiliation first with a local high school and then with a national cultural institution. I had published articles, which I shared with foxhunters, on other local traditions, and a talk that I delivered on foxhunting for a local historical society netted further invitations to attend foxchases.

As I grew more familiar with the foxhunters' world, I realized that certain areas of this male world would always remain off limits. Such areas, however, were not essential to my investigation of how foxhunters constitute the Chaseworld. I found that foxhunters were generally eager to talk about their favorite subject, and their wives often prompted them to tell stories from well-known repertoires. My interest in their stories was not unwelcome. "I got some stories that you probably would like to record," volunteered John Earlin within minutes of my first introduction to him.

And foxhunters devised their own ways to account for my sustained interest in their sport, despite my gender and my paucity of foxhunting relatives. "My mother foxhunted," said Leon Hopkins when Norman Taylor introduced him to me. "She caught the biggest fox I ever saw" (foxchase, January 22, 1986). Robly Champion was reminded of a woman in Delaware who hunted foxes, but on horseback, in Chaseworlds where society is organized differently. "Mrs. DuPont," he said, "down to Delaware . . . she's a Master of Hounds" (interview, September 1979).

The Chaseworld grants glimpses of things arrayed in their proper places: men with their dogs, women with their men, nature with society, peers with their peers. This Chaseworld order may challenge, reorganize, and verify the social and natural orders proposed in ordinary life and in other finite provinces of meaning. A look at the relationship between English-style and working class foxhunting suggests that the different Chaseworlds are not islands unto themselves. Rather, the text of a gregarious pack of hounds in pursuit of a fox can be made to support diametrically opposed views of society. In working class foxhunting we find a radical rebuttal of English-style inscriptions; it is a model for the individual in society, and society in nature, that challenges the aristocratic model.

Dueling Chaseworlds: A Battle of Inscriptions

Both upper and working class forms of foxhunting feature domestic canids on the trail of a wild one, but the English-style hunters who "ride to" pedigreed hounds emphasize horsemanship, while the working class hunters who "listen to" unregistered hounds emphasize dogmanship and their ability to interpret from a distance events at the animal center. Both Chaseworlds constitute unique real estate ventures, impinging on all worlds anchored within hearing distance. But whereas English-style fox-hunters dominate the rolling countryside by riding over it, Pine Barrens foxhunters capture the land in a bubble of sound that shifts and flexes its way across the many surfaces of the forest, some of which include cranberry plantations owned, ironically, by the Pine Barrens version of landed gentry (Berger and Sinton 1985:31).

Through intensified language, costume, and gesture English-style fox-hunters inscribe the Chaseworld with the aristocrat's view of the ideally stratified society, positioning culture at the pinnacle of nature. The English-style hunters display the European notion of the proper relationship between nature and culture, moving culture out over the landscape. Working class hunters, in keeping with a more American notion, immerse themselves in nature. Pine Barrens foxhunters playfully invert the natural hierarchy, inventing a realm in which humans bear animal names and animals, named for humans, are made to enact the egalitarian values of the working class.

Amplifying the contrast through labels and anecdotes, participants dramatize a dialogic relationship between the two styles of foxhunting. According to one well-known anecdote, English-style foxhunters, referred to as "tally-hos" by Pine Barrens hunters, distinguish themselves by the language that gave them this nickname: "We say 'Tally-ho!' not 'There goes the son-of-a-bitch!'"

"They're the upper class," said Jack Davis, of Browns Mills. "We're the lower class" (interview, September 1979).

English-style hunters inscribe social hierarchy and propriety onto every aspect of language, costume, and gesture. A young woman who rides with the Monmouth Hunt Club told me:

> It's a very class-oriented situation. It's the hierarchy. You ride in sections. First comes the Master of the hunt, then the whipper-in and the Mistress of the hunt, and they are, as we used to say, "God Almighty in red." You must wear your uniform and it's a wonderful thing. It's class—you are a gentleman and a lady at all times, and you wear your proper habit, and your horse is properly rigged. (Foxhunt, November 20, 1980)

The "field," as the group of mounted men and women is called ("hunters" in this context designates horses), "rides to the hounds," following them on

Figure 3.7. Cubbing at Unionville, Pennsylvania. Photo by Toni Frissell, October 1953. Courtesy of the Toni Frissell collection, U.S. Library of Congress.

horseback. In contrast, Pine Barrens foxhunters, who "listen to hounds," keep the chase surrounded, anticipating where the fox will emerge from the woods and trying to beat it there with their pickup trucks, which are as ritually invested with meaning as the horse. For English-style hunters, riding to hounds affords an opportunity to test and display equestrian skill and nerve. They relate collectively to a "subscription pack" of registered foxhounds, which are trained and managed by a paid employee. English-style hunters are not individually represented in the pack; rather they are collectively heralded. And for these upper class hunters the language of the hunt is highly stylized, prescribed in published glossaries.[7]

In Pine Barrens foxhunting each hound in the pack is individually owned, and none is registered. Hound performance is stressed over hound pedigree. "I don't go for the looks, I go by how they run," said Donald Pomeroy. "They could be the ugliest dog there is, as long as he can go in there and do his job" (foxchase, November 15, 1980). Dogmanship—the ability to obtain and train good foxdogs—is the skill displayed, not horsemanship. The locus of competition is in the dogs, not in the mode of transportation, though hunters identify themselves with and through their trucks. Each hunter could conduct a foxchase with his own hounds, but the worth of the hounds (and their owners) is best proven in competition. As Norman Taylor put it, "It's in competition that you find out what you've got." The language of the working class hunt—particularly descriptions for hounds' voices—is similarly elaborate, though it varies from community to community.[8] Likewise costuming is governed by unspoken canons approving sensible, warm clothing and boots, topped off by billed caps that usually sport some form of foxhunting insignia.

The upper class sport, which is always conducted in broad daylight, celebrates social hierarchy in the visually rich outer spectacle. There the lead is maintained by those of the highest social rank, where superior equestrian skills underscore social superiority—an instance of quotidian structures leaking into and governing the structure of this ritual as social charter.

In the working class sport, which is often practiced at night, hierarchy emerges in the aurally rich inner realm, where dogs prove themselves superior by their abilities to maintain the lead. The owners of leading dogs bask in reflected glory. But the hierarchy is not static, for hounds in this egalitarian setting are expected to be so evenly matched that all hounds are leaders at one time or another. "If one dog is in the front all the time," said John Earlin, "he is cheating somehow or other. That kind of dog we don't like to keep—one that cheats" (interview, November 21, 1981).

Both styles of foxhunting are intended to cultivate fellowship. "The Field is a most agreeable coffee-house," wrote John Hawkes in *The Meynellian Science*, "and there is more real society to be met with there than in any other situation of life."

'You meet a good class of people foxhuntin'," said Norman Taylor. "I don't care what anybody says" (interview, November 15, 1980).

According to anthropologist James Howe, the argument staged in upper class foxhunting concerns the nature of nobility. Battling it out in that arena are two old antagonists, merit and chance:

> The chase is concerned with a tension or contradiction between ascription and achievement that is common to hereditary aristocracies. While upper-class ideologies stress that social class is a matter of birth and thus unchanging, at the same time they wish to promote the idea that the accomplishments of the upper classes justify their position and that they deserve to be where they are. . . . Such displays advance the proposition that the two senses of the word "nobility" are synonymous. (Howe 1981:290)

But the two styles of foxhunting co-exist as opposing terms in an argument, constructed around the same text of a pack of hounds in gregarious pursuit of a fox. For working class foxhunters the two senses of the

Figure 3.8. Hunters conversing during the Sporting Dogs of New Jersey annual foxhunt in Penn State Forest. Photo by Dennis McDonald, April 1991.

concept of nobility (their word is "honor"—both a noun and a verb) are not synonymous. Unregistered dogs, representing men of blue collars, may prove themselves far superior to registered hounds heralding men of blue blood. Pine Barrens hunters strive to craft superior hounds out of ancestors of unimpeachable behavior and magnificent voices. The occasional sale of such a canine Horatio Alger to a "Tally-ho" is a social triumph for its maker.[9] Thus the finite province becomes consequential beyond itself as this ritual challenges the social structure and occasionally wins.

Notes

1. Mary Douglas laments that "systematic inquiry into how many kinds of construction can be put onto physical nature is not treated as a serious enterprise" (1973:10).

2. Nelson Goodman writes:

Much but by no means all worldmaking consists of taking apart and putting together, often conjointly: on the one hand, of dividing wholes into parts and partitioning kinds into subspecies, analyzing complexes into component features, drawing distinctions; on the other hand, of composing wholes and kinds out of parts and members and subclasses, combining features into complexes, and making connections. (1978:7)

3. Heda Jason describes thresholds between the world of the numbskulls and the normal world as "barriers" (1972:12–17). Katharine Young employs the term "threshold" to refer to openings in such barriers (1987), ports of entry into other realms.

4. Similar battles are waged in England, according to Venetia Newall, who writes:

Hunting is justified as a means of destroying a pest, yet it seems that, whenever numbers are low, foxes are artificially reared. A former Master of the Craven Farmers Hunt raised fox-cubs in his backyard (League, 2) and it seems that in 1822, during a time of scarcity, foxes were actually imported from France. . . . The League Against Cruel Sports has collected photographic evidence to show that lairs are built to encourage foxes to settle and to breed. A number have been found on the Duke of Beaufort's land. Faced with this evidence, the Joint Master and Secretary of the Hunt did not deny it. The Secretary commented: "If it were not for us building artificial lairs and keeping the foxes alive to hunt, they would become extinct and the whole balance of nature would be thrown out." (1983:89)

5. Catering solely to fox fanciers, a mail-order company in Wisconsin named "Foxy" advertises a wide range of goods imprinted with foxes, including doormats, mailboxes, golf balls, bibs, napkins, frisbees, T-shirts, tote bags, letter-openers, playing cards, jewelry, wind chimes, and glassware, as well as figurines, paintings, and photographs (the 1986 Foxy Catalogue, Foxy, 204 West Lawton Street, Edgerton, WI 53534).

6. For a view of foxhunting in Chile as "a form of traditional behavior providing social cohesiveness" see Dannemann (1980:167).

7. For an example of such a glossary, see Watson (1977:220–26).

8. For a glossary of Pine Barrens foxhunters' terms, see Appendix II. For a glossary of terms used by hilltoppers in the southern uplands, see Lyne (1976).

9. In an obituary for Donald Pomeroy, Walt Grekoski mentions this as one of the payoffs for good dogmanship. He writes, "Some of the hunters are rewarded well when they sell a hound who is a good leader to the tally-ho foxhunters in North Jersey" (1986:49).

4. Making the Dogs

Now there's all type of dogs just like there are all type of people.
—Milton Collins (Interview, November 18, 1983)

THROUGH BREEDING AND training, hunters are said to "make" their dogs, painstakingly shaping them to fit the space between nature and society. This process of dogmaking is augmented by dogtalk, the discourse whereby hunters constitute their hounds as Chaseworld characters, mapping human society onto the canine pack, inventing a fictive order among domestic canids and the wild cousin they pursue, embodying in the very form of their discourse the prescribed social etiquette among hounds.

Crafting the Breed

Foxchases would never happen in the wild; in fact, they reverse some aspects of the predator/prey relationship that zoologists ascribe to wild canids. The wild pack evolved in order to hunt cooperatively for game larger than individuals in the pack—game like bison or elk that could provide a meal for the entire pack. Clearly it would be maladaptive for wolves to hunt small, inedible creatures like foxes as a pack. Foxhunting, a contest between cultivated and wild, lawful and lawless, voiced and voiceless, is based in part on the suppression of such natural instincts in dogs, on the triumph of the cultivated response over the natural impulse. Thus one of the most important criteria for a foxhound is that it be "deerbroke"— guaranteed not to pursue deer, the kind of quarry suited to its wild progenitors and their social structure.

The relationship between hounds and foxes has been shaped over the course of centuries, giving rise to a wide array of foxhound breeds. This diversity of breeds reflects differences in philosophies of hunting as well as in the quarry and the landscapes they frequent. Like other media in the plastic arts, the hound breed is malleable, highly responsive to local conditions and changing historical circumstances. Fred Streever's description of the making of the Goodman breed, for example, gives one the impression that the breeder is as much sculptor as matchmaker:

> For the spirit, dash and energy he used the Robertson blood, and when it became too much for their physical strength, he pulled down the turbulent spirit and built up the physical strength with the steadier Walkers. (Streever 1948: 149, cited in Cramer 1990)

And like greenware ready for painting and firing, the breed or strain offers the hunter a hound receptive to "finishing" (that is, training) according to communal standards.

Foxhound breeds and strains vary according to the contexts in which they are used. In the United States there are four very different settings in which foxhounds may perform:

1. the field trial, in which hounds are run competitively, wherein speed and a jealous nature are important;
2. foxhunting with the intent to shoot the fox, wherein a single slow-trailing hound with a good voice is called for;
3. drag hunting, in which very fast hounds are cast on a pre-laid trail of fox scent, and it is speed that counts the most; and
4. pack hunting, in which fifteen or more hounds are cast on a scent, and it is their ability to hunt as a unit that is most valued (American Kennel Club 1985:211).

Like tale types, house types, and other forms of cultural expression, hunting dog breeds are amorphous, and vernacular variants (sometimes termed "potlickers") are continually emerging and receding with little or no official recognition of their passage. For nearly fifty years the Maryland hound, while not recognized as a breed by the American Kennel Club, has been vaunted by hunters in Delaware, Pennsylvania, Maryland, and New Jersey as the breed of choice for pack hunting. Distinctive features are said to include long, floppy ears (which, some say, help to stir up scent), an enhanced packing instinct (which concentrates the music), a tendency toward more meticulous tracking (which prolongs the chase and protects the fox), and manageability. Writing in *Hunter's Horn*, Don Cramer of Chatsworth offers the following description:

> The present day Maryland is a level headed individual. He is basically a medium speed pack hound, although individuals can and do run alone and do

it all. As with most all hounds, if only run with the pack, some do not become independent or pack leaders early on much the same as any other hound. The greatest asset in this territory now is their ability to be handled better than the wind splitters. This in itself, with the highways and constant encroachment upon our running grounds, make this hound a requisite in this area. . . . I have raised, bred, or seen all the present day strains, and the Maryland is without equal and has the true ring of a hound. (Cramer 1990)

The breeding and training of Maryland hounds is governed by a set of specific ideas of what a foxhound should be and do:

1. A foxhound must be "straight fox." That is, fox is the only quarry it will run.
2. A foxhound must "follow the line," which means the terrestrial trail. Following the airborne scent (that is, "winding") constitutes cheating.
3. A foxhound should always "tongue" (that is, vocalize) when it smells the fox, and only when it smells the fox. If a dog knowingly fails to tongue in order to keep the trail to itself (a kind of hoarding), it is deemed dishonest. To tongue on the wrong quarry is considered "trashing." And to tongue with no scent at all is "babbling."
4. A foxhound must be a team player; it must "pack up" and "honor" the hound in the lead. It may not "steal" the trail from the leader, and, when its olfactory glands are resting, it must yield the trail to a hound with the scent.
5. Hounds must be evenly matched. No foxhound should be consistently in the lead or in the rear. Rather, they have to "take turns."

Just as each one of these ideas may vary from one hunting community to another, so may the strains of hounds developed in various hunting communities. And ideas and strains do vary over time and space. Norman Taylor's father and friends, for example, hunted with "universal hounds"— hounds that chased whatever they turned up. Part of the sport for those hunters was to identify the quarry by listening to how the hounds were running. The hunter who shoots foxes may take pride in dogs that learn to outwit the fox, whether by winding it and cutting to catch it, or by deducing the fox's running pattern. The hunter who spares foxes takes pride in his ability to control the dogs by breaking them from the chase at the right time.

The Maryland hound is a regional hound type, bred to run on the Atlantic coastal plain. "He's more adapted to this type of country," said Norman Taylor. "We get some open runnin', we get some heavy runnin', and . . . you can handle 'em a lot better because they're not just a wild dog that wants to take off all the time" (interview, January 22, 1986). In response to the various nuances of the Atlantic coastal plain, subregional inflections of the breed have emerged. The gray foxes and brushy terrain of the Pine Barrens stand in contrast to the red foxes and open fields of Maryland, where gray foxes are considered trash. "It takes a slightly different hound here than in Maryland," said Hubie Driscoll, of West Creek. The Maryland hound as a breed provides hunters in both states with the desired packing ability and "big voices," but individual hounds are selected to match variations in local terrain. Speed is an asset for hounds pursuing swift red foxes over open fields; it is a liability for hounds unraveling the tangled course of the slower gray fox through pushcover, ganderbrush, and swampland. Under those conditions it takes, as Hubie Driscoll put it, "a neat, careful dog." Whereas hunters themselves may read the open fields of Maryland for signs of red fox, the scruffy Pine Barrens understory yields this information only to "cold-nosed" hounds able to tongue a track that is eight hours old. Such requirements turn out to be complementary, according to Hubie Driscoll, who observed that Maryland hunters often favor the younger dogs for speed, while Pine Barrens hunters appreciate the experienced noses and moderate gait of older dogs who will chase their gray foxes but are unlikely to catch them.

In the absence of an official registry for Maryland hounds, hunters try to breed and keep hounds that will run together, while satisfing individual aesthetic considerations. "Everybody's got their own way of breedin'," said Donald Pomeroy. In the course of generations of experimental breeding, physical features like ear length, conformation, and tail type have come to be linked with patterns of behavior. In theories about what makes a good foxhound, features that hunters find most aesthetically appealing become intertwined with the hounds' ability to tell the story properly. "Ear length always meant a lot to me," said Don Cramer. "The dogs with longer ears tend to have heavier notes." Those heavier, "ringing" notes are linked to the ability to stick to the trail and pack up. "Grandpop used to say, 'The longer the ears, the colder the nose, the gentler the disposition,'" said Hubie Driscoll (telephone conversation, April 2, 1991). Such hounds are deemed less likely to kill the fox. John Earlin, for instance, avoided short ears, long hair, and a curled, thick, or flagged tail. Short ears and a flag tail are often cited by Pine Barrens foxhunters as hallmarks of the Walker hound, which is known more for speed and cunning than for its vocal and trailing abilities.

In hunters' conversations about breeds, the Walker often emerges as a foil to the Maryland hound. The Walker, a breed developed in Kentucky and recognized by the American Kennel Club, is enormously popular throughout the South among coonhunters and foxhunters.[1] Milton Collins offered this contrast:

> The Walker has little ears instead of big ears, and a flag tail, and he carries his tail up over his back. If you notice, Suzie drops hers. A Walker, he's a proud dog, but we don't have 'em up here, because they cover so much ground. They just *lace* a fox and they run him out of the country. We have the slower dogs with more noise.[2]

Pine Barrens foxhunters claim that the Walker is far more competitive and aggressive than the Maryland hound; it is an asocial if not downright antisocial being, disinclined to pack up. Said Norman Taylor:

> We've tried Walkers in this area, but the Walker hound is more or less a dog that wants to hunt wider from you, and we just don't care for 'em. . . . A Walker hound likes to, they just like to beat each other, I'd say. They're not satisfied to get right in the pack and run as a pack. (Interview, January 22, 1986)

And John Earlin:

> I have had Walkers and don't like 'em. See they run different from this type of dog. These dogs will run together, and every one of those likes to be ahead. If a dog was comin' up here that had it, the Walkers wouldn't even bother with that dog. They'd try to steal it away from him. (Foxchase, November 15, 1980)

However, Walker antecedents are not entirely shunned. Breeding a little Walker into a Maryland hound is said, for instance, to produce a "tough, tight foot." But hunters monitor each other for incompatible breeding practices. "My son-in-law likes a fast pack of dogs," said one hunter.

> He's always trying to get 'em to go faster, and I told him one day, I said, "Look, I wanna tell you somethin', and I don't wanna hear no goddam gripes outa you. Next thing you know, these dogs are gonna start to catchin' foxes. (Interview, November 21, 1980)

Hunters who hunt together have to keep compatible hounds. Hunters with chronic "deer dogs" are pressured to get rid of them. As an incentive, fellow hunters may help them replace the undesirable dogs with others.

Thus two hunters agreed that a third would have to get rid of his deer dogs before he could join any more fox chases.

"I thought [he] was gonna come up and go runnin' with us," said one hunter to another.

"Get rid of them three deer dogs he's got first," the other reminded him.

"Okay, yeah," agreed the first.

"Then we'll give him some good ones and we'll get him goin' again," the second promised.

There are networks for the redistribution of undesirable dogs. "If you have a hound that runs too fast or something like that," explained Norman Taylor, "there's other people runs faster than what we do, then we'll move that hound to a foxhunter who's running a lot faster than what we are" (interview, January 22, 1986). A fast dog or a deer dog is "moved away," not given to one's hunting companions. "I might as well keep him as let Junie Bell have 'im," said Norman, "cause he's only gonna dump him in on me. So therefore you're better off movin' him out of the area" (interview, January 24, 1986). This could mean moving the hound to a state like Virginia in which hunting deer with hounds is legal, or moving it deeper into South Jersey where poaching remains a time-honored tradition.

Whereas foxhunters account for their breeding practices in aesthetic and moral terms, zoologists view the process in evolutionary terms. According to zoologists Lorna and Raymond Coppinger, folk practitioners of animal husbandry have unwittingly shaped dog breeds over the centuries through a process that zoologists call "neoteny"—the arresting of a breed at a juvenile stage in its development (Coppinger and Coppinger).[3] Neoteny inhibits the development of domestic dogs into wild adults, suspending them in one of four "metamorphic" stages between infancy and adulthood: adolescents, object players, headers-stalkers, and heelers. Progressing through these stages, a canid learns each of the behaviors it needs to assimilate in order to hunt as a wild adult. Physical attributes, linked with stages of development, betray the stage at which a domestic breed's development was arrested. For example, aggressive breeds such as the German shepherd and Doberman pinscher, displaying alert ears and short hair, are more mature and apt to function as attack dogs. Gentler breeds like the Saint Bernard and Golden retriever manifest puppylike features into adulthood, including floppy ears and long hair.

The Coppingers observe that "hunting" breeds are actually misnamed, for hounds are "object players" bred for low aggression and a strong packing instinct more typical of puppies than of hunting adults. Breeds that are "stuck in the object play stage tend to exhibit more juvenile submissiveness . . . and are more easily trained than dogs farther along in the maturation process" (1982:72). In other words, perpetual canine adolescence makes the domestic packhound easier for hunters to handle.

The evolutionary model is, of course, one way of accounting for differences between breeds. When held up to the Coppingers' model, Walkers appear to be at a more advanced stage in the metamorphic process. But hunters who complain that Walkers are too wild tend to characterize them as socially regressive beings who will cheat to get where they want to be. In contrast to the Maryland hounds, who are satisfied to stick to the trail, who "don't want to get up and taste their quarry," as Don Cramer put it, the short-eared Walker's "desire is to catch it" (telephone conversation, February 15, 1991). Maryland hounds, with their long ears and ringing notes, their abilities to run together and stick to the trail, have evolved as the breed that best tells the story of Pine Barrens hunters, foxes, and landscapes.

Dogtalk

Crucial both to sustaining the form of something as fluid as a hound breed and to keeping track of the regional repertoire of hounds is dogtalk, a kind of discourse for which foxhunters are well known in the community. It is in conversation with other hunters that the breed is conceptually fixed. Through dogtalk hunters continually monitor their "making" of dogs and packs, determining what constitutes desirable traits like "intelligence," "voice," and "bottom" (that is, endurance), and undesirable traits like the tendency to "wind," "trash," or "babble."

The ability to engage in dogtalk is prized among foxhunters. "He was always ready to talk foxhounds," wrote Don Cramer, in praise of his deceased colleague Ernest Bennett, of Port Republic, "and could do so for hours, for it was his great interest in life" (1991). Through dogtalk, hunters keep track of the steady stream of unregistered hounds flowing into and out of the region, and of career foxhounds that bounce around among hunters within the region as well. Over the course of a two-hour conversation I heard a group of hunters discuss dozens of individual dogs, litters, and breeders. Through dogtalk, too, hunters debate, challenge, and verify can-

Figure 4.1. Bob Hayes and hounds investigating a "miss." Photo by Dennis McDonald, April 1991.

ons for making dogs, arguing over which dogs best exemplify those canons, weaving together the repertoire of hounds and the community of hunters, establishing what is acceptable in terms of looks and behavior, determining what is most desirable in a foxdog.

In this inimitable form of discourse, foxhunters develop and exercise the metaphors that not only render explicit the multiform links between dogs and men but shape the pack into a microcosm of human society. Social dynamics among hounds are made to resemble those inherent in family life, the military, the workplace, the worlds of sports and music, and other spheres wherein humans collectively labor to achieve a common goal.

Music emerges as the most highly elaborated metaphor,[4] elevating canine interactions to the status of an art form. The notes of hounds are highly differentiated through language that mixes terms from the realm of music with terms used to discriminate vocal behaviors in a variety of species, including humans. Thus hounds squall, yell, holler, speak, sing, and so forth. "I can recognize almost every dog that I keep by its voice," said Norman Taylor.

> I got a dog I call Mike and he's got a real bass note, and you can tell him in a fox chase because he's just got a good coarse bass note. And then I have two or three screaming dogs which I like to hear. They're real high-noted tenor voices. And then you get different double yells and you get some dogs with a long drawn note. (Interview, January 22, 1986)

In making a pack a hunter strives for a diversity of voices, according to Norman:

> I think the average hunter likes to mix up his voices in his dogs, like you have in a band or anything like that. You don't want all bass dogs, and you don't want all real soprano dogs, but you like to hear the voices mixed up so they sound good to you. (Interview, January 22, 1986)

Norman Taylor also likened the pack to a ball team. Two hunters trading dogs, he once said, are like team owners trading ballplayers. "You're trying to better yourself, and so is he. What you need for your pack's like what he needs for shortstop or second base, something like that" (interview, November 23, 1980). Indeed, hounds are inscribed as athletes in other ways as well. They must run frequently in order to stay in shape, for example. And Milton Collins saw in his hounds the physique of a boxer or wrestler. They should be, he wrote, "wide in the chest, thin in the withers, like a broad-chested, thin-waist fighter" (letter to author, March 1986).

Individual hounds contribute in various ways to the accomplishment of the canine society. Hounds, like people, can be loyal, ambitious, trustworthy, lazy, jealous, and sneaky. "Hitchhikers" are hounds that let others do all the work. "Loungers" are immature and undisciplined in their approach to the trail. "It's like having a teenager in the lead," explained Don Cramer. "They think they know what they're doing, but they don't. Yet they carry everybody with their enthusiasm." A hound that is "dead game" is one that "gives everything he can. Like one of the family—he's always ready to help you." One hound was nicknamed "The General." "Every time he shows up," said Don Cramer, "he takes charge" (telephone conversation, February 15, 1991, and foxchase, November 18, 1983).

Dogs are said to develop reputations among each other for reliability. "If you got a dog that gets noisy," said Norman, "that's babblin noisy, and just not—tongue where it belongs, dogs learn that dog and they won't honor it, yeah" (interview, January 25, 1986). Other hounds, lacking in confidence, may succumb to peer pressure. This was the case, according to John Earlin, when several of his reliable hounds ran silently with the pack, even though they knew better:

> Certain dogs wasn't opening up because they were going backwards. They
> knew they were going backwards, but they went with 'em anyway, because, I
> suppose the noise was too much for 'em. They just carried along with the
> crowd. (Foxchase, November 15, 1980)

The society of hounds also has its deviants, who cheat and go crooked,
and whose front-running positions resemble ill-gotten gains. "We don't like
a dog that's what I call a cutter," said Jack Davis. "He leaves the track and
runs around to the front and tries to get ahead." Even these can be made to
serve a purpose, however. Jack Davis spoke of a dog named Harry with a
mixture of pride and chagrin:

> He was slippery that's what I called him. But he was the best dog I ever seen to
> start a fox. He was a great dog but he wasn't honest. To tell the truth, I'd get
> another one just like him if I had the chance. (Interview, November 21, 1980)

Despite his failure to perform as a team player, Harry was kept as a
specialty dog for starting foxes. Jack Davis's ambivalence about Harry
evinces the deep-seated tension in the Chaseworld between competition and
cooperation. Although the admiration and envy of one's peers and the
achievement of communitas with them are seen as mutually exclusive goals,
the possibility of attaining both is an idea that dies hard. Like Harry himself,
hunters may be tempted to see how far they may go before others will blow
the whistle on the compromise of ideals. Harry provides a comic illustration
of this sort of moral bet-hedging, as we will see later in this chapter.

Hounds are not only likened to humans, they also are apt to be cast as
morally and intellectually superior beings. "In my opinion," wrote Don
Cramer, "any town that has more people [including teen-agers] than
hounds and dogs, is no fit place to live" (1990). And Norman Taylor, exalting
his favorite hound, put it this way: "You could put Lead in a line with a
hundred people, and he'd have more sense than seventy of them" (interview,
January 24, 1986). This kind of thinking is playfully reinforced in the hunters'
assumption of animal names for CB handles, which contrast with the human
names often given to hounds. Through names for hounds, hunters further
crystallize their network, documenting their society through additional
inscriptions, which further amplify the metaphors of dogtalk.

Hound Names

The solidarity achieved by men through their dogs is reflected in the system
of naming whereby the hunters keep track of scores of unregistered

hounds. The intermeshing of hound and human identities is illustrated in link-chain recitations that account for hound origins. Said Norman, offering an account of where his hounds came from: "Smoke, I know he's out of Stafford's Jim dog, yeah. Sailor was bred by Jeff Powell. Becky and Lil, they were bred out of a dog that Sharpie had, they were out of a dog by the name of Chico. Janie and Pat are out of Bull and Bull is one of Jakie's dogs (interview, January 24, 1986). Hound names designate genealogical and social location, and can barely be recited without reference to it.

In the poetics of hound naming lie concealed mnemonic devices for keeping track of hound lineage and relationships.[5] Thus Randall Stafford named three littermates Coffee, Tea, and Cocoa; Donald Pomeroy named a pair Left and Right; and Robly Champion tagged three consecutive sets of pups Slip and Slide, names that alliteratively describe hound movements in chases as well as blood relationships. Norman Taylor paired sets of sibling pups as Nip and Tuck, Jack and Jenny, Punch and Judy, and Speck and Spotty. "Things like that keep the litters in mind," he explained.

Other content may be encoded into the names, such as the year of birth or a veiled reference to the man who supplied the pups. Thus in 1985, when Halley's Comet was on the horizon, Norman named two puppies that he bred Halley and Comet. Joe Albert purchased a pair of puppies from a man afflicted with shingles and named them Shingles and Jingles. Many of the names become an ad hoc index to the hunting community, overtly linking pups with the men who bred them. Donald Pomeroy's Freeman came from Freeman Taylor, and a number of hunters have "Jake dogs" from Jake Meredith, Sr. Norman Taylor appropriated nicknames from the Stafford family to name a trio of siblings Snap, Chunk, and Bull. "And Johnny Earlin named one Norman every now and then, come out of me," Norman said (interview, January 24, 1986). Other names allude to idiosyncratic aspects of a hound's appearance or behavior. Thus small dogs bore the names of Shorty and Peanut; smiling dogs became Smiley and Grinner; and odd-looking dogs were named Funny-Face and Blockhead.

Names for hounds contrast markedly with names for house dogs. The maintenance of hounds at a greater social distance from humans than that at which house dogs are kept makes the application of human names from the community acceptable, since, as Lévi-Strauss notes of birds, the hounds function as a metaphorical human society (Lévi-Strauss 1966:182). He further argues that dogs incorporated into the household relate metonymically to the human sphere and are therefore issued names conventionally reserved for dogs (Rover, Bowser, Spot, Blackie, and the like) or human names not in use by members of the community. To name a domestic dog after the head of the household would engender confusion.

It would be interesting to examine the thematic series displayed in a more complete sampling of hound names. The primary series, of course, suggests a metaphorical human society: Maude, Kate, Becky, Lil, Janie, Jennifer, Norman, Freeman, Topsy, Bricky, Jakie, Bull, and so forth. But other series cross-reference the sport with other symbolic realms and conceptual systems. In this regard the naming of hounds appears to be, as Lévi-Strauss notes of totemic naming systems, the detotalization of a cosmological order or subsystems within that order. My notes suggest the following additional series: canine morphology (Spot, Curly, Funny-Face, Blockhead); transportation (Wheelbarrow, Locomotive, Driver, Sailor); music (Siren, Bugler, Screamer, Music, Singer, Basie, Rock, Jazz); aristocracy (King, Queenie, Prince); and beverages (Coffee, Tea, Cocoa, Liquor, Bitters, and Whiskey). (Milton Collins, a methodist minister opposed to drinking, changed Whiskey's name to Biscuit.)

Hounds' names taken as a whole constitute a potent trove of information to be protected; the classified nature of this information, like the stranger who could not hear music in hounds' voices, is the topic of an anecdote told about strangers in the presence of them. When asked by a stranger (always a woman in the versions I heard) for the names of his dogs, the protagonist resorts to names that are not names to avoid divulging his dogs' identities. In Jack Davis's version, told to his wife Ann and myself, Jack Davis the character is talking with a customer in the saloon he kept at the time:

> I told a woman in the bar—at that time I had twenty some [hounds]—and she said "What's their names?" And I said "The males are 'Son' and the females are 'Bitch,' and I call 'Son of a Bitch!' and they all come!" She said "You think you're damn smart don't you?" (Interview, November 14, 1980)

The anecdote concerns a verbal prank that turned a woman's request for information into an occasion to use strong language under the guise of answering her question. The prank may be seen, using Mary Douglas's term, as a "joke rite" comprising in essence "an attack on control" (Douglas 1968:371), an effort to subvert conventions governing both social differentiation and conversation in mixed company, the latter being an aspect of the way in which gender is socially constructed. In defiance of the raison d'être for names, Davis uses names to designate gender rather than social location. He then goes on to ignore the presence of two genders in the human sphere by using language that, while acceptable in male company, may be deemed inappropriate in mixed company.

Among themselves, and with their families, hunters may use the word "bitch" as a technical term, bracketing out its negative connotations in the society at large. The metaphorical value of the term is cast into relief in the presence of strangers, particularly women, which in turn heightens the sense in which the term constitutes a barrier between insiders and outsiders. Hunters are not only authors of the realm, but gatekeepers who can admit strangers or deny them access if they try to enter through the wrong portal.

Mouth and Sociability

Canons for hound discourse are echoed in the human arena where, with talk for the sake of talk about chasing for the sake of chasing, hunters constitute the Chaseworld. Mary Douglas points out that "Sets of rules are metaphorically connected with one another, allow meaning to leak from one context to another along the formal similarities that they show" (1973:13). Rules for interaction among hounds are metaphorically linked to rules for interaction among humans in the hunters' inscriptions of hound utterances as "saying," "speaking," "telling," "talking," and the like.[6] A comparison of rule structures governing use of "mouth" among hounds and hunters reveals some of the meanings recovered by hunters through the Chaseworld.

Hounds' voices materialize the trail, an ineffable pattern of pheromones, into something they can "own," "move," "lose," "wiggle," "straighten," and "craft." As Norman Taylor graphically illustrates the ownership, "When you hear one start right up sharp he's sayin' 'I got it! I got it! I got it!' And you'll hear 'em all come at him and get in with him" (interview, January 24, 1986). But the ownership is temporary, for hounds are supposed to share the trail. "Your best dog isn't always in the front," as John Earlin put it.

> If one dog is always in the front, he is cheating somehow or other. That type of dog we don't particularly like: one that cheats, because it takes the music outa your pack. In other words, say they're runnin' out here and the dog come out here and run down the road and grab the fox, he, to me, is of no value. (Foxchase, November 15, 1980)

Hounds are required by dint of sheer physiology to "take turns," a phenomenon that Patricia Dale-Green describes in her book on dogs and doglore:

> After two minutes' continuous sniffing of a strong scent, hounds suffer from nasal fatigue, so when working they give their noses rest periods. During a run some hounds will be working and throwing their tongues, while others merely follow running mute. The whole pack take turns, so there is never a time when all are resting at once. (1967:21)

Onto this episodic olfactory apprehension of hounds the hunters map conventions for turntaking. Thus is the democratic ideal of shared power manifested in a pack that follows a rotating leadership. The hunters' distribution of the conversational turf epitomizes the ideal, even as they discuss it.

"Nobody likes the hind end," said Jeff Powell.

"Don't wanna be in the back, huh?" responded Jake Meredith.

"I don't mind bein' in back the first couple rounds," Jeff Powell averred.

"They can't all be in the front, can they, Jakie?" Norman Taylor teased.

"Not very well," laughed Jake.

"Some of 'em's gotta get back a little," Norman added.

"Take turns," supplied Jake.

"Yeah, they gotta take turns," said Norman. "You wanna get the kind that take turns."

"If they all get in front at one time," said Jake, "there's somethin' the matter" (storytelling, July 14, 1990).

Hounds, like human conversationalists, are supposed to lend a voice to the proceedings, speaking when they have something to tell about, otherwise remaining silent unless lending support to the hound in the lead. Such support should be judiciously rendered. "Sometimes a hound will tongue to favor another dog," said John Earlin.

> But it shouldn't happen too often. You want a dog to tongue when he smells the fox. If he's comin' up behind him, it's all right—every dog gets slurred—but you don't want him tonguin' a steady stream goin' up there. If he hollers once in a while tryin' to get there, that's perfectly all right, but you don't want him goin' "woofwoofwoofwoofwoof" all the way up behind him. (Interview, November 22, 1980)

Hunters govern their own conversational turntaking with canons for true sociability. Narrating the chase in the egalitarian fashion of sociable talk,[7] they often emphasize agreement over content. Such interchanges have an almost staccato rhythm, and utterances of more than two sentences in the purely sociable exchange are rare. In this human version of allelomimesis,[8] everyone present is obliged to contribute. Much of the talk is directed toward turn-taking, toward equitable distribution of conversational turf. Exchanges are characterized by invitations, echoes, elaborations, and rephrasings, as in the following evaluation of the inner activity, drawn out over four turns at talk:

[Invitation]
    NT: He didn't run as wide as a lot of foxes though. Jesus! He was a nice fox to run wasn't he?
[Echo]
    HS: Oh yeah wonderful fox to run.
[Elaboration]
    HT: Ran a three or four mile circle there.
[Rephrasing]
    NT: Yeah, he was running that one area. (Interview, October 17, 1986)

Hunters narrate the Chaseworld collaboratively; their ability to complete and adumbrate each other's utterances is a hallmark of their shared understandings.[9]

    DT: He come out, hit the blacktop road, and run up the road a ways to try to
    HS: outfox the dogs.
    DT: Yeah, that's what he's tryin' to do, yeah. (Foxchase, January 25, 1986)

    JB: Now what he's done before, he goes in and fools around in there, and then he'll come back. And where he's gonna come out is
    DT: anybody's guess
    JB: yep. (Foxchase, January 25, 1986)

Exalting the other hunter, and deflecting flattery away from oneself, is a stylistic feature of the discourse whereby hunters construct each other as equals.

JE: Pomeroy, those dogs of yours are botherin' mine right out.
DP: I doubt it. I doubt that very much. You've been runnin' 'em every
day. (Foxchase, November 15, 1980)

The hunters build what Georg Simmel calls "an ideal sociological
world" in which "the pleasure of the individual is always contingent upon
the joy of others; here, by definition, no one can have his satisfaction at the
cost of contrary experiences on the part of others" (1971:132). Sociable
talk—talk for its own sake—emphasizes form over content, freeing its
participants from the hierarchies that burden the interactions of everyday
life.

Correspondences between dogs and humans are clearly articulated in
rules governing use of mouth. The term "sport" is used to frame the mock
attacks of men upon men, as well as the pursuit of foxes by hounds. "It's just
a lot of sport," said Robly Champion. "Nobody gets mad at nobody, we
ride one another. Tom'll say, "Boy, I seen your dogs a-comin', they're
gonna bring up a lousy fifth" (interview, September 1979). Where teasing
breaks down, or becomes insulting, the world of communication collapses.
As Mary Douglas points out, "The barriers between finite provinces of
meaning are always sapped either by the violent flooding through of social
concerns or by the subtle economy which uses the same rule structure in
each province" (1973:13). Hunters who violate canons for sociable discourse
topple the Chaseworld, whose foundations rest in part on the correct use of
"mouth" in both hunters and dogs.

Jack Davis, speaking to Ann Davis and myself, said, "You know, Mary,
there's an awful lot of trouble with foxhunters, because you like your dog, I
like my dog, she likes her dog, this guy over here likes his dog, and you can't
run one of those dogs down or the next thing you know—I've seen 'em get
down there—five-six-seven-eight trucks—next thing you know'd be a
damn fight."

"You've seen fights happen?" I queried.

"Oh yeah!" Jack Davis replied. "I've seen fights."

"Do they ever come to blows?"

"That's what he means!" said Ann. "Come right to blows! Not tongue
fights but fist fights!"

"And it'll always be happenin'," Jack emphasized, "by just somebody's
mouth that shouldn't be runnin'" (interview, November 14, 1980).

Invaded by hierarchical concerns from the world of everyday life, the
Chaseworld pauses or vanishes altogether as its authors emerge from the

realm to repair breaches in its framework. Such invasions lay bare some of the metaphorical links between Chaseworld conventions and the everyday structures they borrow.

Like the well-worn chisel handle that shapes the workman's hand, the hounds' behaviors effect the contours of hunters' talk. On the trail of good fellowship, hunters mirror the turntaking of hounds. Honoring each other, casting about for stories in conversation, they chime in with an affirmative chorus.

"I remember," says Norman, "when Jack had Harry and Johnny had the Black and Tan." He chuckles, as do others who remember.

"Johnny said he'd pick up—" Jeff begins, spying an opportunity to tease the older hunters.

Norman looks for corroboration from his own generation. "He practically owned the place down here, didn't he, Jake?"

"I don't know," Jeff jumps in, "because I wasn't alive then, but he's told me about it, and he said he'd jump a fox for you boys, and you'd lose it, and he'd have to turn the dog back out so you could find the fox again. Said Jack and you guys—Norman wouldn't even pick him up. He said he'd pick him up and they'd lose him before they'd get to the next road!"

This is greeted with shouts of laughter.

"He could jump you a fox, boy," says Tom Driscoll, the oldest in the room next to Nick Harker.

"So could Harry," says Norman. "Harry would jump you a fox."

"Yeah, they could find fox," echoes Jake.

"Jack always told me," elaborates Tom, "he says, 'Look. I used to come down here day after day and never jump a fox till I got Harry.'"

"Mmhm," Norman supports him.

"And he'd get him a fox," says Tom.

"He'd jump a fox," says Norman.

"I remember him," says Jeff. "I seen him in operation."

"You could see him anytime in operation," says Tom emphatically, "but *not in back*. He might be in back, but he was gonna be in front when he come across the next road."

"He was gonna shortcut on the front dog," laughs Norman.

Jeff remembers a scene. "I was with you in them briars down there, and Jack Davis was there—I was just a kid—and the dogs was a comin' runnin'. And we'd seen the fox, and we walked up the road and: 'Here comes a deer! Listen to it!' And it was crackin' in the brush, and (laughing) here comes Harry! And he never said a word!"

"Yeah," Jake says, "that's him, never said nothin'."

"Yeah," says Norman, to a background of laughter.

"Boy, but he could get you a fox," says Tom Driscoll.

"After he crossed the road you could hear him," says Jake.

"Yup," says Tom.

"Seventy-five yards or more," says Jake.

"He'd open up," adds Norman.

"Yeah, he'd tongue then," Jake continues, "and then they caught up to him."

"Yeah," says Norman.

"And then they'd—" says Tom.

"When they caught up to him," Norman picks up.

"He'd—he'd—" Tom begins.

"He'd shut up," Norman finishes.

"He'd know where that next road was and he'd be around there goin' with him," Tom finally jumps in.

"Yep," Jake punctuates it.

"That's the kinda dog I want," says Jeff Powell.

"I went to Jack and Johnny wantin' to know who he come from," says Norman.

"Yep, I know where he come from," says Jake.

"Leavey," Norman says.

"Yep," says Jake.

"Leavey, he come from," Norman repeats.

"And the bitch they got with him," Jake begins.

"Was a good bitch," Norman finishes, as Jake is saying, "Ain't never been a better one ["Better one," echoes Norman] born than that one."

"That's right, yeah," says Norman.

"Yessir," says Jake.

"She was a good bitch," Norman reiterates, "Yep, she come from Leavey."

"Wasn't no—" Hubie Driscoll begins.

"Never been any better than her," Norman muses.

"M-mm," says Hubie, "She didn't do one thing wrong and she could trail a fox right down the road. Just pick him out."

"And they also got the gyp that Bobby Bell got two little blue tick bitches out of," Norman remembers. "What did he call 'em, the little ones that Kenny got?"

"Oh," says Ted Goff, who has been quiet. "Kathy and—"

"Kathy, yeah," Norman confirms.

"And Deena," Ted adds.

"There wasn't nothin' wrong with them, was there Ted?" Norman invites.

"No sir there wasn't," Ted responds.

"They was *good* gyps," Norman emphasizes.

Collaboratively constructing an ideal realm, hunters weave a dense tapestry of utterances about dogs. Exchanging and rehearsing knowledge to which they as a group are uniquely privy, they complete each others' thoughts, yield to the next speaker, honor the one with the story, and lend voice to choruses of affirmation and teasing in ways that are not merely interruptions but rather intensify and enhance their edifice of talk.

Notes

1. The Walker breed dates back to the 1850s, when Walkers and Maupins living in Madison County, Kentucky began outcrossing their English foxhounds to obtain a breed capable of capturing the red foxes that were moving into the area. They prided themselves on the result: a line known for its "self-reliance, cold noses, refusal to pack, and a fondness for skirting" (Longrigg 1975:194, cited in Marks 1991:95). For a helpful capsule summary of the development of the Walker line, see Marks (1991:94–95).

2. This is not to say that those who use Walkers elsewhere intend to kill their quarry, but rather that Walkers, initially bred to negotiate the steep and rocky slopes of the Kentucky uplands, have an unfair advantage over foxes on the coastal plain. Walkers are credited with the sort of behavior described by Frank H. Reynolds in a story he told to Herbert Halpert:

> Henry Webb of Pasadena told me this—told it for the truth. He was a fox hunter this Henry Webb, and he'd go out and start this fox. This fox would go to a tree that leaned over the creek, go up the tree and jump on the other side of the creek. That would fool the dog. He did that several times.
>
> Then he went out one morning, the dog hit a trail, and he jumped him. This dog did a lot of barkin' to get the fox goin'. He made so much noise, then stopped barking, that he thought the fox was treed. Well, he couldn't find the dog so he went out in the road that leads from Pasadena to Webb's Mill. There he saw the dog's track where he'd gone towards Webb's Mill. He figured the fox had gone across the same place, so he went there, and the dog had the fox. The dog had figured the same way and got him going, then beat him to the tree and caught him. (Halpert 1947:361)

3. In an article in *Smithsonian* magazine, Lorna and Raymond Coppinger describe their search for a dog that would protect sheep in the United States from

predators. Their search ended in the mountains of Yugoslavia where shepherds were using a dog that differed radically from the Border collies of the British Isles. Whereas the dogs in the British Isles related to sheep as prey, the Yugoslavian breed related to them as family. The sheep-herding dogs from the British Isles look and act like predators, while the sheep-guarding dogs from Europe look and act like sheep. For more on the breeding process, see Coppinger and Coppinger (1982). I am grateful to Gerald E. Parsons for bringing this article to my attention.

4. Hunters are not alone in their inscription of canine vocalizations as music. Animal ethologists do the same, speculating that the music making of wild canids functions as a rite of bonding. Writing of "the dawn and dusk choruses of coyotes and jackals, and the choirs of wolves," Michael Fox theorizes that these may "serve a territorial function, informing other groups of their presence. Solitary howls of wolves may be used for location of (or by) conspecifics, and may also be calls for assembly" (Fox 1971:429–30). Citing the observations of Lois Crisler, he further elaborates the music metaphor, describing a field technique of natural history that recalls the participant observation of ethnographers:

> . . . the mechanics of the wolf howl or song as a kind of ululation, the tongue being drawn up and down in the mouth like a trombone slide, and on a long note, the tip of the tongue is curled against the roof of the mouth. The notes are shaped by altering the tension of the cheeks. If she [Crisler] sang with the wolf on the same note, the wolf would shift a note or two. Wolves, she concludes, seem to avoid unison singing and instead prefer chords! (1971:170–71)

5. Duncan Emrich has written about conventions governing hound naming in Maryland (1972), and James Salter (1888) outlined the poetic strictures imposed on hound namers in Great Britain more than a century ago. I want to thank Herbert Halpert for bringing both articles to my attention.

6. These inscriptions fall under Goffman's heading of "laminator verbs": speech acts that enclose messages about events in a different realm (Goffman 1974:505; Young 1987:226–28), in this case, the Chaseworld.

7. Georg Simmel writes that, in the truly sociable interchange:

> . . . personalities must not emphasize themselves too individually. Where real interests, cooperating or clashing determine the social form, they provide of themselves that the individual shall not present his peculiarities and individuality with too much abandon and aggressiveness. (Simmel 1971:130)

8. "Allelomimesis" is the term used by canine ethologists to describe the tendency of certain canine species to run together in large gregarious packs (Fox 1971:204).

9. Katharine Young, in a consideration of joint storytelling, observes that "Chiming in to complete another person's utterance, whether competitive or collaborative, discloses shared understandings" (1987:184).

5. Inscribing the Fox

Foxes aren't called foxes just for the name, you know—they're *foxy*!
—Ann Davis (Interview, November 21, 1980)

HISTORICALLY THE fox is a newcomer to the ancient practice of coursing with hounds. Throughout the Middle Ages the fox was deemed unworthy to grace the coats of arms occupied by other quarry with whom aristocrats were pleased to associate themselves. Considered not only inedible but unsavory in character, foxes were classed as vermin, not game. Red foxes and foxhunting came to this country via Great Britain, where eighteenth-century nobles began chasing foxes when the stag (*Cervus elaphus*) had been nearly extirpated. Anthropologist James Howe argues that foxes were only drafted into the chase because no other creature in Great Britain's forests could support a chase on horseback. English-style foxhunting, he argues, has little to do with foxes, creatures that have nothing to contribute to aristocratic identities.

Yet the notion that hunting fosters an empathetic relationship between hunter and quarry is widespread. "The pursuer cannot pursue," writes Ortega y Gasset, "if he does not integrate his vision with that of the animal" (1972:124). In the course of integrating one's vision with an object of pursuit, one aspires to think like the fugitive. "I've often wondered to myself," said Jack Davis, pondering the mystery of fox consciousness, "'wonder what they think of when they hear that pack of dogs trailin'?'"

"After them poor little foxies," said his wife, Ann.

"I often thought to meself, wonder what the hell they think?" Jack repeated.

"And what do you answer?" I asked.

"I don't know!" he exclaimed. "I ain't *got* the answer!" (interview, November 14, 1980).

The more resourceful and wily the fugitive, the greater the esteem in which he is held by his pursuers, who would only diminish in stature themselves if bested by half-wits and underlings.[1]

The fox—indeed a very different quarry from the stag—is inscribed by the subjects of Howe's study as "artful rogue," "rare old sinner," and "the chartered free-booter of our fields and forests." Such terms, Howe suggests, make the fox sound more like a charming poacher than a noble lord of the forest (1981:295). But perhaps the fox offers something other than nobility to its pursuers, who must spend at least some time imagining the world through vulpine eyes.[2]

While the fox is not the paradigmatic equivalent of the stag, as a symbol—an emblem lavishly inscribed on its pursuers—it still has to work for its living. The question is, how is the fox rendered a suitable object of pursuit in particular contexts, and how does identification with foxes square with the identification with hounds, which are in opposition to foxes?

Anthropologist Edmund Leach theorizes that English foxhunting, which he terms "a barbarous ritual surrounded by extraordinary and fantastic taboos," sprang up partly as a way of coming to terms with an anomalous, liminal beast. He averred that for the English the fox is so anomalous as to be the sole occupant of its class, a creature poised at "the borderline between edible game and inedible domestic animals" (Leach 1964:52).

Because animals employed in human rituals so often appear to be anomalous, anthropologists have theorized that rituals take shape around a creature's marginality as a way of mitigating its threat to cherished cultural categories. In this view, between-ness is powerful, whether it is embodied in the liminal phase of ritual (Turner 1977), the marginality of tricksters (Babcock-Abrahams 1975), or the anomalousness of cassowaries (Bulmer 1967). Anomalous creatures are thought to possess creative, intermediary powers that can be unleashed and controlled through ritual means. Laden with qualities from both sides of categorical boundaries, such creatures traverse symbolically the problematic borders between self and society, masculine and feminine, nature and culture, and, at another level, order and chaos.

But anomaly is not a given-in-the-world, or even a given in worlds beyond a particular province of meaning (Halverson 1977:515). Foxes are not inherently symbolic, but rather are inscribed as such. The fox of foxhunters is a Chaseworld character, an anomalous creature somewhere between dogs and cats. And the scale, as we will see, is a sliding one.

Chaseworld Foxes

Chaseworld foxes are uniquely located within the social and natural order. Foxhunters constitute the fox in part by lowering and raising the level of contrast between foxes on the one hand and dogs and cats on the other. These modifications of the fox are sensitive to shifting political and ideological contexts. Clyde Kluckhohn observed that "when a culture as a whole changes rapidly its myths are also substantially and quickly altered" (1942: 56). Faced with declining fox populations and rising public antagonism toward hunting, Pine Barrens foxhunters have abolished the kill from the chase. Accordingly they have withdrawn the fox from the category of vermin, doing so partly by strengthening its links with dogs and cats.

When hunters routinely killed foxes up until the early 1960s, they often accounted for their sport as a means of varmint control. "People used to think the fox was an awful outlaw," said Leon Hopkins (foxchase, January 22, 1986). Loathing of foxes was so pervasive that one naturalist blames the fox's renowned craftiness on centuries of human aggression against its kind: "As a result of contact with man [red foxes] have developed a cunning that now connotes the name fox with the acme of cleverness" (Walker 1975:1156). The bounty on fox offered by many states (including New Jersey until the early 1970s) supported the view of foxes as vermin; they were widely despised, and fair game for anyone. However, now that the bounty on foxes has been lifted, and hunters regularly call off their dogs to preserve a depleted resource, we find the fox has been rewritten as a kinder, gentler trickster.

The idealized fox of Pine Barrens foxhunters is a well-respected trickster, a full-fledged Chaseworld accomplice; unperturbed by the hounds and fully in command of the situation, the fox is "game" in the best sense of the term as it is often applied to hounds and humans. Foxes like Old Sage and Fireball epitomized this ideal. "Freeman and I," recalled Norman Taylor, telling the story to Hank Stevenson, John-John Earlin (John Earlin's grandson and namesake), and myself:

"We run some of the first red ones we had around here, and we had one that we called Fireball. We used to always start him in the Laps, and he would run up into Buckingham. Went way up above Danny Brit's cabin and back again. And you could run that fox all day, I'm tellin' you. He'd almost let dogs look at him, and you could run him all day.

"And John [Earlin] he—it was on New Year's Day, and he overslept. He came by with a whole load of dogs, and we was runnin' right there in the laps. We said, "Get 'em in there!' And he threw 'em all in, and we run that fox till just about dark, and, Christ! What dogs was left—there wasn't a whole buncha dogs was left, and they come out on the railroad.

"And we was loadin' dogs, and that fox sat down on the railroad watchin' us. That's the truth. He just run right down the railroad a ways and set right there on his behind, and watched us loadin' dogs. I said, 'John, what do you think of that?'"

"He must've been in shape," said Hank Stevenson.

"Fireball!" pronounced Norman.

"He was an in-shape fox," repeated Hank.

"Yup," Norman concurred.

"Whatever happened to Fireball?" I asked.

"I never knew," replied Norman. "Probably somebody killed him or something, yeah. But we had him there for about three years, that same fox. Yeah, he was a nice one" (interview, October 17, 1986).

Even in the 1950s, when Fireball was running, hunters did not like to see such a fox destroyed. But the fox is a contested creature over whom hunters, trappers, and animal rights activists continue to vie for hegemony. State fish and game regulations allow deerhunters to kill foxes if they have not taken any deer, and trappers are permitted to take foxes in snares. Thirty years ago the verminous status of foxes supported foxhunting; now, however, foxhunters find their sport threatened by negative public opinion not only about hunting but about foxes as well. In a single stroke foxhunters manage their own enemies and the enemies of foxes by deflecting the ire of animal rights activists toward those who kill foxes for livelihood or sport. Hunters now systematically peal away the fox's image as a marauder of poultry and rabbits (the quarry of other sportsmen) to reveal a benign creature who thrives on nuts and berries, field mice and snakes.

Robly Champion, playing to the strong local revulsion against snakes, pronounces the fox an excellent means of snake control. For the benefit of rabbit hunters, however, he emphatically minimizes its impact on the rabbit population. "Are there people around here who think the fox is a varmint they'd just as soon be rid of?" I asked him.

"Lots of people," he answered.

> But I love to rabbit hunt, and I still say that right where you got fox the thickest you got rabbits the thickest, and I can prove to anybody that the fox waits till the meat gets rotten before they start to eat it. It spoils. And, like snakes, I've watched—I've taken *pictures*. I used to sit at the pit . . . and watch these little foxes, and they'd come out there and the mother'd bring 'em a snake. You oughta watch them eatin' that snake. (Interview, September 1979)

The opportunistic character of the fox in flight is made to extend to its wide-ranging, omnivorous appetite. "A fox'll eat most anything," said John

Earlin. "He'll eat cranberries, he'll eat acorns, he'll eat mice, he'll eat crickets. He'll eat most anything at all. He'll eat rabbits, he'll eat birds" (interview, November 22, 1980). And if a fox does take a few cherished birds now and then, it is really no worse than a dog or a cat, according to Jack and Ann Davis.

"Do gray foxes eat rabbits?" I asked them.

"Oh yeah," replied Jack, "but I think a gray fox is more into woods mice."

"I think the fox is accused of some things it don't do," said Ann. "It'll rob nests, birds 'n' quail 'n' grouse."

"No, I don't believe they do, Ann," her husband corrected her.

"Not near as much as a skunk or a mink," she capitulated.

"Well, a cat would do it," conceded Jack. "A dog would do it" (interview, November 21, 1980).

This quarry, so close in substance to its predator, is inscribed as inedible. The close identification of foxes with dogs and cats, which are in turn closely associated with humans, is one of the bases for deeming foxes inedible, making the proscription against eating foxes a likely extension of the taboo against cannibalism.

"Do people ever eat foxes?" I asked Jack and Ann Davis.

"Noooo!" exclaimed Jack.

"Too strong, like a dog or a cat," Ann explained.

"Too strong!" echoed Jack.

"See," said Ann, "one of them belongs to the cat family, one belongs to the dog family" (interview, November 14, 1986). Thus simile gives way to synecdoche in the hunters' reclassification of red and gray foxes as dogs and cats respectively.

At another level, inscriptions of the fox as trickster raise the degree of contrast with the honest, team-spirited hounds. This contrast echoes in a way the scheme whereby naturalists arrange wild canids along a dimension of sociability, locating the competitive, unsociable foxes at one end and the gregarious wolves at the other. Foxes, "type I" canids, do not mate for life, have a very loose social structure, and hunt independently, stalking quarry smaller than themselves. Wolves, "type III" canids, are thought to be the progenitors of pack hounds. They mate for life and dwell in complex, socially stratified packs (Fox 1975:431–36).

Foxhunters' inscriptions of the fox as wild and wily, and of dogs as cooperative and honest, implicitly draw the contrast along the same axis. Foxes, seen as solitary, uncooperative creatures who drive each other out of their territories, are not team players. Foxhunters often depict the fox as a creature who enjoys the opportunity to put the pack to the test, who shatters the hounds' teamwork through trickery.

Such allegations, which have stood for centuries, have wrought for the fox a compelling image that is difficult even for naturalists to shake. One naturalist complains that folklore has contaminated his field of inquiry: "Accounts of the cunning and extraordinary reasoning ability of red foxes have become so firmly entrenched in our folklore that one has difficulty conducting an objective study of the animal" (Ables 1975:233). And Konrad Lorenz, the eminent animal ethologist, impugns folk scribes for encapsulating bad natural history in proverbs:

> Strange what blind faith is placed in proverbs, even when what they say is false or misleading. The fox is not more cunning than other beasts of prey and is much more stupid than wolf or dog, the dove is certainly not peaceful, and of the fish, rumour spreads only untruth; it is neither so cold-blooded as one says of dull people, nor is the "fish in water" nearly so happily situated as the converse saying would imply (Lorenz 1952:22).

Foxhunters, in turn scandalized by what they see as the naturalists' misclassification of foxes as canids, argue that foxes are not very doglike. They criticize the inconsistency of naming a creature *vulpes* and placing it within the canine taxa. For both, however, the fox does not quite fit into the category assigned it. By foxhunters and at least some naturalists, the fox is construed as a creature "between," mostly between dogs and cats.[3] The question to take up here concerns the nature and function of this betweenness, so characteristic of tricksters, jokers, and other liminal beings.

The Case of the Feline Fox

Popular natural histories of foxes, of great interest to foxhunters, make much of the animal's feline qualities. "This canid hunts like a cat," remarks one writer in *Natural History Magazine* (Henry 1980). And a prominent English-style foxhunter theorizes that "The vulpine surely provides the link between the worlds of the canine and feline" (Watson 1977:36). Having accepted the ground rules that group foxes with dogs, naturalists and others then proceed to marvel at the fox's undoglike features: its contractile pupils and its scent glands, its tree-climbing abilities, its giving birth to "cubs," just like lions, tigers, leopards, and other felids. One author suggests that the use of "cub" to designate young bears as well is "merely another of the anomalies already mentioned." Concluding that "whenever Nature draws a straight line, she smudges it," he implies that such lines are givens-in-the-world, not cultural inventions (Burton 1955:612).

While hunters elsewhere ponder the catlike behavior of red foxes, Pine Barrens hunters who chase mostly gray foxes claim their quarry is the most catlike of all, intensifying its status as an anomalous creature. "The way I put it," said Jack Davis, "the red fox is in the dog family, and the gray fox is in the cat family."

"You can see it in the Latin names," said Norman Taylor, using the naturalists' own scheme against them. "They aren't even in the same family." Norman and others point out that the gray fox, *Urocyon cinereoargenteus*, leaves a small, catlike track in contrast with the doglike pawprint of the red fox, *Vulpes fulva*. While red foxes climb only leaning trees, the gray fox, equipped with semiretractile claws, can climb to the tops of telephone poles. Just as cats have smaller litters than dogs, so gray foxes are less prolific than red ones. Norman and Caroline Taylor cited a pet red fox that ran rabbits alongside beagle dogs, and a pet gray fox that took readily to kitty litter (interview, November 23, 1980).

"The gray is in the feline family," said Norman Taylor. "The red is in the canine family. No way will they interbreed. . . . They're definitely different families. A cat would nurse a gray fox in a second. We never have tried to nurse a red fox on a cat. I know for a fact a cat will nurse a gray fox."

"The gray one," said Caroline Taylor, "you can train easier to use the cat box. The red fox is harder. We never did get Snoopy trained to use the litter box. He would use it, but you couldn't depend on him all the time" (interview, November 23, 1980).

Jack Davis contrasted their eating and breeding habits to support the sundering of foxes into two different animal families:

> I don't have any proof, but they tell me that a mouse will make a gray fox a meal, whereby a red fox eats a lot. Then on top of it, a gray fox has a small litter—two or three, and a red fox is liable to have seven or eight. (Interview, November 14, 1980)

Chaseworld behaviors are made to uphold this distinction. Red and gray foxes are in fact said to be so different that some hounds will run one but not the other. Gray foxes are easier to catch than red foxes, according to Norman Taylor:

'Cause they're not as big and they don't run as fast, and believe it or not they don't go in a hole like a red fox. You get *him* tired out, *he'll* go in a hole. He knows where all the holes are. He'll get in one. Now a gray fox'll climb a tree, like one of these trees here. He'll climb right up it just like a cat if you get runnin' him too hard. (Foxchase, August 12, 1982)[4]

A possible reading of the dog/cat :: red fox/gray fox equation relates to differences between human men and women within the Chaseworld. That is to say, inscriptions of red and gray foxes parallel to a degree inscriptions of men and women. Generally, in our culture, as a large stockpile of metaphors indicates, dogs are regarded as masculine while cats are seen as feminine. Wives and husbands are said to fight like cats and dogs. Men can be leaders of the pack, gossipy women are said to be catty. When Elvis sings, "You ain't nothin' but a hound dog," he is singing about a man. "Kitty" is a woman's name. There are also plenty of exceptions, but Konrad Lorenz himself evinces the widespread, unconscious view of dogs as male and cats as female when in the preface to his *Man Meets Dog* he assigns gender to dogs and cats:

> The whole charm of the dog lies in the depth of the friendship and the strength of the spiritual ties with which he has bound himself to man, but the appeal of the cat lies in the very fact that she has formed no close bond with him, that she has the uncompromising independence of a tiger or a leopard while she is hunting in his stables and barns; that she still remains mysterious and remote when she is rubbing herself gently against the legs of her mistress or purring contentedly in front of the fire. (1955: x)

But whether a fox is a he-fox or a vixen, hunters inscribe it as male when the hounds are chasing it. Thus the gray fox's felinity is particularly jarring, as is its behavioral proximity to a taboo quarry that hounds sometimes mistakenly run.

Norman Taylor told a story of how he once accidentally cast his hounds on a cat and the chase ended up in the basement of a Whiting resident. The proscribed location for cats, gray foxes, and women is close to the home. Hence the feral cat's status as a pollutant in the woods, described by Jack Davis above, and its close association with the hearth, nicely described by Lorenz:

> The purring cat is, for me, a symbol of the hearthside and the hidden security for which it stands. I should like no more to be without a cat in my home than to be without the dog that trots behind me in field or street. (1955: x)

Gray foxes are said to stay close to home, in contrast to red foxes who wander far afield. Said Norman:

> This gray fox, he lives right here, and about the only place he's gonna run is between Reeves's Bogs here and the big swamp here and over in these briars and back, where a red fox, he has no home. You start him and he could go anyplace. Ten, fifteen mile from here. (Foxchase, January 25, 1986)

Hounds are masculine tools for achieving male solidarity, which by definition excludes women. "I only want a hound dog, not a sweetheart," sang Joe Albert, in a parody of the 1930s hit by Eddie Jones:

> For sweethearts only make you blue.
> Sweethearts make a promise, then they'll break it.
> That's a thing a hound would never do.[5]

Though Joe Albert never went down that lane, most of the other foxhunters in this study did, and they often presented foxhunting as a thing not entirely within their wives' ken. Oscar Hillman reported that his wife asked him, "Don't you ever get lonely up there in the woods?"

"I've got the dogs," he answered. "They're my buddy and I'm their buddy."

The system dividing males from females does not extend to hounds. Female hounds, alluded to as "gyps" (more polite) and bitches, are otherwise inscribed no differently from male hounds and are expected to run and behave as males in the Chaseworld.

Central to the male sphere is the pursuit of action, "chancy tasks undertaken for 'their own sake'" (Goffman 1967:239). Action always entails risk, and neither women nor gray foxes are inscribed as risk takers. Women who hunt do so in the context of the family structure, accompanying a male relative who runs hounds. And by and large, when women have jurisdiction over dogs, they are house dogs, not hounds. Once, when Norman Taylor offered to give his wife, Caroline, a hound on the condition that she take it hunting, she refused on the grounds that it would disrupt her relationship with the family pet (foxchase, August 12, 1982).

Interestingly, in the Pine Barrens, where it is the preferred beast of the chase, the gray fox is more anomalous than the red fox. Perhaps the feminization of the gray fox places it closer to nature, a position universally occupied by women (Ortner 1974). Thus located, it becomes superior in its capacity to mediate nature and culture, a task also assigned to women.

Figure 5.1. Joe Albert at his "Homeplace," a hunting cabin in the Forked River Mountains. Photo by Carl Fleischhauer, May 1980. Courtesy of the American Folkife Center, U.S. Library of Congress.

Anthropologist Sherry Ortner points out that the universal assignment of women to the home relates to their work as primary caregivers for young children, whom they must socialize and cultivate (Ortner 1974). Here we might recall that the term "fox" is metaphorically applied to both men and women, with very different connotations, an instance of the fox's capacity to bridge those polarities.[6] Whereas foxiness in females implies physical beauty, foxiness in men implies an ability to manipulate reality in order to deceive. At a concrete level, the fox brings nature within the hunters' range;

at a metaphoric level, it orchestrates for them a display of culturally constructed reality, calling attention, through its ability to deceive hounds and to resist the structure imposed on it by hunters, to the vulnerability of that reality.

The desire for contact with nature is a powerful motivating force in foxhunting. The fox is not only the conductor of their canine symphonies, but an animal guide on whose trail hunters witness natural events and are astounded by them: the whippoorwill with eyes like balls of fire, the pregnant rattlesnake in the brush, the wild beehive suspended from a pine bough, the uncanny call of a deer for its mate, the explosive percussion of a courting grouse. "There are so many wonderful things happening," said Milton Collins, "that they don't all come to mind" (interview, December 18, 1980). Bursting through the structure of the foxchase, Nature dramatically intervenes in Culture, raising the curtain on unexpected scenes and vignettes, wresting the hunters' attention away from foxchases, daydreams, and sleep.

"I'll tell you," said Jack Davis, "they'll make you think in the night when you're there." The topic was whippoorwills.

"Jakie and I was there to Papoose, and we was settin' there, and the dogs was runnin'. There's a big swamp there—cranberry bogs, swamps—they was runnin', we listened to 'em, moon was just as bright as day.

"And Jakie, he don't pull up long 'fore, that's it, he's asleep. I'm settin' there, listening to 'em, got my flashlight in me hand, and that stinkin' damn thing lit close as that stove, let out 'WHIPPOORWILL!!' And it raised me up, Jakie raised right up: 'What the hell was that?'"

"Could you see it?" I broke in.

"I shone me light right on it," Jack declared.

"Their eyes are like little balls of fire," said Ann.

"Just look like fire," Jack emphasized. "But I'm tellin' you, Mary, settin' there in the quiet night, now, and he was settin' there quiet and everything—it gives you a funny thrill, now don't you think it don't" (interview, November 21, 1980).

David Wilson suggests that untoward events in nature have the same impact on their witnesses as great works of art or religious experiences have on the connoisseur or mystic. The effect is one of freedom from form, of release from ordinary experience.

> To come face to face with a flying spider or a rattlesnake in the road unhinges habit and intensifies awareness, just as stumbling upon an ancient rune does,

or encountering a burning bush. These uncommon phenomena throw the settled world into disarray. . . . Everyday meaning and value become problematic. Close attention must be paid and care taken if one is to make sense of it all, and if the world is to make sense still. (1978:1)

As a backdrop for such events, the Chaseworld itself takes on the cast of the Ordinary.

Seen as being closer to nature than men and hounds, women and foxes are more ambiguous, more intermediary. The tasks of bringing nature to culture—such as giving birth, rearing young children, of preparing food— are generally assigned to women, while the more abstract work of sense-making, of making categories and assigning contents to them, is left to men. Ortner writes:

> . . . women tend to enter into relationships with the world that culture might see as being more "like nature"—immanent and embedded in things as given—than "like culture"—transcending and transforming things through the superimposition of abstract categories and transpersonal values. (1974:82)

The fox's incorporation of male and female aspects enables an interesting reversal to take place in the Chaseworld. In the Ordinary it is the women who, by dint of their bodily cycles and functions, are often perceived as being closer to nature. Thus positioned, they serve as intermediaries, integrating nature and culture, heart and mind. Within the Chaseworld, which excludes women and thus places them at a greater distance from nature than men, men become intermediaries who experience and present nature to their audiences. These audiences, of course, include women. In the Chaseworld, independently of women, men named for animals achieve contact with nature through the androgynous fox.

The fox at the Chaseworld's center, neither wholly dog nor wholly cat, mediates the oppositions it embodies: male and female, nature and culture, home and abroad, sociable and unsociable, food and not-food, insider and outsider, concrete and abstract. As a catlike dog on the margins of society, the fox also threatens the reality that rests on such agreed-upon distinctions.

The Fox and the Joker

An omnivorous, androgynous, anomalous creature, a dishonest beast on whom the entire reality of the Chaseworld is centered, the fox fits the classic trickster paradigm. In this contest between order and chaos, the fox is clearly the antistructural figure whose trail engenders the music. He endeavors to silence this music by giving the hounds a false picture of the trail, by falsifying their impression of reality.

In its creative/destructive dualism, and in its assumption of the role of dupe as well as of fabricator, the fox (taken here as the sum total of its presentations by Pine Barrens foxhunters) offers a version of the archetypal trickster described by Paul Radin in his classic study:

> Trickster is at one and the same time creator and destroyer, giver and negator, he who dupes others and who is always duped himself. He wills nothing consciously. At all times he is constrained to behave as he does from impulses over which he has no control. He knows neither good nor evil yet he is responsible for both. He possesses no values, moral or social, is at the mercy of his passions and appetites, yet through his actions all values come into being. (1972: xxiii)

No longer depicted as the evil marauder of the henhouse, or the hapless victim of the hounds, today's ideal Chaseworld fox emerges as a supremely conscious being, remarkable for its ability to manipulate context.

This marginal creature at the heart of the Chaseworld has a standard repertoire of tricks. "Oh they have all kinds of tricks," said John Earlin. "They'll run right along up a path and then turn right around and run back it. And the dogs'll go right on up it and there'll be nothing there (foxchase, November 15, 1980).

Foxes have been known to stop abruptly and let a pack of dogs rush over them, giving themselves a good lead in the opposite direction before dogs get wise to the ploy. Norman Taylor called this behavior "skulking."[7] "I seen him skulking," he reported, "where he'd try to run right back through the dogs" (interview, October 17, 1986).

Each fox has a stock routine, which lends itself to the development of a Chaseworld character whom hunters can identify. As Norman Taylor put it:

> We can actually tell the foxes we're runnin' by the area he runs in, and the roads he takes, the crossin's he makes, yeah, so when you get a fox you've run a lot you can almost tell where he's goin' to go. (Interview, January 22, 1986)

A gray fox at Reeves' Bogs, for example, is known to run in a circular pattern, the kind of pattern that lends itself to listening and seeing. "This fox," said Norman, "he belongs to run here, and he's going to run between here and over them briars, I'll tell you that right now" (foxchase, January 25, 1986).

On another occasion, Norman characterized a new fox, predicting its Chaseworld habits. "So Pomeroy run that fox last night that I run today," he said, reporting to his wife Caroline and myself. "Accordin' to Leon he done the same thing with him: he lost 'im in the road. Now he's gonna be a bad fox to run. He's gonna do that every time."

"Sure," said Caroline. "He knows how to trick you."

"Yeah," said Norman. "There's no scent on that blacktop road, the dogs can't smell him" (foxchase, August 12, 1982).

Foxes are seen to interact with hunters in ways that are aggressive and manipulative. They go to the hunters to be rescued from hounds, and they "laugh" at the hunters when they've worn the dogs out. "This is probably an old fox, an old he-fox that's been here all his life, and knows every briar patch and every inch of the woods," said Norman Taylor of a fox that confounded his hounds. "A young fox wouldn't do this to you" (foxchase, January 22, 1986). And of an uncooperative quarry John Earlin commented, "You can't take a picture of this fox. This fox won't let you" (foxchase, November 15, 1980).

Hunters portray foxes as calculating beings. "Have you ever seen a fox hide and watch the dogs go by?" I asked Jack Davis.

"I actually saw one in a blueberry field," Jack replied.

> I was settin' in the truck, just about from here to the fence over there. It was a red fox, come over and come down this row of blueberries, and right opposite to me the fox stopped. And this man had two dogs, was runnin' it slow. They come "Baroo! Baroo! Baroo!" And after a bit, when they hit the row where this fox was in, and the fox turned around and trotted down another row.
>
> They wasn't botherin' him. They was a couple old dogs, runnin' him slow. But it was comical to sit there and look, he'd sit there, and had his head turned around watchin' up the row for them dogs to come to the end of the row. (Interview, November 21, 1980)

Creatively negating the constraints imposed on it by the Chaseworld, the fox shifts the balance of power, turning the Chaseworld's terrestrial trail rule to its own advantage. The fox tricks not only the dogs, but the hunters who inhabit the dogs. "Why is it so hard for a dog to catch a fox?" I asked Norman Taylor. "Why?" he answered:

> Because the fox has got a lot of tricks to do, and he's [the dog's] gotta follow every inch he does. First of all he's gotta get up underneath him and get him

runnin' hard. And then you gotta outwind him. You gotta outrun—you gotta
have more wind than the fox has, once you get him runnin' hard. And by doin'
that you can't miss him anyplace, otherwise that fox is gonna rest up on you.
(Foxchase, August 11, 1982).

The smarter the fox, the more he rises to the level of noble adversary, a role
traditionally played by favored quarry, the sort whose qualities hunters may
transfer to themselves. "Hunters come to imitate their quarry," writes
Ortega y Gasset (1972:125). Do foxhunters imitate foxes? If so, how and to
what end?

In one story told by Jack Davis, Davis becomes an extension of the fox,
serving as an accomplice who aids the fox in duping another hunter and all
of the dogs. The story is actually about two fabrications, an animal fabrication and a human one in which it becomes nested. In the story, both
fabrications follow the classic pattern of the practical joke. This pattern,
according to Richard Bauman, has five parts: orientation, setup, trick
event, discrediting of fabrication, and evaluation (1986:45). To illustrate
parallels between the fabrications, I have identified these parts of the
pattern in brackets, assigning roman numerals to the fox and lower case
letters to Jack Davis.

The discussion among Jack Davis, his wife Ann, and myself has turned
to smart foxes. Davis, a skilled raconteur, has a way of inserting his listeners
into the Chaseworld, of conjuring the dogs into the dining room, placing
the fox just outside the window and the road beneath our feet. "I'll tell you,
Mary," says Jack, anticipating the story he has to tell, "they're pretty damn
smart. They're pretty damn smart now.

[I. Orientation]
They'll fool you. I was up there one time with Jakie. The dogs are
trailin' off here, I'm standin' on the road. Jakie's over with the dogs and
I'm listenin' to 'em. All at once I hear somethin' scratchin'. I go "What
the hell's happenin'?"
[II. Setup]
And I looked right out oh just about maybe a little farther than that
holly tree is out there, and there's this fox goin' up a tree. The tree's—
oh maybe a little higher than this ceiling, you know what I mean—and
he got right on top of it and I'm standin' there watchin' him. Now
them dogs hadn't gotten where he got out of his bed fresh and he was
up that tree. And they come out there rarin' and Jakie at that time was
younger and boy he come out a-runnin'.

Figure 5.2. Jack Davis of Browns Mills. Photo by the author, September 1983.

[III. Trick event]
 You know what the funny part was? The dogs couldn't go nowhere.
[a. setup]
 He says "What the hell" he says "is wrong?"
 "What do you mean?"
 "Well where the hell did the fox go?"
[b. trick event]
 "I don't know," I says, "they lost him."
 "Well hell they couldn't lose him."
 So I let it go a minute or two.
 I said "Don't you know where that fox is?"
 "No—where?"

[c. discrediting of human fabrication]

    I pointed. (Davis points to the holly tree outside the window)

[d. evaluation]

    "Well I'll be goddammed" he says. So he walked up the road this
way with the dogs to get 'em away from it,

[IV. Discrediting of animal fabrication]

    and I chased it out of the tree. But the next time it went over in the big
swamp and that was the end of the chase.

[V. Evaluation of animal fabrication]

    But they will do that once in a while, but very seldom. They don't do it
very often" (interview, November 21, 1980).

In this account, Jack Davis opportunistically seizes on the fox's trick,
using it to play one on Jakie. Through the similarity in rule structures,
Davis implicitly draws a parallel between the two tricksters, the fox and
himself, both of whom manipulate Chaseworld information in a way that
produces confusion and discomfiture in their victims.[8] That Davis models
his behavior on that of the fox suggests that this worthy adversary is a
potent resource for identity building, as a brief look at the relationship
between the story and its setting shows.

This story is anchored in a conversation to which it contributes a
point, which is that foxes are smart enough to fool you. But that is not the
entire point, for this fox, smart enough to fool other human beings and
other canids, did not fool Jack Davis, who was, as it turns out, smart
enough to fool Jakie. Jack Davis's demonstration of wit in the Chaseworld
strays into the Storyrealm, where it enhances his image as a canny hunter.
The story illustrates one way in which inscriptions of animal players and
events in the Chaseworld come to have bearing upon their human witnesses in the conversational realm.

This sort of prank is often recounted in stories. Though the hunters'
behavior is not always so neatly aligned with the fox's, it is analogous.
Jokers, like foxes, are benign tricksters deemed remarkable for their abilities
to manipulate and control their situations through joke rites (Douglas
1968).[9] In the joke rite, whether invented on the spot or constituted in
anecdotes, the joker disinvents the social structure in which he is implicated, substituting for it a structure of his own invention[10] (Douglas
1968:365).

Inveterate jokers, foxhunters overturn structures of reality as capri-
ciously as foxes distort their own trails, substituting structures of their own

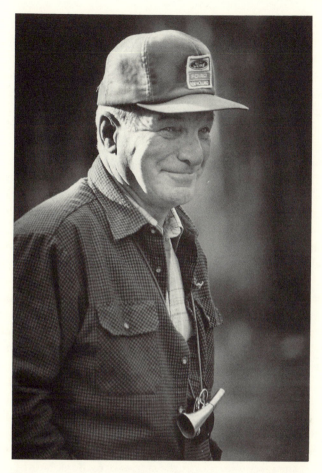

Figure 5.3. Bob Hayes of Port Elizabeth. Photo by Dennis McDonald, April 1991.

design. "Mary, you want to see a foxhunter's trick?" Oscar Hillman asked me, during a foxchase.

"Yeah, sure," I said. "A foxhunter's trick?"

"Look here," said Oscar, pointing to a muddy can attached to the tailpipe of Bob Hayes's pickup truck. "That's a can of baked beans tied on there," he laughs incredulously.

Bob Hayes begins elaborating. "Damn right, Mary, when you want a hot can of beans, you just take a screwdriver and take that can off! The tailpipe is always hot, so the beans stay hot!" He waits for the laughter to subside and continues: "I tell you what. I always kept a couple cans of beans on my manifold—"

"Uh-huh," laughs a skeptical bystander.

"—and that's good. *But*—the way they make these new trucks nowadays, the can of beans slips down and gets into your throttle control, and here I'm goin' down the road around sixty mile an hour with a can of beans, and got my throttle wide open, and I turn the key off and my steering wheel locks! So I put 'em on the tailpipe now."

Oscar Hillman and others standing nearby are mightily amused at Haysie's "trick," which turns out to reside not so much in the attaching of a cylinder to his exhaust pipe—whether to protect the pipe from ruts or to have a hot meal handy—as in Haysie's ingenious devising of alternatives to convention (foxchase, April 7, 1991).

Often in stories of themselves and each other, hunters appear as jokers, celebrated for pulling one over on a stranger or a warden or a fellow hunter. Like foxes they have stock routines, which are made uniquely available to them within the Chaseworld and which become hallmarks of foxhunting personalities. More than one hunter appeared as protagonist in stories of the stranger who was unable to hear hounds' voices as music, and of the woman who forced a hunter to curse in front of her in order to answer her question about hounds' names.

Like the fox, the joker is an enemy of boundaries, a font of creative negation and possibility relocated in the Chaseworld from the edge of things to the center. Within the Chaseworld, the paradoxical figures of foxes and jokers unexpectedly illuminate reality from novel angles, revealing hidden possibilities and meanings. As we will see in the following chapter, it is the joker who frames the stories of foxhunters as lies. Denying his own discourse, the joker whimsically cancels reality, like the fox whose entropic mission is to stifle the music for which his trail is the score.

Notes

1. The psychology of this perverse respect for the fugitive from justice was aptly stated by David Cyr, the U.S. Postal Inspector assigned to the trail of Tom Billington, a savings and loan official who had fled into hiding with millions of dollars he had stolen from his institution. "It's funny how you feel like you know someone when you're in pursuit," says Cyr. "There's a kind of intimacy builds up, but it's only one way. You think you're thinking like him. . . . I guess we'd like to believe that he's very smart and clever, because if we don't, if we're dealing with a

buffoon, then what does that say about us?" (Gup 1991:13; used with permission of the *Washington Post Magazine*).

2. In Great Britain, the days of the noble lords have passed, and with them the noble quarry. Might not the changing historical context for hunting be reflected in the inscriptions of the quarry noted by Howe? Consider that the noble lords were divested of their deer with the help of poachers (epitomized by Robin Hood), and that the descendants and would-be descendants of these noble lords, in full pursuit of the "charming poacher" (whose colors, incidentally, they have appropriated in their costumes), are sometimes taken to court for trespassing on the lands of ordinary people. Might such inscriptions euphemize and thereby trivialize the trespassing of aristocrats? For a discussion of the fierce controversy surrounding the trespassing of foxhunters in England, see Newall (1983).

3. Roger Abrahams points out that foxes "are not alone in this in-between-ness," noting that animals focused on in other realms of hunting (e.g., raccoons, possums, squirrels, badgers) similarly achieve "a kind of ritual elevation" within the vermin-game (i.e., killable) kingdom" (personal communication, August 1989).

4. This view of red and gray foxes is upheld among those who practice this kind of foxhunting elsewhere. Stuart Marks collected the following statement from a foxhunter in North Carolina:

> The gray fox—from the scientific name you'd know the gray fox is more or less a member of the cat family, he's a feline. And the red fox is from the dog family, he's a canine. . . . For instance, a gray fox can climb a tree, the red fox can't. The gray fox is a lot like a cat, he sneaks around like a cat, and if you get one and he's an older fox that's been run some, he might come out of there and make a two mile circle, but he's gonna get back in a swamp to really do his thing. The red fox, he just knows he can outrun them. He'll just get out in front of them and outrun them. (Marks, tape transcription of interview on October 4, 1979)

5. Joe Albert, who played washtub bass with a Waretown-based group called "The Pineconers," sang this in concert on May 20, 1980. Permission from MCA Music Publishing company to reprint some of the lyrics from Eddie Jones's song, "I Only Want A Buddy, Not A Sweetheart," is gratefully acknowledged.

6. Compare, for example, the implications of the "foxy lady" epithet with those inherent in monikers for political and military leaders such as "the Swamp Fox" (Francis Marion), "the Red Fox of Kinderhook" (Martin van Buren), and "the Desert Fox" (Erwin Rommel). For more on such metaphoric uses of the fox in society at large, see Hufford (1987).

7. Interestingly, "skulk" is the obsolete collective term for a group of foxes.

8. This squares with Bauman's definition of tricks as:

> enactments of playful deceit in which one party or team (to be called *trickster*) intentionally manipulates features of a situation in such a way as to induce another person or persons (to be called *victim* or *dupe*) to have a false or misleading sense of what is going on and so to behave in a way that brings about discomfiture (confusion, embarrassment, etc.) in the victim. (1986: 36)

9. "The joker," writes Mary Douglas, "is by no means anything like a taboo breaker whose polluting act is a real offense to society." Like the ideal fox, the joker "has a firm hold on his own position in the structure" (1968:372).

10. Mary Douglas defines the joke rite as "a play upon form" wherein "something formal is attacked by something informal" (1968:365).

6. The Chaseworld Anchored in Stories

You dasn't tell too many of them lies, or they'll catch you in one.
—John Earlin

FOXCHASES ARE NOT the only enclaves through which hunters and their audiences enter and inhabit the Chaseworld. Opportunities for peering into the Chaseworld are plentifully lodged in the realm of conversation. Outside foxchases, foxhunters lavish a great deal of attention on the Chaseworld, continually shaping and refining it, sometimes entering it over such thresholds as photographs, home movies, audiocassette recordings of chases, and journal entries. Often in the realm of conversation they open it up through stories.

The Chaseworld, which *can* be attended to outside stories and foxchases, is most vividly conjured and inhabited when constructed as an enclave, that is, in Schutz's words, as a region "belonging to one province enclosed by another" (1970:256). In Katharine Young's phenomenological model of storytelling, the participants first set up an enclave that she terms the Storyrealm. The Storyrealm occurs within the realm of conversation, itself an enclave in the Ordinary. The storytellers then move through this enclave into a reality located in another time and space, the Taleworld (1987). In foxhunting stories, the Taleworld *is* the Chaseworld.[1] In order to construct and maintain the Chaseworld as an alternate reality in conversation, the hunters have to frame what they are doing as storytelling. Continually shifting their attention from the Storyrealm to the Chaseworld and back again, the hunters conjure the Chaseworld.

Though the hunters work at maintaining and conveying the Chaseworld as a discrete reality, the Chaseworld is hardly an island unto itself. As Mary Douglas writes, speaking in general of finite provinces of meaning:

> There is a tendency for meaning to overflow and for distinct provinces to interpenetrate. Schutz has argued that there are separable, independent, finite provinces of meaning. But this becomes implausible when one observes the same formal rules being applied from one range of experience to another. (1973:13)

As foxhunters suggest in their comparison of hounds to storytellers, fox-hunting and storytelling are analogous rites for conjuring society. In both foxchases and stories about them, the Chaseworld comes to mirror the occasion of its conjuring. An examination of the relationship between the Chaseworld and these occasions provides clues to the Chaseworld's variable meanings. Meaning leaks from the Chaseworld into its social settings through metaphorical connections between Chaseworld characters and those in attendance at foxchases and storytelling sessions like the one we are about to consider.

Narrative Boundaries and Frames

In conversation, hunters can orient to the Chaseworld outside stories, but it is through stories that they conjure and inhabit it.[2] Though the Chaseworld is a world that goes on beyond its horizons in stories, within the Storyrealm it has beginnings and endings that mark the initial and final events in a sequence. The Chaseworld is anchored in a Storyrealm that is in turn set apart from the stream of conversation by boundaries that identify what the hunters are doing as storytelling.[3] Within these boundaries, conventions governing ordinary conversation are suspended, and the raconteur emerges.

BOUNDARIES

Storyrealm boundaries, set at the level of the utterance, function to mark the storytelling as a distinctive event within the conversation surrounding it. Storyrealm boundaries comprise openings and closings, and prefaces and codas. Within the Storyrealm, the Chaseworld is set apart as a realm in a different time and place through additional boundaries, Chaseworld beginnings and endings.

An opening launches the story as a distinct event in the conversation, classifying the event as storytelling:

NT: This is a good one. You gotta listen to this.

NH: I got a better one than that!

A closing signals that the story is over, forming a transition between the Chaseworld (the past) and the Storyrealm (the present) in which it is anchored. It serves to emphasize the distinction between the Chaseworld and the Storyrealm:

NH: Those were some days.

NT: They were the good days.

It can also form a bridge between stories:

NT: That's got Tom thinkin'.

A preface can herald a particular story in conversation, signaling that a story is about to be told, and indicating what it is about or what it will illustrate:

JD: Foxes are smart. They'll fool you.

TD: How about the time you let the foxes out of the warden's truck!

And:

NT: Did he ever tell you the one about Fireball?

Taking the form of abstracts, some prefaces serve to summarize or entitle their stories:

JE: How about the joke he used to tell that Aunt Ramona told at the funeral—the one about—
NT: Oh yeah, "John the Dog," yeah—

JE: I have another story, about—a story I would call "The Fox in the Bush."

A coda punctuates the Chaseworld ending, often by recapitulating the salient features of the Chaseworld. It bridges the gap between the Chaseworld and the realm of conversation by moving listeners back toward the present, emphasizing that there is nothing more to tell in that story; the point, which may explicitly recall the anticipatory preface, has been made.

JD: But they will do that once in a while, but very seldom. They don't do it very often.

NT: Yup, you get one like Moe every now and then.

Within the Storyrealm, Chaseworld beginnings and endings mark the start and conclusion of the sequence of Chaseworld events, set in a different time and space:

[Chaseworld beginning]
    JD: I was up there one time with Jakie.
. . .
[Chaseworld ending]
    JD: But the next time it went over in the big swamp and that was the end of the chase.

FRAMES

At a different level of analysis, the hunters frame the Chaseworld with orientations and evaluations, which were defined in Chapter 2. These locate the Chaseworld in time and space and characterize its inhabitants. In stories, a single utterance can perform multiple functions, serving, for instance, simultaneously as boundary and frame:

[Preface/Chaseworld Beginning/Personal/Temporal Orientations]
    TD: First time I ever seen a red fox, I was with Johnny.

Thus an utterance can function to open the Storyrealm while beginning the Chaseworld and orienting listeners to Chaseworld person and time. Hunters also use orientations and evaluations to vivify the Chaseworld, rendering it immediate through the use of tense markers.

ORIENTATIONS

In telling stories, hunters often map Chaseworld time and space onto the Storyrealm through spatial and temporal orientations that turn "there" into "here" and "then" into "now:"

[Spatio-temporal orientation—there and then]
    JD: I was up there one time with Jakie.
[Spatio-temporal orientation—here and now]
    The dogs are trailin' off here, I'm standin' on the road.

Hunters also conjure Chaseworld space by borrowing features of their immediate surroundings:

[Spatial orientation]
>   TD: They were from here to that dogpen. [He points to the kennels, which can be seen through the window.]

Within the boundaries of the Storyrealm, the hunters conjure the Chaseworld, inhabiting it as various characters, invoking its distinctive spatio-temporal matrix. Reproducing the Chaseworld's sounds and utterances, hunters act out the behavior of Chaseworld characters, including the canine players. Thus Tom Driscoll quotes his dogs ("Yupyupyupyupyup!") and emulates the fox's speedy departure ("Whoosh!"). Tense markers help to muffle the distance in time between the Storyrealm and the Chaseworld. The narrator often shifts to the historical present when framing utterances lodged in the past: "I said . . . he says . . . ," while keeping the Chaseworld loosely anchored in the past:

[Past]
>   TD: And I said to this here one old guy, with Walkers, "How did them there pin-eared dogs get turned loose?"

[Present]
>   He says, "What do you mean, 'pin-eared dogs?' "

[Past]
>   I said, "Like them you got on that string there."

"Laminator verbs" like "says" and "said" (Goffman 1974:505) are sometimes dropped altogether as the narrator enacts a dialogue between Chaseworld characters:

>   JD: He says, "what the hell," he says, "is wrong?"
>   "What do you mean?"
>   "Well, where did the fox go?"
>   "I don't know," I says, "they lost him."

Eliminating the laminator verbs, which enclose messages about events in another realm, has the effect of narrowing the distance between the hunter-as-narrator and the hunter-as-Chaseworld-character, thus vivifying the Chaseworld.[4]

Personal orientations link characters in the Chaseworld with people in the Storyrealm. Since these stories are personal experience narratives, most are presented as eyewitness accounts, so that the narrator himself pivots between the Chaseworld and the Storyrealm. Through personal orientations, the storyteller may also heighten the relevance of the Chaseworld for listeners who do not appear as characters in it. Younger hunters, like Charlie Jameson, Jeff Powell, and Hubie Driscoll, do not appear in many of the stories in the session we are about to consider. Thus, to heighten the relevance of one of his stories for them, Tom Driscoll introduces the character Pat Heinrichs, who owned the dog Moe, as "Hubie's grandpop."

EVALUATIONS

Katharine Young observes that conversationalists manage the distinction between Storyrealm and Taleworld through the use of two sorts of evaluation (1987:55–60). The first kind focuses on the stories as stories, classifying the utterances as truth, lies, insults, or good stories (well told):

> NT: That's the truth!

> NH: I got a better one than that!

> HE: But that's a good one. We love to tell that one on John.

The second kind focuses on events within the Chaseworld:

> NT: That's unusual for a red fox.

> JE: But that was the sorrowful part of the foxchase.

Thus, *story* evaluations call attention to the nature and structure of the Storyrealm in this time and place, while *Chaseworld* evaluations focus on events transpiring in another time and place (Young 1987:60). Chaseworld evaluations manage attitudes toward events transpiring within the Chaseworld, keying them as amazing, funny, sad, frustrating, wonderful, and so forth. Chaseworld evaluations tell the audience what to think or how to feel about characters in the Chaseworld:

> NT: That Apie was a hunter though.

Chaseworld evaluations can be delivered by characters in the Chaseworld as well as by participants in the Storyrealm. Thus Jake Meredith points out that it "didn't bother Apie" when his brother John cussed his little Black and Tan, and Tom Driscoll the character disparagingly refers to the "pin-eared [Walker] dogs" of a hunter who did not have the sense to realize that this particular chase belonged to the dog Moe.

The Story Session

We are seated in the living room of Jake Meredith's hunting cabin, a one-story structure just south of Chatsworth named "Three Bridges Shanty." The New Jersey Sporting Dogs Association holds its monthly meetings here, but our present gathering is less formal than those meetings. It is attended by eleven hunters who have come at Norman Taylor's invitation to talk about foxhunting with me for the book I am writing. I have met most of these hunters on foxchases throughout the Pine Barrens north of the Mullica River over the past ten years: Junie Bell, Jake Meredith, George D'Andrade, Jeff Powell, Don Cramer, and Charlie Jameson. The names of others are familiar: Ted Goff, Hubie Driscoll, Tom Driscoll, and Nick Harker. These hunters, ranging in age from late thirties to mid-seventies, represent several generations of foxhunters. The Chaseworld they conjure covers a span of seventy years and includes a peep at circumstances a decade hence, when hunters gloomily forecast the sport's demise.

It is late afternoon. The smell of coffee wafts in from the kitchen, where Caroline Taylor and her mother are chatting with my husband, who is minding our infant daughter. A table in the center of the room is piled high with potato chips and dip and doughnuts, next to a cooler full of sodas. To launch the session I explain that I am writing a book and am interested in stories about foxhunting. Some of the hunters express their hope that such a book might foster a better public understanding of foxhunting. I secure permission to turn on my tape recorder, and soon the talk splits into three or four simultaneous conversations. With no further prompting from me, the hunters erupt into dogtalk. The hubbub of conversation is overwhelming. Sometimes there are as many as six men speaking at once to the persons next to them, while at other times all turn their attention to the same scene or theme. I think of foxhounds sniffing out the trail in couples and trios until one announces a discovery, at which point the others rush to join him.

Seated in Jake Meredith's hunting cabin and surrounded with signs of the Chaseworld, the hunters are physically removed from the Ordinary. On one wall is a photograph, by Leonard Lee Rue, III, of a New Jersey gray fox climbing a tree. Not far from the cabin are kennels filled with Jake Meredith's foxhounds, whose voices occasionally stray into our awareness. The ambience is gleeful as hunters punctuate the narratives of those who briefly gain the floor with full choruses of affirmation, incredulity, teasing, and laughter. In a realm of conversation orienting toward the Chaseworld, stories emerge within which Chaseworld vignettes unfold.

Many of the stories are collaborative, issued in rapid-fire succession by hunters who share the same rhythms of speech. Between pauses, sets of thematically linked stories take shape, bounded by dogtalk and commentary designed to enhance understandings of Chaseworld characters and places. Now and then the hunters venture beyond the Chaseworld, lured there by Chaseworld characters who were, for instance, professional ballplayers or great skaters. The floor is often ceded to the two oldest foxhunters, Tom Driscoll (age 73), and Nick Harker (age 75), who begin their stories amid anticipatory chuckles from the others. On the heels of stories about John Earlin's "Black and Tan" and Jack Davis's "Harry," the Storyrealm pauses, and Jeff Powell invokes the next cluster of stories by soliciting a story from Nick Harker, who lives on Story Street in New Egypt, a road named for his grandfather, Story Harker. It is easy to see how this large, bearded man with twinkling eyes and a full shock of white hair acquired the CB handle of "Santa Claus."

[Personal orientation]

NT: She was the mother of that pair, I took 'em up to Jake when they was puppies, and, uh, they got runnin' a rabbit and he sold 'em to Kenny.

JM: Mhm

NT: They were small, they weren't real big.

(Pause)

[Storyrealm opening]

JP: Well Nick, you gotta tell us some lies now.

(Laughter)

NH: No!

(Laughter)

NH: I'm too young for you guys!

JP: You know more lies than we know.

(Laughter)

NH: No, I'm too young.

Following this playful negotiation, Nick Harker (who, after refusing to tell a lie, promptly stretches the truth about his age) begins orienting toward the Chaseworld:

[Temporal, personal and spatial orientations]
> NH: I was foxhuntin' when you didn't have a car! I walked from New Egypt to Snag.[5] Used to walk with dogs.

[Storyrealm opening]
> JP: Well tell us about it!
> NH: No!

(Laughter)

[Orientation]
> Used to walk with 'em.

[Chaseworld evaluation]
> JP: They must've been awful slow dogs!

[Storyrealm evaluation]
> (Laughter)

[Orientation]
> NH: Then you guys with all your money didn't want my dogs to run, so I'd keep 'em on a rope till you got the fox up, layin' in a ditch, and then cut my dogs loose. And they'd [Nick's dogs] say, "He's here! He's here!" Yeah!

[Chaseworld evaluation]
> (Laughter)

STORY 1

[Preface]
> And I'd show 'em somethin' too!

[Orientation]
> They was mongers!

[Chaseworld beginning—personal, temporal, spatial orientations]
> Old Kevin Potter and them and Sandy was down there one day, and I laid in the ditch with them two dogs, and I cut 'em loose.

[Chaseworld ending]
> They shot eighteen times that day at the fox. I shot at it four times—I got on a hassock and shot up in the air when he went by.[6]

[Personal orientation]

I never killed a fox in my life. Never killed a fox. I loved to foxhunt, but I never killed a fox.

[Coda]

And all the great shots in New Egypt was there and they shot eighteen times that day,

[Story evaluation]

that's the truth

[Coda]

at that fox. Eliot Bell killed it the next day, yeah, in Snag.

[Closing/temporal orientation]

Yeah, they were (pause) some days.

STORY 2

[Chaseworld beginning—spatio-temporal orientation]

TD: We had a foxchase over in back of the Forked River Mountains, you know, and they brought them Walkers in.

[Personal orientations]

And Hubie's grandpop had a little black dog—

NT: oh yeah, bought it from Apie—

TD: he got it from Apie—and he was over there that day

NT: yeah, I know the dog—Moe! Moe! Yeah! I had dogs there

TD: and Chunk, Snap, and Bull and all of us was there

NT: yup, yup

[Chaseworld—spatial orientation]

TD: and we hadn't put a dog out, and Britton and I sit there on the open bank and pretty soon I heard Moe comin' down through there, he was a-comin',

[Temporal orientation—present]

and these guys begin to cut them there small-eared dogs loose, you know,

[Temporal orientation—past]

and was goin' over the pines, under the pines, and everywhere, and they never caught him, he put him in the tree himself.

[Personal orientation]

NT: Who? Moe

TD: Moe did.

[Truth evaluation]
>   NT: Mhm
>   TD: And we went in and shook him out and they let him go and they said to Pat, "Let him go!" So they let him go and they made a loop and they went way down.

[Temporal orientation—present]
>   Pretty soon here come Moe back with him,

(Laughter)
>   pushin' the dogs on him.

[Temporal orientation—past]
>   And I said to this here one old guy, with Walkers, "How did them there pin-eared dogs get turned loose?"

[Temporal orientation—present]
>   He says, "What do you mean, 'pin-eared dogs?'"

[Temporal orientation—past]
>   I said, "Like them you got on that string there. What's the matter with that dog's runnin' that fox?"

[Temporal orientation—present]
>   He says, "You got any in there?"

[Temporal orientation—past/Chaseworld ending]
>   I said, "Don't want any in there. I'm listenin' to him!"

[Evaluation]
>   NT: (chuckles)

[Coda]
>   TD: Boy, he was runnin' the fox that day.
>   NT: Who, Moe—he'd take the fox away from you.
>   TD: Yessir.
>   NT: He knew how to take the fox away from you.

(Laughter)

[Personal orientation]
>   TD: Old John used to cuss at Apie's little Black and Tan.

[Chaseworld coda]
>   NT: He'd take it away from you.

[Chaseworld evaluations]
>   JM: That didn't bother Apie
>   NT: Right.
>   JM: He just laughed.
>   TD: He got another and he took it back, s'posed to be a son, looked like him. Took it back to him.

[Coda/temporal orientation—present]

NT: Yup, you get one like Moe every now and then.

TD: Boy, that was—

[

[Personal orientations]

NT: That Apie was a hunter, though. He started more fox'n Johnny could, and with nothin'.

JM: Yeah, but he was *up* four o'clock in the morning. Johnny was in bed.

JP: Be up when it was zero.

NT: Yeah. Every morning, he'd get up before daylight and go. Rain, shine, or what.

JP: Johnny jumped a lot of—when he had good dogs, he jumped a lot of fox.

STORY 3

[Preface/Chaseworld beginning—personal/temporal orientation]

TD: First time I ever seen a red fox, I was with Johnny.

[Spatial orientation]

Goin' through the woods, was about that much snow. These three dogs that he had was ahead of us. Goin' trailin'. Pretty soon he stopped, he said, "You see him layin' right there!" That fox laid up there.

[Truth evaluation]

NT: Yup

[Chaseworld ending]

TD: That fox laid up and the dogs come darn near up on him before they jumped him.

[Chaseworld evaluation]

JM: Hm!

[Closing]

TD: That's the only time I ever seen a fox do that.

[Chaseworld evaluation/temporal orientation—present]

NT: That's unusual for a red one though, 'cause they usually get out quite a ways ahead of you

TD: Yep, they'll see the fox.

[

NT: snow bein' on, yeah.

[Coda]

TD: There was snow about that deep

[

NT: there was snow

TD: and he points to him—he said (whispering) "See that fox! See that fox there!" And I said, "Where?" "See him layin' right there?" And there he was, layin' right on a little hassock, and "Whoosh!" Away he went.

STORY 4

[Chaseworld beginning]

NH: I was with Johnny one day when they was pinnin' the fox so hard that the fox come right out and laid down in the road there.

[Story evaluation]

That's the truth.

[Chaseworld ending]

Johnny broke them dogs off, crackin' whip, bangin' on that truck.

[Truth evaluation—preface]

NT: Well Jakie'll verify I've caught foxes ahead of the dogs when they was runnin' 'em.

JM: Mhm

NT: Gray fox—

[

JM: Yeah.

[Orientation]

NT: when the fox are tired out, just run right in there and catch 'em ahead of the dogs.

[Invitation]

Couple times you was with us, wasn't you?

STORY 5

[Preface]

JM: Yeah—when we was up Butler Place you caught two one day—

NT: two, ahead of the dogs, alive.

[Chaseworld beginning]

JM: Freeman run around there in that—

[Spatial orientation]

what was that field they called there? Ahead of Butler Place where them old apple trees was—

[Chaseworld ending]

he run one down there and caught that one.

[Closing]

NT: That's got Tom thinkin'.

[Coda]

JM: Caught two.

STORY 6

[Preface/temporal orientation]

TD: How about the time you let 'em out of the warden's truck!

NT: (chuckling)

[Personal orientation]

TD: Adams, wasn't it?

NT: Yeah, Salty Adams.

[Chaseworld beginning]

TD: He pulled up there—

[Orientation]

and he had three of 'em, wasn't it? Wasn't it three in the back?

NT: Yeah, whatever he had in the box.

[Chaseworld]

TD: We took him down the road you know, and Norman opened the gate,

[Ending]

and out went the fox.

NT: I let the foxes out of his truck.

[Coda]

TD: He never said a thing, did he?

NT: He didn't know they wasn't in there when he went home, but he never mentioned anything.

TD: Didn't know they was gone.

[Evaluation]

NH: (chuckling)

[Personal orientation]

NT: Yeah, yeah—he used to be the state trapper.

[Evaluation]
    NH: (laughing)
    NT: Hah!
    TD: Boy oh boy.
    NT: Yeah.
    TD: Had some fun, didn't we?
[Closing/temporal orientation]
    Them days.
    NT: Yep.
(Pause)
[Preface]
    NT: Remember the night when we lost all of our dogs, and we built a
    big fire down there on top of Benny Caddy's there?
    . . .

This conversation, which proceeds from one set of thematically linked stories to another, is "story-dominated" (Kirshenblatt-Gimblett 1974:291–93; Young 1987:101). Some important differences between this occasion and occasions when stories were told to me by one foxhunter deserve note. None of the stories on this occasion were spun out as seamless texts by individual raconteurs, as may be the case when a foxhunter tells stories to his wife or to an ethnographer or when he records them for posterity as John Earlin did. Though the older men led many of the stories in this session, there were no dominant storytellers, as there were in my field interviews, where I requested information and recorded long narrative texts. I will examine some of the implications of this contrast later, following an inquiry into the relationship between the Chaseworld and the Storyrealm on this particular occasion.

THE STRUCTURE OF THE STORY SET

Though four of the stories have central narrators, the densely collaborative nature of the session is striking. Here the hunters' comparison of foxhounds to storytellers seems especially apt. Honoring each raconteur as he picks up the thread, hunters continually jump in with orientations, evaluations, and codas, echoing each other right on the beat. The set begins with an invitation from one of the younger foxhunters, Jeff Powell, to the oldest one in the room, Nick Harker, who obliges with a story that becomes a formal and thematic resource for the five stories that follow. The fifth and sixth stories are jointly narrated, first by Norman Taylor and Jake Meredith and then by Norman Taylor and Tom Driscoll, who match form, content, and understandings in a dramatic display of the shared community of experience that enables them at times to speak almost with one voice.

Stories that follow other stories, termed "following-on stories" by Goffman and Labov, may relate to their preceding stories as either "serial stories" or "second stories (Young 1987:81). Serial stories, according to Young, tend to be stories by the same teller that "pick up elements from first stories and play them out in different arrangements," while second stories "pick out relations between elements, that is, actions, or what Vladimir Propp calls functions, and work them into the story." (1987:81). Where participants are as closely related as these foxhunters are by common experience, they can cooperatively produce serial stories as well as second stories, whether the primary teller is the same or not.

The six stories in this set are serial stories, thematically linked as stories about the same elements—hunters, foxes, and dogs. They are also formally linked in the manner of first and second stories by two actions: (1) nonpedigreed foxhounds start foxes and provide good chases, and (2) hunters spare foxes or release them. Nonpedigreed foxhounds include Nick Harker's "mongers," Pat Heinrichs' "Moe," and Apie Earlin's "nothin'." The story set unfolds as hunters select elements and actions from the first story by Nick Harker and play them out, ultimately elaborating on the function of sparing foxes. (Though Nick Harker says the fox that showed itself eighteen times was killed the next day by Elliot Bell, these stories focus on contact with foxes by hunters intent on sparing them.) In all of the stories the fox comes within reach of the hunters, who release it by (1) not shooting it, (2) shaking it out of the tree, (3) calling the dogs off, (4, 5) catching the fox before the dogs get to it, and (6) freeing the foxes from the warden's truck. Thus each story in the set follows from the one preceding it, demonstrating its appropriateness to the occasion by replicating relations among elements. The interplay of serial and second stories patterns the session, with serial stories expanding the Chaseworld and second stories structuring the Storyrealm. "Thus," as Young writes, "serial stories point toward the Taleworld, transparencies to the events the story is about. Second stories point toward the Storyrealm, shaping the relationship between stories, and, by extension, between storytellers" (1987:96).

Through serial stories that are also second stories, the hunters establish a trail, if you will, connecting the stories. They do so by elaborating on two of the points that Nick Harker makes in his first story, while remaining in the time period he establishes, which is a long time ago, when Tom Driscoll, Pat Heinrichs, Norman and Freeman Taylor, Jake Meredith, and

Apie and John Earlin hunted together. The first point is that Nick Harker's "mongers" could really run a fox (which is often the point of foxhunting stories). The second point is that Nick Harker could enjoy foxhunting without ever killing a fox, though he had the means at his disposal. A series of permutations follows. Tom Driscoll elaborates on Nick Harker's first point, matching Harker's account with an account of the exploits of the dog Moe, who belonged to Hubie Driscoll's grandfather, Pat Heinrichs. Hunters on that occasion return the fox to the chase by shaking it out of the tree. Norman sets the stage for the third and fourth stories through personal orientations that link the dog Moe to Apie Earlin. The hunters then move through personal orientations that elaborate on the relationship between Apie and John Earlin, and contrast them as hunters, returning the stage to Tom Driscoll, who illustrates Jeff Powell's assertion that John Earlin jumped a lot of fox with an account of a red fox that showed itself to Earlin's dogs (Story 3) this time in the beginning of a chase. Nick Harker, returning to the thread of hunters who don't kill foxes, offers an eyewitness account of how John Earlin broke his dogs from the fox's trail (Story 4). Norman Taylor and Jake Meredith match this with an account of how Norman and Freeman rescued two foxes ahead of the dogs on the same day (Story 5). The set closes with an account, jointly narrated by Norman and Tom, of how Norman rescued three foxes from the state trapper (Story 6).

ELEMENTS AND FUNCTIONS LINKING THE STORIES

1. a. "Mongers" make a fox show itself eighteen times.
   b. Nick Harker and his friends shoot eighteen times as the fox goes by, but do not kill it.
2. a. Pat Heinrichs's "little black dog," Moe, proves himself superior to Walkers.
   b. Tom Driscoll, Pat Heinrichs (Hubie's grandpop), Norman Taylor, and others shake a fox down from the tree so Moe can chase it some more.
3. John Earlin and his dogs give Tom Driscoll his first glimpse of a red fox.
4. John Earlin breaks his dogs to protect the fox.
5. Jake Meredith, Freeman Taylor, and Norman Taylor catch foxes before the dogs can get to them.
6. Norman Taylor (in the presence of Tom Driscoll) releases foxes from the back of the warden's truck.

Figure 6.1. Jake Meredith, Norman Taylor, and Jeff Powell at "Three Bridges Shanty," Jake's hunting cabin near Duke's Bridge. Photo by the author, July 1990.

The set progresses, from stories of dogs as heroes who start foxes and really run them, to depictions of men as heroes who save foxes from their dogs. The set closes down with a surprise twist. Exemplifying a pattern that Katharine Young notes is characteristic of closing stories, the story "harks back to and reiterates what its teller perceives as thematic to the storytelling occasion" (1987:142). In the last story the dogs disappear, and in their stead is the warden, who becomes a foil for Norman's trick. The interpolation of the warden presents an interesting reading of the foxchase, aligning the dogs with the forces of law and order against the fox, with whom the hunters make common cause. Norman's trick on the warden suggests a subversive alliance with the anti-structural creature at the heart of the Chaseworld, an alliance that is not unusual for the hunters.[7]

Leakages and Meanings

As in Jack Davis's account of the trick he played on Jake Meredith (see Chapter 5), the stories here draw an implicit parallel between human and animal players in the Chaseworld through human replications of animal actions. Meanings that leak across the boundaries between stories also stray from the Chaseworld into the Storyrealm, where we find, as Alan Dundes wrote of riddles, "the structure of the context (social situation). . . is paralleled by the structure of the text used in that context" (1980:25). At several levels the stories explore the complex interrelations of hunters and foxes. The notion that hunters identify deeply with their quarry is repeatedly asserted in the literature on hunting.[8] A close look at how participants in the Storyrealm replicate Chaseworld functions reveals one way in which this identification with the fox may be played out.

There are two realms in the storytelling session: the Storyrealm and the Chaseworld. Central to each is a paradoxical figure: in one it is the joker, in the other, the fox. As analogous rites for conjuring the Chaseworld, foxchases and stories about them both conjure as well the circle of fellowship, where rules governing turn-taking among hunters parallel those governing turn-taking among hounds. Like hounds constituting the trail of the fox in a canine chorus, the hunters structure their experiences in stories. But hunters also emulate the relationship between hounds and foxes, through the auspices of jokes, anti-rites that attack the very order they ritually invoke.

As ritual structures, both foxchases and stories about them contain within themselves a liminal phase, which, as Victor Turner observes,

> provides a stage (and I use this term advisedly) for unique structures of experience (Dilthey's *Erlebnis*) in milieus detached from mundane life and characterized by the presence of ambiguous ideas, monstrous images, sacred symbols, ordeals, humiliations, esoteric and paradoxical instructions, the emergence of symbolic types represented by maskers and clowns, gender reversals, anonymity, and many other phenomena and processes which I have elsewhere described as "liminal." (1986:41)

The liminal phase of the foxchase takes shape around the fox's trail. In the foxchase, the fox is clearly the antistructural creature, whose trail engenders music. He endeavors to silence this music by misrepresenting his trail, thereby falsifying the hounds' sense of reality. When he succeeds in losing the dogs, he capsizes the Chaseworld.

In storytelling sessions, the Chaseworld is summoned up by hunters without the assistance of hounds or foxes. In the Storyrealm the antistructural position is occupied by the joker. In the hunters' sociality the joking relationship looms large, and the role of joker is available to anyone spying an opportunity to step into it. Like the fox, the joker calls the shots. As the fox befuddles the hounds by making his trail appear nonexistent, the joker declares that the storyteller is lying, asserting in effect that none of this is really happening.

In this particular storytelling session, it was Jeff Powell who continually framed the stories as lies. When I asked him why, he replied, "If you ever meet a foxhunter who tells you he never told a lie, he's lyin' to you."

"Not Nick," said Norman Taylor, by way of illustration. "He never told a lie, did you Nick?"

"No," Nick Harker returned, to a roomful of chuckles (July 14, 1990).

Foxhunting stories are shot through with what Katharine Young calls "truth evaluations" (1987:55), which storytellers use to frame Chaseworld events as having really happened and thus to justify the telling of the story. The preponderance of truth evaluations in foxhunting stories, however, plays as well to an assumption built into the genre that the truth is likely to be stretched.

TD: I ain't a-kiddin' you.

JA: It's the God's honest truth and I hope I drop dead if I'm lying.

NT: It's the truth. That's really what happened.

JD: I could tell you a big story, but I don't believe in it.

DC: They'll think we got stories, just like the fishermen.[9]

The hunters' insistence that the stories are true narratives of personal experience and the jokers' repeated declaration that they are lies generates the paradox of Epimenides, the Cretan who said that all Cretans are liars. In this instance the paradox is stated thus: [All things within these brackets are false: this is the truth].

The joke rite dissolves the Chaseworld, shifting the attention of the hunters to their own social relationships as they playfully attack one another. The alignment that hunters take up with foxes in the Chaseworld is paralleled in the Storyrealm, where, as jokers presiding over joke rites, they topple the structure of their own discourse. The joke, according to Mary Douglas, is "a play upon form" wherein "something formal is attacked by something informal." (1968:365) Jokes, then, are anti-rites, disorganizing the order and harmony imposed by rites of sociability like storytelling and foxhunting. Joke rites, whether performed by hunters or foxes, disrupt the orderly flow of events. Thus, in an atmosphere of high jinks, Jeff Powell lures Nick Harker into the liar's seat, only to immediately cancel the meaning of what Harker has to say:

> NH: We used to walk with 'em.
> JP: They must've been awful slow dogs!

The session was peppered with such overturnings of meaning, which abruptly wrest attention away from the Chaseworld to the Storyrealm, to the relationships among those within it, and to the caliber of the joke rites performed. The conversation turns to an unsavory Chaseworld character.

[Personal orientation]
> TD: We never hunted with him. He was a *ratty* fellow.
> NT: Ratty?
> TD: You knowed him, didn't you?
> JM: Yeah, I seen him a few times. I never hunted with him.
> TD: He hunted over here in all these roads. He had different names
> NT: that's right
> [
> TD: for 'em and everything.
> NT: Yeah, he hunted here a lot.
> JM: Never knew where them dogs was. He was always huntin' your dogs, wasn't he?
> NT: Yeah.

[Chaseworld beginning]
> TD: Tater and I used to come up, one time,
> JM: always huntin' for 'em

[Spatial orientation]
> TD: he was huntin' on the Plains, right there on the turn, you know, the white road that goes up? And it was in summertime. Russ and I stood there, and Tater and I walked up the road listening to him, and I felt somethin' bitin' me, and,

[Storyrealm—truth evaluation]
> I ain't a-kiddin' you,

[Chaseworld ending]
> them fleas was that thick in that road. It was *just black* up there up that stretch of road!

[Chaseworld evaluation]
    All: (shouts of laughter)
    Mm!
    Mm!
    Oh dear!
[Joke rite]
    JP: Don't think it's any better for me sittin' next to him!
[Storyrealm evaluations]
    All: (explosive laughter)
    NT: Mary's got that on tape, Tom!
    All: (louder laughter)
[Story opening]
    NH: Hey Fleaman! I can tell you a better one than that!
[Chaseworld beginning]
    We had a guy named Bill Grubby
[Storyrealm]
    JP: Got me scratchin'!
    [
[Chaseworld]
    NH: in New Egypt and he was foxhuntin' and we asked him why he
    came back so late, and he said he come up to Sandy Crossway and run
    into snow fleas so *high up* that his
[Storyrealm—truth evaluation]
    JP: SNOW FLEAS?!!
    [
[Chaseworld ending]
    NH: wheels got stuck right into the snow fleas and he couldn't pull
    out. He was there *all night*—
[Chaseworld evaluation]
    All: (laughter, hoots, howls, thigh slapping)
[Coda]
    NH: all night, couldn't get out, the snow fleas was so thick, there to
    Sandy Crossway, yeah. Heh. Heh. Heh-heh-heh.
[Story preface/Chaseworld beginning]
    TD: Well, I'll never forget the first time I seen Snap and Bull,
[Evaluation]
    All: (background chorus of residual and anticipatory chuckles).

The subject of the first flea story was not a member of the circle of
fellowship, and Tom Driscoll attempts to account for this with a story. He

is supported by others who help illustrate his point that the man was "a ratty fellow," an outsider who used idiosyncratic names for roads, who hunted for other men's hounds, and whose own hounds were infested with fleas. As Tom Driscoll gets to his point, the joker strikes, engendering disorder. Invoking fleas from the Chaseworld into the Storyrealm, Jeff Powell causes the map to invade the territory in a way that confuses rather than clarifies, resulting in a startling comparison between Tom Driscoll and the hounds of the man he was criticizing.

Nick Harker's following-on story of the snow fleas encountered by a man named—felicitously if not improbably—Grubby, implies that Tom Driscoll's story was not altogether on the side of truth. Drawing a parallel between Tom Driscoll the narrator and Bill Grubby the character, Nick Harker rescues "Fleaman" from his fleas by recasting Driscoll's story as fiction.

Paradox is precipitated by the message "this is play," which is, according to Gregory Bateson, "an attempt to discriminate between, or to draw a line between, categories of different logical types" (1955:48). Within the boundaries of the play frame, behaviors that would not be tolerated under other circumstances are sanctioned. Having bracketed their behavior as play, the hunters engage in lying, bragging, and mock attacks on one another, with the understanding that these things do not mean what they would outside this setting.[10] The same frame confers immunity upon the joker, whose disruptive comments are in a sense, as Mary Douglas points out, "the comments of the social group upon itself. [The joker] merely expresses consensus" (1968:372). Calling attention to the paradoxes that must be ignored in order to sustain reality, the joker topples the Chaseworld.

These commentaries on the form of sociality that holds together the Chaseworld constitute a move toward greater abstraction. "Jokes, being themselves a play upon forms, can well serve to express something about social forms" (Douglas 1968:270). Just as foxes attack the form that hunters impose on them, hunters use jokes to attack the forms they create, to loosen the constraints governing sociable interaction. Conventions governing the maintenance of face are openly tweaked; they are playfully violated and then reinstated. Douglas points out that, through the joke rite, something under control in the social structure attacks the source of control, changing the balance of power. In the cases under consideration, the joker subverts meanings, pulling the rug out from under the speaker, making the speaker appear to confess to having slow dogs or to having fleas himself, or recasting the "true" story as fiction by proclaiming it a lie.

Figure 6.2. Tom Driscoll of Tuckerton. Photo by Dennis McDonald, April 1991.

Framing their behavior as fictive, hunters can reverse their own meanings as well as those of others, issuing mock insults which they then recant. Complaining about the bias of this particular storytelling session toward the old days, Jeff Powell leads the hunters in a litany of the present-day obstacles for dogs:

[Storyrealm]
   JP: All's you people do is talk about dogs forty years ago. They had a
   lot easier runnin' than they got now. Wasn't all the motorcycle paths 'n
   firelines.

[Temporal orientation to Chaseworld]

> GD: That's *true*. You gotta be a heck of a lot better dog today than they was then.
>
> NT: Oh yeah, it's harder runnin' today, because motorcycle lines and roads.

[Spatial orientation]

> JP: I'm just talkin' 'bout places the fox goes. Down in Maryland they run 'em through houses and trailer parks (laughing)
>
> JM: gettin' worse everyday
>
> GD: bow 'n' arrow hunters up every tree, snowmobiles

[Storyrealm]

> DC: yeah, you better write that book soon,

[Temporal orientation]

> 'cause five or ten years from now
>
> JP: might be no foxhuntin'
>
> [
>
> TD: we might not be here.

[Spatial orientation]

> JP: There ain't gonna be too many places to go.

[Personal orientation]

> MH: Do you have many younger guys huntin'?
>
> TD: Just me and a couple others.

(Laughter)

> NT: Other than Jeff and Charlie Jameson I don't know a young fella that's foxhuntin', do you?
>
> HD: Hey I'm not *that* old!

[Storyrealm/joke rite]

> NT: Well you're not foxhuntin' for god's sake!

[Storyrealm evaluations]

> All: (Uproarious laughter)

Norman's rejoinder to Hubie Driscoll, which intentionally distorts the meaning of Hubie's remark, has turned everyone's attention away from the Chaseworld as they begin to evaluate the impact of the joke on various members of the audience, including myself and Jake Meredith, who is Hubie's regular hunting partner.

> HD: Don't tell her that! She thinks I'm a foxhunter!
>
> NT: Jakie—I got Jakie laughin' now!
>
> JP: Yeah, he liked that!

NT: He liked that!

JP: What's he [Hubie] gonna do with that dog I just sold him? He just give me a hundred, said, "I want somethin' to beat Jakie with!"

(Laughter)

NT: That's a dirty blow, Hubie.

With this last remark, Norman restores order, in effect taking back what he said, making it plain that nothing was meant by it. The bite, to use Gregory Bateson's analogy, did not denote what it would have outside the realm of play (1955:43). The hunters then close the window on their society opened up by the joke and return their attention to the Chaseworld.

The relationship between hounds and foxes offers only one of many possibilities for replication in the Storyrealm. The joking sociality that takes hold when hunters gather was not present when a lone hunter told stories before an audience consisting of myself and his wife. Differences in texts relate to differences in the sociality to be achieved by conjuring the Chaseworld. Stories told to me in my early interviews with Jack Davis, John Earlin, and Joe Albert, for instance, were marked by the appearance of strangers whose positive responses to Chaseworld events I now take to be instructions from the foxhunter to the outsider in his audience, as in the following story by Jack Davis:

[Preface]

JD: And when you tell people somethin', a lot of people act like they think you're lyin'.

[Chaseworld beginning]

I used to have a fella and his wife come in the bar, and I'm goin' foxhuntin' all the time, and they were makin' a joke out of it.

So one night I took 'em, him and his wife, and that fox almost run under his feet. He says to me

[Chaseworld evaluation by character]

he says, "There goes the son-of-a-bitch!" I swear, Mary, it was four foot from him.

[Chaseworld evaluation by narrator]

Well after that it was comical.

[Chaseworld ending]

Somebody would be talkin' about how we only used foxhuntin' just to go, and he used to say, "Like hell they do! Goddam if they didn't put the fox right under my feet anyhow!" (Interview, November 14, 1980)

Notice that Davis has to do much of the work of constructing this realm himself, furnishing its frames and boundaries, alluding to the expectation that lying goes on, and evaluating the Chaseworld, mostly through a Chaseworld character. The witness's remarks are instructions to the audience for what Harvey Sacks terms "hearing-as" (cited in Young 1987: 59)—in this case for hearing the story as remarkable and true, and for viewing the protagonist as a clever fellow.[11] Since a foxhunter's wife already knows what to think about foxhunting, the instructions were intended for me.

This, of course, reinforces what is now axiomatic among folklorists, that performance contexts, including the ethnographic one, bear heavily on the making of texts and their meanings. For the solitary foxhunter invited to hold forth before an audience consisting of his wife and an ethnographer, storytelling still provides a way to shape the relationships among those present in the Storyrealm, but the relationships are of a different sort. When a group of foxhunters tells stories about foxhunting, it is conjuring not only the Chaseworld, but a circle of fellowship, telling itself a story about itself (Geertz 1972:448), exploring its own worldview and values. In the circle of male fellowship, the joke rite emerges as a metacommentary on rites that conjure not only the Chaseworld, but reality in general. Calling into question the necessity of social forms, the joker alludes to their vulnerability as well, and to the power of words to invoke and revoke the world (Bauman 1986:77).

Like the fox, the joker departs from the path of predictability, veering off to explore hidden possibilities. The joker, a "minor mystic," in Douglas's phrase, is a master of reality, revealing its contours to those implicated in his antirites, which in the presence of other jokers may spiral off into anti-antirites. For example, the flea stories above may be seen as a skirmish in an ongoing war of the wizards. Jeff Powell invokes the fleas from the Chaseworld onto Tom Driscoll in the Storyrealm. Nick Harker hurls them back through a fabrication that implies they never existed in the first place. Reminding his fellows that none of this is really happening, the joker engenders in them "an exhilarating sense of freedom from form in general" (Douglas 1968:365).

Chaseworld foxes, like jokers, exhibit a keen sense of human formality, an uncanny sense for animals. Fireball, the fox who "liked to be run," seemed to know when the chase was really over. Standing on the railroad one New Year's Day, watching the hunters load their dogs after a nine-hour chase, Fireball scored the last word. "I'll never forget it," said Norman

Taylor. "He had dogs tired out, we had the box *full* of dogs, and they was tired out, didn't want to run no longer, and he was down there just laughin' at us." Paradoxically situated at the Chaseworld's heart, the marginal figures of foxes and jokers issue its parameters, bidding it to be and not to be, collapsing it into mirth.

Notes

1. It is not my purpose here to detail fully how Storyrealms and Taleworlds are constructed, but to show how the conjuring of the Chaseworld in stories is similar to its conjuring in foxchases. For a thorough explication of narrative structure and of the phenomenological theory and issues involved, see Young (1987).

2. Related to this necessity is Goffman's distinction between "reports," which simply tell about something that occurred in the past, and "replayings," which are stories into which hearers can "empathetically insert themselves" (1974: 504).

3. The following discussion is indebted to William Labov, who first identified prefaces, codas, and orientations in narrative, and to Katharine Young, who thoroughly elaborated on them in a chapter entitled "Edgework: Frame and Boundary in Narrative Communication" (1987:19–68).

4. The hunters' use of the historical present, also termed the "dramatic present," to render the Chaseworld immediate, squares with the traditional hypothesis that the historic present functions to make narratives more vivid. Nessa Wolfson, in a study of the alternation of past tense with the conversational historical present, concludes that "CHP alternation occurs only in a specific type of narrative which we have called a performed story; one which contains features such as dialogue, asides, expressive sounds, motions and gestures, and repetition. We may see this kind of narrative as a structured performance in which the switching between past and present tenses has the function of organizing the narrative by setting off one act sequence from another" (Wolfson 1982:105) The present study suggests that as a strategy for conjuring the alternate reality, the tense alternation also enhances the necessary distinction between Storyrealm and Taleworld.

5. Snag is the name of a cedar swamp that flanks Route 539 south of New Egypt, now located within the boundaries of Fort Dix Military Reserve.

6. While the others, from whom Nick Harker was separated, may have been shooting *at* the fox, Harker was simply shooting into the air to signal the fox's location to those who were not in the swamp. The account illustrates Harker's desire to spare the fox even when it was not popular to do so.

7. Katharine Young's use of this method to show how a storyteller presented himself as a trickster on one occasion suggested this direction to me (see Young 1987:146–56).

8. James Howe writes that "Hunters in many societies, both primitive and modern, implicitly identify themselves with at least some of the animals they pursue,

and by killing them, they symbolically transfer certain of their qualities to them-selves. A similar kind of identification holds in war, with the concept of the *noble adversary* whose sterling qualities confirm one's own" (1981:293).

9. Joe Albert alludes to the expectation that foxhunters make exaggerated claims in the concluding lines to his poem "A Foxhunter's Life in a Camp in South Jersey" (See Figure 1.5). His concluding lines constitute a kind of trick on the reader:

> Then you feed the dogs and start the fire
> So when you read this story don't call me a ——

Having inserted the reader into the poem through the empathetic "you" and thus established shared understandings between the poem's reader and speaker, the speaker corners the reader into admitting that the events described in the poem are true.

10. The message, according to Gregory Bateson, is "This is play." In such a context, he writes that "Paradox is doubly present. . . . Not only does the playful nip not denote what would be denoted by the bite for which it stands, but the bite itself is fictional" (1955:43).

11. This strategy of embedding evaluations deeply within the narrative, which was discussed briefly in Chapter 4, serves to deflect potential charges that the narrator could be bragging and stretching the truth. It is a potent means of self-presentation in that the narrator can indirectly portray himself as the cause of a skeptic's amazement, distancing himself from his own claims to greatness by placing the claims in the mouth of a Chaseworld character.

7. Cosmos Out of Chaos:
Memoirs of a Foxhunting Trickster

When we contemplate and construe our experiences, building up an explanation for Self and Universe, we make Cosmos out of Chaos.
——Barbara Myerhoff, *Number Our Days* (1978: 222)

I have a tape up at the cabin of some of my experiences.
——John Earlin

AS A MEANS OF access to the Chaseworld, stories offer several distinct advantages over foxchases. Through stories the past becomes a frontier for exploration, for hunting and capturing not foxes but experiences, which are actually created, masterfully crafted, in the telling.[1] Through stories told in the course of a single conversation hunters can explore a realm spanning sixty or seventy years as they draw occasionally on received memories from the previous generation, leap backward and forward in time, and allow older relatives and friends who have died to speak as co-inhabitants of this realm. Reflecting on the Chaseworld in stories, hunters imbue it with meaning.

The capacity of stories to reconstitute the past is of particular significance for elderly foxhunters not able to hunt as freely or as frequently as they did when younger. For them the Chaseworld provides an attractive alternative mode of self-presentation, a means whereby they can author themselves as Chaseworld characters, key players on a stage shaped by them with authority and precision.[2] Recurrent and enduring in form, conjured repeatedly over many decades of a long life, the Chaseworld offers the elderly hunter a potent means of organizing his life from a single point in time, a way of constituting himself as a character who modulates throughout the course of that life while remaining essentially the same person.[3] The Chaseworld thus becomes a buffer against discontinuity as well as isolation, a means both for conjuring sociality and for gathering together bits of the self lodged in the past, rendering it whole, and portraying it to an audience.[4] Identities given form within the Chaseworld flow out through Storyrealms to take hold in the Ordinary. As a way of garnering audiences, foxhunting stories also can provide hunters with a social currency beyond the Chaseworld's circumscribed borders, attracting not only other foxhunters, but grandchildren, nonfoxhunting members of the community, journalists, and the occasional ethnographer.

This chapter considers a storytelling session that John Earlin committed to tape when he was in his seventies. That he undertook this project as an elderly man suggests that the recording was actually a kind of life review project,[5] a definitional rite related to the task of self-integration in later life. Barbara Myerhoff points out that life crises trigger rites of self-definition and that ritual provides the necessary reflecting surfaces for the task (1978:222). The rites for conjuring the Chaseworld are, in her terms, "definitional ceremonies . . . performances of identity" (1978:32), whereby hunters build for themselves a collective face, firmly locating themselves within society, and society within cosmos. Similarly the autobiographical project can constitute a self-definitional ceremony for the individual (Myerhoff 1978:222).

John Earlin's Tape of Stories and Its Audience

Hunters do not always go hunting in groups. While it is important to go together because, as Norman Taylor put it, "it's in competition that you find out what you've got," foxhunters also find it necessary to go alone, as Jack Davis put it, "so we can find out the notes of our dogs." By the same token, a hunter may tell stories as a soloist, rendering coherent his own vision of the Chaseworld and his position within it.

One evening in the mid-1970s John Earlin set about such a task. "From nothin' at all," as he put it, marveling a little, he filled an audiocassette tape with forty minutes of stories about foxhunting. He told me about this tape the first time I met him, during a foxchase. "I have a tape up at the cabin of some of my experiences," he said.

"Any chance I could come hear it?" I asked.

"You certainly can," he replied. "My cabin is right up this road. Go straight up this road across the railroad, across the tar road, and go on around where the road is wore, follow the electric poles and come right to my cabin. That's Pasadena" (foxchase, November 15, 1980).

John Earlin's cinderblock cabin in the abandoned railroad town of

Pasadena was for many years a haven for hunters in the forest; a spring-board for chasing foxes, driving deer, and hunting rabbits; and a setting for playing cards and spinning yarns. "We'd play rummy all the time," said John Earlin's teen-aged grandson and namesake, John-John, recalling his so-journs there during rabbit and deer season, "and he thought he was the champion of Pasadena, and of course there's nobody in Pasadena, so he probably was. And we'd play, and he'd tell me story after story" (interview, October 17, 1986).

The cabin is set on a thirty-five-acre tract of woodland and field, together with a large kennel for foxhounds, a stable, a grazing area for the horses, and a jumping course. The entire ensemble is brought together under the name "Foxchase Farm," as a sign near the entrance proclaims. When I arrived later that evening, John Earlin played the tape for me, as he must have played it for many others, because he silently moved his lips to his own recorded voice, mouthing the words, which I recorded as he'd uttered them several years earlier.[1] (A transcript of the stories appears in Appendix II.)

"What made you decide to do it?" I inquired when we'd finished listening.

"Well," he said, "one day I had the recorder there and I said to myself I wanted to do it. Often I just sat there and whittled 'em off here. Bobby was outside there, and he never did come in. He just stayed out there, and he said, 'That man's crazy. Goin' nuts. Talkin' to himself' " (interview, November 15, 1980).

But he was not really talking to himself, as the recording makes clear. Undaunted by solitude when his muse struck him, John Earlin conjured Storyrealm as well as Chaseworld. An audience is essential to the self-definitional rite; it is a reflecting surface to aid the initiate in his quest for self-awareness. John Earlin's use of the story idiom together with an imaginary audience is significant. This audience, in providing a reflecting surface, assists the recovery of meanings that, as Alfred Schutz put it, "only become visible to the reflective glance" (1970:63). Thus John Earlin presents himself as a storyteller in an imaginary Storyrealm: "I'd like to tell you a story that I just remembered." He sustains this illusion throughout, continually re-minding his audience that he is telling stories: "But that wasn't all of *this* story"; "So that is the second story about Snuffy."

And he orchestrates listener response, leading his audience along an emotional itinerary of amazement, approval, disapproval, sorrow, fascina-tion, amusement, admiration, and empathy. "Well that's a real interesting

Figure 7.1. John Earlin's cabin at "Foxchase Farm" in Pasadena. Photo by the author, November 1986.

story," he tells them, "and I believe you should like that." Or, "I think that was showin' a lot of sportsmanship, and we owe everybody a hand." He makes his stories pointed by conjuring a curiosity for his audience, which he then satisfies: "And, I mean to tell you, you want to hear a man that really was mad, that was Ben!" According to the feedback he gets from his imaginary audience, John Earlin unfolds as an interesting, funny, and sporting fellow, who has lived long and witnessed much.

The audience John Earlin has in mind is an intimate one, as the consistent absence of such contextual information as surnames, dates (with one exception), and precise locations implies. In several instances he hedges his bets, qualifying a name as a nickname and clarifying locations: " 'Webby,' as we called him"; and " 'the Jersey Plains,' they call it." But he does not say that Webby is the nickname of Clarence Webb, nor do his orientations acclimate listeners to the terrain. The biographies of John Earlin's intended witnesses overlap significantly with his own. His ideal listeners know who Norman, Freeman, Jake, Ben, Bert, and Snuffy are, and that the North Branch is in Lebanon State Forest, not the Forked River Mountains. This audience, familiar with the terrain "four or five miles from the cabin" in all directions, shares with Johnny his esoteric vocabulary for Chaseworld topography and events. He is not talking to strangers.

Telling his stories alone offered John Earlin some distinct advantages over the storyteller holding forth to a live audience of familiars. In contrast with the stories rendered at Three Bridges Shanty, the taped stories are remarkable for both their quantity and their individual length. John Earlin's Chaseworld is not subject to the whims of conversational collaborators, who might inhibit his control over sequence, content, and duration. Ensuring his ability to tell what he wants to tell without interruption, Earlin eludes the joker.

In time the tape has reached its intended audience, where it has taken on a life of its own, expanding Earlin's Chaseworld exponentially as a topic in countless conversations. Others in the community, familiar with the tape and its genesis, repeatedly drew my attention to it. The tape, it turns out, actually circulates among hunters and their friends. My interest in foxhunting seemed to remind them of the tape. "There's a hunter around," said Donald Taylor, when I first met him on another foxchase five years later. "Well, he's sick now, he's dyin' of cancer. His name's John Earlin. He made a tape a few years ago. I don't know whether I still got it at home or not, but I think you'd like to hear that. It's pretty good. He talks of Norman and Freeman, he talks of goin' to Delaware, havin' a couple of chases down there. It's pretty interesting" (foxchase, January 25, 1986).

In conversations I had with foxhunters over the years, references to the tape always triggered more stories relating to their mutually constructed world of foxhunting, with hunters offering their own abstracts, versions, and second stories.[6] The universe of discourse generated by the recording seems unlikely to close as long as foxhunters who appear as characters in it are alive. In the conversation at Jake Meredith's cabin, Jeff Powell suggested the hunters get together to listen to the "tapes of Johnny Earlin's."

"Get everybody to sit 'n' listen to 'em," he said. "We could laugh."

"What have they got on 'em?" inquired Hubie Driscoll.

"Just tellin' stories about goin' to Corny's or Bill Passwater," said Jeff. "Just one story after another. One story he talks about him and Jack Davis goin' up—someone bet Jack the night before he could catch a fox."

"Yeah, up at South Branch," said Norman. "Josie Anderson, yeah. Josie, he took the fox outa the tree, didn't he? Yeah, I was with 'em."

"It tells about when Snuffy first come there," added Jeff. "There's another story he tells about Snuffy, too."

"Johnny had some stories," said Jake Meredith (storytelling session, July 1990).

"From nothin' at all" John Earlin conjured a Chaseworld around which fellowship continues to take shape. His stories are a reflecting surface for his fellow hunters, who concede that the stories are true, inasmuch as any story told from a single vantage point can be true. "He told 'em his way, which was alright," avered Jack Davis. "He was makin' the tape" (interview, November 14, 1980).

Like his cabin, John's tape of stories has become not only a threshold to the Chaseworld, but a touchstone as well. "It says so on that tape of Johnny's," said Norman Taylor, in support of his own memory of an event recorded there (interview, January 24, 1986).

In his recording, John Earlin catches up and parades before his audience many of the Chaseworld's intrinsic themes: the thrill of owning the hound in the lead, the embarrassment of owning a hound that won't perform, the tragedy of the loss of a good fox, the satisfaction of witnessing astonishing events in nature, the irreconcilable tension between the desire to be best, and the desire for good fellowship. In John Earlin's Chaseworld, human and animal passions are on display, and their consequences are explored. Hunters overestimate their hounds, are victims of their own overweening pride, lose their tempers, prove their loyalty, and provide each other with sterling companionship. John Earlin learns, and vicariously so do we, what it would be like to be a fox attacked by hunting dogs. What John Berger calls "the narrow abyss of non-comprehension dividing humans from animals" (1977:504) is spanned by hunters who issue commands to foxes and chickens, and by a hound who reads the mind of its master.

The Story System

Like the collectively rendered stories at Three Bridges Shanty, John Earlin's solo stories form an integrated system, demonstrating continuities of character, time, and place. The sequencing is roughly chronological as John clusters stories around characters with whom he hunted during certain eras in his foxhunting career. He repeatedly asserts the logic of this sequencing: "I'm going to tell you another story about Ben and I"; "A lot of these stories are about foxhunting in New Jersey, but here's one about a Delaware foxhunt"; "So that is the second story about Snuffy"; "Well, we're back in Jersey now and in 1955 I seed some land for sale up in the northern forest."

The stories are structurally interrelated through replications of actions. Such replications, as we saw in Chapter 6, allow meaning to seep across the boundaries between stories (Douglas 1973:13; Young 1987:101). John Earlin's Chaseworld is by turns orderly and disorderly. By replicating formal relations among elements, he uses later stories to correct aspects of the world gone awry in earlier stories.[7] In this way he introduces and explores themes endemic to the Chaseworld: the problem of how to achieve and sustain fellowship, the deep ambivalence about the death of the fox, and the boundary between human and animal consciousness.

In its fluctuations between states of order and disorder, Earlin's Chaseworld universe resembles the worlds of tricksters and marginal figures in general (Babcock-Abrahams 1975:168). The session progresses from stories that introduce a number of disorders to stories in which these disorders are resolved.[8] John Earlin's story session demonstrates a gradual movement forward and upward: from the disintegration of the first chase, which culminates in the disgraceful capture of a fox by a hound that never entered the chase, to the final, supremely orderly gesture of Blockhead the hound, who uncannily discerns and dispels John's confusion about the Chaseworld's outcome; from John's failed attempt to rescue a fox in the second story to Freeman Taylor's successful liberation of the fox in the fifth; from human relationships fraught with discord in the fourth, eighth, and ninth stories, to the good fellowship at the breakfasts in Delaware (tenth story) and the fabulous friendship with Snuffy (eleventh, twelfth, and thirteenth stories).

In his stories, John Earlin endows the Chaseworld with meanings both explicit, through his evaluations of events, and tacit, through his structuring of the session. On the whole, the stories constitute an exploration of the Chaseworld's basis in good dogmanship, sportsmanship, and fellowship, depicting their gradual achievement over the course of John Earlin's life as a hunter. A closer look at the structure of the session reveals a marked difference between stories in the first half. which largely introduce disorders, and stories in the second half, which portray an orderly realm capable of withstanding threats to that order.

Between the two halves of the session we find the intensely disturbing deaths of two prized foxes. The deaths occur much to the chagrin of hunters who in his other stories are not at all displeased to see foxes die. As John Earlin's stories compellingly demonstrate, no single meaning may be attached to the death of the fox. Over the course of the fourteen stories the fox's death represents a variety of things, including money, hubris, the superiority of hounds over nature, the superiority of New Jersey hunters over Delaware hunters, the inability of hunters to control hounds, and injustice in several guises. But the deaths of foxes midway through the session seem unusually catastrophic, causing sorrow and turmoil among the hunters with something at stake in the foxes' lives.

These deaths are closely linked with the sequence about hunting in Delaware, which constitutes a watershed in the series. Before and after the episodes in Delaware, the Chaseworld is a different place. Prior to the trip to Delaware, the world is awry: one dog catches a fox without having joined in the chase, another inexplicably disappears, and John Earlin's pack savagely throws him to the ground in an effort to wrest the fox from his arms. And even when the pack is running well, relations among men appear less than felicitous: Ben loses his temper, Jack Davis accuses John of trying to subvert his effort to win a bet, and hunters in the first two Delaware stories exhibit rancor and hostility. In the final Delaware story and those that follow it, the Chaseworld is a fairly flawless realm, inhabited by good dogs, good sports, and good fellows.

The session closes by drawing attention back to the introductory theme, a pattern evinced in the collaborative session described in Chapter 6 (Young 1987:142). In the final story, the death of the fox becomes a means for the hound Blockhead to bridge the gap between human and animal consciousness, to repair the breach caused in the first story by John's errant Black and Tan. The confusion in this story is over whether the Chaseworld has ended. Blockhead proves that it has, thus providing Chaseworld and Storyrealm with closure while reiterating a central theme, the disparity between human and animal consciousness.

Meanings: Animals and Human Identity

Of particular interest in a consideration of the Chaseworld as a resource for self-definition is the role played by animals in the shaping of human identity. Imposing form on "the inchoate pronouns of social life" is a process that, as James Fernandez writes, "has for millennia turned to the animal world" (1986:35).[9] In Chapter 6 we glimpsed foxes and jokers in relation to a group defining and commenting on the society it achieves. John Earlin's Chaseworld is similarly studded with human and animal tricksters. Do the Chaseworld's animal players become predicates—"primordial *points de ré-père*," as James Fernandez calls them (1986:32)—in John Earlin's quest for identity? And how might this process be further assisted by tricksters, both animal and human?[10]

Identification with the quarry is one of the paradoxical mysteries of hunting. Ortega y Gasset describes this identification as "a mystical union with the animal . . . that automatically leads the hunter to perceive the environment from the point of view of the prey, without abandoning his own point of view" (1972:124). John Earlin's association with the fox in this series occurs at the most visceral and cerebral levels, progressing from the physical to the metaphysical. The association begins in the second story, wherein John learns what it must be like to be a fox attacked by dogs. Reversing the outcome of the second story, the hunters' rescue of the fox in the fifth story takes on the hue of a redemptive act. The association between hunters and foxes is deepened and clarified in the post-Delaware stories through replications whereby John and Snuffy reconstitute and transcend the conditions that destroyed the fox. What the fox lacks is culture, and it is through the culture of the Chaseworld that hunters invoke and triumph over forces that threaten their reality. Imitating the fox, John Earlin and Snuffy transcend the Chaseworld's inherent paradoxes as jokers.

At the chronological heart of his Chaseworld, the death of the fox in the bush, with whom Earlin has come to empathize, and whom he admires, becomes in a sense the destruction of the hunter. Here Earlin takes us to the brink of an "abyss" that Victor Turner ascribes to ritual, a depth that is infinite and defies comprehension. Ritual, writes Turner, "is a transformative self-immolation of order . . . in the subjunctive depths of liminality. . . . Only in this way, through destruction and reconstruction, that is, transformation, may an authentic reordering come about" (1980:160).

The "reconstruction" begins, aptly enough, with John Earlin's consumption of massive quantities of food, and it continues "back in Jersey" with the building of a cabin and an exemplary friendship. Hounds do not figure at all in the tenth story, which celebrates fellowship centered around the sharing of food. The cause for amazement in this story is John Earlin's tremendous appetite, which he likens to that of an elephant. For the sake of politeness, John Earlin eats a second breakfast, consisting of ham, potatoes, sausage, and fourteen eggs (interestingly, the number of stories in the session).

This story pivots between stories of bad fellowship and stories of good fellowship. The incorporation of massive amounts of food in order to be polite might be seen as an initiatory rite, marking the crossing of a threshold between "higher" and "lower" selves, which Berger and Luckmann point out are "respectively equated with social identity and presocial, possibly anti-social animality. The 'higher' self must repeatedly assert itself over the 'lower,' sometimes in critical tests of strength" (1967:182–83). For the sake of fellowship, John Earlin puts his stomach to the test, and his colleagues are greatly amused.

Following these breakfasts, John Earlin returns us to New Jersey, where he erects a firm center of order for the Chaseworld in the form of a small cinderblock cabin. In his story system, orderly gestures arise in response to disorders depicted in earlier stories. The cabin with its attendant kennel is, as we have seen, a powerful Chaseworld threshold, a shelter for hunters and their hounds. The building of this cabin, and the subsequent fellowship with Snuffy are actions that replicate and triumph over conditions that brought the foxes down. Whereas the foxes in the seventh and eighth stories perish because of inadequate cover, John Earlin builds a cabin that becomes a Chaseworld bulwark.

The cabin enables him, in the stories that follow, to provide hospitality, food, and shelter to the circle of foxhunting fellows, and he promptly expands the circle with the introduction of James Fisher, who is given the Chaseworld name of "Snuffy." John's friendship with Snuffy commences with the sharing of "a heck of a stew," which Snuffy, echoing John in Delaware, welcomes with a gratifyingly large appetite. The friendship progresses over the series from the initial sharing of food to the sharing of the cabin each weekend, and goes on to the sharing of dog kennels, dog boxes, and, ultimately, the same state of mind.

Through the later actions of Snuffy and John Earlin, the "fox in the bush" comes to constitute the joker in a previous incarnation. The parallel suggested here between foxes and hunters is borne out in a closer comparison of Snuffy's behavior with that of the fox in the bush. In the seventh story, this fox attempts to defend himself, contriving an unusual stalemate for the chase by attacking the dogs from his small fortress in a ground oak bush. In the manner of the joker, the fox attacks the formal order of the Chaseworld with an informal, improvised order of its own (Douglas 1968:370).

In the twelfth story, a quotidian rite of passage threatens to cancel the weekly rite of fellowship—the exchange of greetings and the sharing of food—between John and Snuffy. One Friday evening Snuffy announces to John that he is to be married the following Thursday. John's response, hardly congratulatory, is one of total concern for the Chaseworld: "Well, that'll break your record, won't it? You won't be here at seven o'clock Friday night." Thus a quotidian rite that places men within the controlling sphere of women is pitted against a Chaseworld rite of male solidarity. Snuffy protests that his wedding will not prevent him from meeting John the next Friday. John's challenge is thus a critical test of Snuffy's commitment to the Chaseworld, a test which Snuffy passes with honors.

Describing the role of the trickster as cultural protector, Barbara

Babcock-Abrahams writes that "Trickster is a sacred being and the founder of the ritual and ceremonial life of his society precisely because he violates taboos for the profit of his group" (1975:164). Though he violates no taboos, Snuffy emerges here as a culture hero who breaks with social norms in the quotidian for the sake of the Chaseworld. Like the joker who uses the informal to attack the formal, Snuffy forces quotidian conventions to accommodate to the Chaseworld. The Chaseworld emerges as an institution at least as powerful as marriage.

In the next story—the penultimate one of the session—Snuffy is cast as a full-fledged joker. Again Snuffy protects the Chaseworld, this time through an attack on the formal constraint that a question from a stranger imposes on him. Snuffy has gathered both his hounds and Johnny's hounds together in his pickup. The large number of hounds packed into a small space attracts the attention of a stranger, who asks him how many hounds are in the truck.

In violating the social dictum to mind one's own business, the stranger invades Snuffy's privacy, and by extension, John Earlin's, for the hounds of both hunters were implicated in the stranger's question. Information about hounds, as I have indicated in Chapter Four, is zealously guarded by hunters. Moreover, the stranger posed his question at one of the Chaseworld's transitional junctures, when hounds were loaded but not sorted. Thus, while the interchange was taking place two packs of dogs and their owners were held between states of reality. The threat also could be one with very real consequences. If, for example, the stranger should turn out to be a "do-gooder" (animal rights activist), he could complain that foxhunters treat their dogs inhumanely. At any rate, the stranger's question imposes on Snuffy an obligation to respond, and he evades this moral pressure through a bit of word magic.

Snuffy's smart answer, the raison d'être for the story, invents another meaning for the stranger's question. According to his answer, the question becomes, "How many dogs do you have in there [as opposed to outside of the truck]?" In his display of verbal wit, Snuffy demonstrates "the transformative capacity of speech" (Bauman 1986:77), emerging again as a culture hero who cleverly defends the Chaseworld, this time through the enactment of a joke rite.

If Earlin's story system can be said to document a progression from a "lower" disorganized self to a "higher" organized one (Berger and Luckmann 1967:182), the penultimate story about Snuffy defines that higher self as a joker. In the Snuffy stories, John Earlin turns our attention to the hunters' capacity to erect and sustain the reality in which their essential identities are rooted. Poor dogmanship, unsportsmanlike behavior, and the absence of fellowship and good will can all threaten the Chaseworld. These disorders can be addressed through attention directed specifically toward the Chaseworld's contents: hounds, humans, and foxes. But the Chaseworld is an alternative realm of play. And play, by its nature, requires that players progress beyond facility with the contents of the alternative realm to facility with its frames.[11]

The Snuffy stories extol this facility, celebrating the ability to manipulate frame as well as content, to summon reality as well as to cancel it, to use the Chaseworld as a stronghold against the Ordinary. Overcoming threats to the Chaseworld entails the development of mastery over reality, the ability to summon it forth or cancel it. And traipsing the boundary between being and not-being are the paradoxical figures of foxes and jokers.

Thus, where the fox in the bush has failed, Snuffy succeeds. Like the fox in the bush, Snuffy substitutes the improvised order of the Chaseworld rite for postnuptial convention. Like the fox in the bush who throws off its assigned role as fugitive to become an assailant, Snuffy rewrites the script imposed on him by a stranger, substituting an anti-structure for the one the stranger proposed. Like the fox in the bush, Snuffy resists outside authority, calling attention to the "made-upness" of the rules, to the arbitrary nature of cultural categories (Moore and Myerhoff 1977:17). In both stories—that of the fox in the bush and that of Snuffy's wedding—the extraordinary behavior of the trickster constitutes the reason for telling the story. "It was amazing to see a fox . . . I'm just amazed about it." Yet more astounding to John Earlin than anything he has ever witnessed is Snuffy's postnuptial appearance at the cabin: "And I was never so surprised in my life—to see Snuffy on the night after he got married."[12] Like the fox in the bush, only more so, Snuffy astonishes John Earlin.

The ability to conjure Chaseworlds—to make culture—is what distinguishes humans from animals.[13] Built into these cultural forms are references to their vulnerability, to the abyss over which humans, making meaning, perform their high-wire acts. Where the fox in the bush cannot quite muster the resources to prevent its own annihilation, humans, through culture making, offer superior resistance. Storytelling is one such mode of resistance, particularly for the elderly, for whom narrative comprises a powerful means of tackling "the challenges of discontinuity," a means of inscribing the self and its milieu "on the threshold of disappearance" (Kirshenblatt-Gimblett 1987).

The story of Earlin's journey toward mastery of self and Chaseworld contains an accounting both of his education into the realm and of the revelations that demarcate stages in his development. With these revelations comes the increase in self-awareness that attends the witnessing of untoward events both in nature and in culture: the assault waged upon him by his dogs, the cleverness of the fox in the bush, and his own gargantuan appetite, reflected back at him through a story told by another Chaseworld character.

Detailing such moments before an audience, the initiate of the self-definitional rite comes to cross what Myerhoff terms "the delicate but crucial threshold between merely being and being a man, a sentient human being, *knowing* himself to be" (Myerhoff 1978:221–22). Enroute to this threshold, John Earlin explores the meeting places of human and animal consciousness, and investigates associated forms of jeopardy. Worse than loss of life is loss of face and of being. Cultural structures like ritual and narrative, those declarations of "form against indeterminacy," serve as vessels that hold these intact (Moore and Myerhoff 1977:8, 16).

Anthropologists and others have written about the transfer of qualities from quarry to hunter almost as though it were a form of magic, mostly sympathetic, but in some instances contagious as well. Ortega y Gasset defines hunting as "an imitation of the animal" wherein "a contagion is immediately generated and the hunter begins to behave like the game" (1972:124) in an effort to get as close to the animal as possible. James Howe alludes to the metaphorical transfer of qualities, whereby medieval aristocrats could incorporate the nobility of the stag or the warriorlike fierceness of the boar through the slaying of the beast. In the case of foxhunting, the transfer of qualities operates at a far more abstract level, and at times the magic itself becomes an object of contemplation.[14] The forces binding humans into society are no less mysterious than the gravity that keeps them from falling into space. The Chaseworld, itself a feat of legerdemain, becomes a means of fathoming the mysteries behind the appearance, endurance, and disappearance of worlds.

Notes

1. Alfred Schutz writes that "Only from the point of view of the retrospective glance do there exist discrete experiences. Only the already experienced is meaningful, not that which is being experienced" (1970:63).

2. Katharine Young writes that the alternative mode of self-presentation afforded by stories "may be especially attractive to old people whose presentations of self in everyday life may come to seem to them circumscribed. Stories about the

past reconstitute for them a realm of events in which they were far livelier than they are now. And one over which they exercise a far more delicate and absolute control than they ever did when they inhabited it" (1987:199–200).

3. As Jeff Todd Titon points out, "The problem of how much a person may change without losing his or her identity is the greatest difficulty facing the life storyteller, whose chief concern, after all, is to affirm his identity and account for it" (1980:290).

4. Offering coherence in place of fragmentation, an alternate reality like the Chaseworld is a powerful resource for self-definition in the postmodern era. "Identity," write Berger and Luckmann, "is objectively defined as location in a certain world and can be subjectively appropriated only *along with that world*. Put differently, all identifications take place within horizons that imply a specific social world" (1967:132).

5. For more on the forms and functions of life review projects see Kirshenblatt-Gimblett (1987) and Hufford, Hunt, and Zeitlin (1987).

6. For instance, when I asked Norman whether he was considering making a similar tape of stories, he responded with a story about himself and John Earlin, in which John figures as an unwitting source of chaos:

NT: Yeah, one of these days I might. I'll never forget one time Johnny Earlin was down on the Plains—no, Webb's Mill, and that was big country in them days. And believe it or not, he had a dog—I must've been about sixteen, seventeen years old, and I said, "I'll catch that dog runnin' deer, John."

So I took right off through the woods after the dog, and when I finally caught the dog, and I took a switch and switched it, and I put it on a lead, and I started back to Johnny. I figured he would be where I left him, so I called and nobody answered. I called and after a while he blew his horn. So I went for the horn. I got pretty close to where the horn was, and he made up his mind that I must have been on the other side, and he went all the way around to the other road. So when I got back here he blew his horn on the other side.

So, "I gotta be lost." So I turned around when he blew his horn and I went the other way, and then he blew it some other place. So I walked out there in the ground oaks, leading that dog for about two hours, and every time I got close to the road he'd go the other direction.

So I come out, "Jesus, Johnny! Why don't you stay still in one spot? I come out here lost, and tryin' to find the road, and you're blowin' your horn all around here!"

MH: You were lost?

NT: Yeah, I wanted to go the shortest route to the car, and when he was blowin' his horn I started that way, and in the meantime, when he blew it again, he was in back of me.

MH: Was he lookin' for you?

NT: He was lookin' for me too! I was so far that he couldn't hear me, but yet I could hear his horn. I said, "I'm goin' around in circles here, but instead it was him movin' the car. (Interview, January 24, 1986)

7. These later stories relate to the earlier ones as "second stories" which are, as was discussed in Chapter 6, "stories by a second teller parasitic on stories by a first" that "replicate certain formal relations between elements and so have the property of structuring the narrative discourse or Storyrealm" (Young 1987:101).

8. In its examination of various forms of order and disorder, John Earlin's stories resemble the classic trickster cycle, which tends to "begin with a statement of order followed by its dissolution and, thereafter, by an examination of forms of disorder" (Babcock-Abrahams 1975:168).

9. James Fernandez writes that

in the growth of human identity, the inchoate pronouns of social life . . . gain identity by predicating some sign-image, some metaphor upon themselves. These pronouns must, in [G. H.] Mead's [1934] terms, become objects to themselves, by taking the point of view of "the other," before they can become subjects to themselves. This becoming an object, this taking the other, this predication upon the pronoun, is a process that has for millennia turned to the animal world (1986:35).

10. Some scholars have linked the trickster with primitive cultures and early stages of socialization in childhood. Others argue that the trickster is a product of highly sophisticated minds, a tool for mediating cultural contradictions and transcending social constraints (Lévi-Strauss 1955; Babcock-Abrahams 1975). For a review of conflicting hypotheses about the trickster, see Abrams and Sutton-Smith (1977), and Babcock-Abrahams (1975).

11. Susan Stewart writes, "Through play an organism does not learn so much the content of categories of behavior as that there are sorts and categories of behavior, and that such sorts and categories can be manipulated, can support each other, transform each other, or cancel each other out" (1979:31).

12. For a consideration of some of the dynamics placing hunting and marriage at cross purposes, see Marks (1991:160–65).

13. Thus Victor Turner terms us "animals with culture" (1977).

14. Mary Douglas suggests that "the achievement of consonance between different realms of experience is a source of profound satisfaction" (1968:375). Authoring the Chaseworld, or any other inherently satisfying realm, issues from what scholars have seen as a human imperative to symbolize (Langer 1942:41), to play (Csikzentmihalyi 1975), to express the unfathomable (Turner 1962:87, cited in Douglas 1968:375), and to explore the relation of thought to experience (Douglas 1968:375).

8. Epilogue

WINTER WANES AND the Pine Barrens quicken with the signs of new life. The spring peepers are in full chorus, piping from the edges of tea-colored streams, and whippoorwills fill the April nights with their undulating cries. By day the pine warblers, returning north, resume their trilling in graceful monotones, harbingers of the blueberry blossoms that will soon flood the air with their sweet scent. And brooding foxes and lengthening days portend the close of another season for chasing foxes.

The season's end is ceremonially marked with a big chase in Penn State Forest, near Three Bridges Shanty. Members of the New Jersey Sporting Dogs Association have come from as far away as Cream Ridge and Port Elizabeth, each with two or three favorite hounds to cast with the pack. I have come with two photograpl.ers, commissioned to capture the foxchase on film. Oscar Hillman and Bob Hayes are here; so are Jake Meredith, his uncles, Norman and Freeman Taylor, and Caroline Taylor. The gathering also includes Leonard Duffy, Tom Driscoll, Bud Anderson and his son Ray, Jake Reuter and his brother Bud, Alvin Stafford (son of Snap), Dadio, and Paul "Possum" Sooy. The red fox they jumped in the Briar Hole is now leading forty or fifty vociferous hounds through the swamp they call Papoose and around the cranberry bogs at Sim Place.

The air around the swamp's dark water is clean, penetrating, and astringent, seasoned with wiffs of cedar. A hound trots in from the woods with a bone in its mouth, to the amusement of those who see it. "That fox made a lap down there," says Tom Driscoll, "and it come back, and it went acrosst, and that may be where them dogs is headin'." A sense of the fox's pattern having been thus established, attention diverts from the pack, and the air is quickly enlivened with the sound of male camaraderie, of spectacle in full swing while the dogs are running. Tom Driscoll spies a man he hasn't seen in years. "I know that man, from way back," he says, approaching him. "I know you," he greets the man. "Didn't you buy a dog from me one time?"

"I bought one off you," says Dadio, "I bought that, what the heck was her name, a little white dog—my buddy bought the blue tick—"

Figure 8.1. Foxhunters gathered for the Sporting Dogs of New Jersey Association's annual foxhunt, near Sim Place, southeast of Chatsworth. Photo by Dennis McDonald, April 1991.

"The blue one, yeah," says Tom Driscoll. "That's the one he wanted. That one you bought was no damn good. Was never any good."

"She used to run," Dadio says in her defense.

"Did she run with you?" Tom Driscoll asks. "Well she was young, that's when we broke up the pack—and he bought Jenny."

"We bought three of 'em," Dadio recalls. "I bought Jenny and the white one."

Driscoll is intrigued. "Didja? You had Jenny—did you ever get her to run?"

"Sure!" says Dadio.

Walking down the road past the line of pickups, past the men arranging and rearranging themselves in trios, pairs, and by the half-dozen, one glimpses the profusion of spritely repartee and dogtalk, the murmurings of men at the Chaseworld's rim, orienting to their world and appreciating what they have wrought.

"I spent a thousand dollars apiece for them dogs," says Jake Meredith, "and them son-of-a-bitches wasn't worth ten cents."

This draws laughter from Leonard Duffy and others, leaning on a pickup, listening.

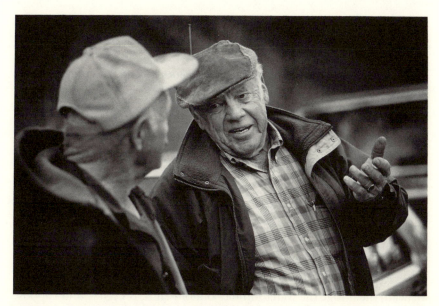

Figure 8.2. Jake Reuter and Leonard Duffy. Photo by Dennis McDonald, April 1991.

"That fox was in here," Jake continues. "And as soon as they made the first miss, they'd trail right straight back to you, both of 'em, just a-tongin' like they was—and they wasn't worth ten cents, and I damn near got a speedin' ticket, and if the guy hadn't a got talkin' to me, and been decent, he coulda given me a ticket."

Leonard Duffy chuckles.

"And I spent a thousand dollars," Jake reiterates,

"A thousand dollars and a fine," supplies Leonard Duffy.

"And they wasn't worth the gasoline to go get 'em," concludes Jake.

Farther down the road, the gnats, drawn out by the warm weather, draw commentary. "When the gnats come out like this in the spring," says Bob Hayes, "that's when the herring start running. That's what them old timers always said."

"Yep," said Oscar Hillman, "That's what they always said."

"They oughta be runnin' pretty good this morning then," said Bob Hayes.

The hunters guffaw loudly at this.

Later, Oscar Hillman would savor the wit of his colleague. "Did you get that on the tape?" he would ask me. "What he said about the herring? That was pretty good. 'They oughta be runnin' pretty good,' yeah."

Standing on the bridge, peering into Papoose waters, Norman Taylor and Jake Reuter lament the fox's enemies—the trappers and the rabbit hunters. "But there's worse things on rabbit in the woods than the fox," Norman points out. "You take your mink and weasel, they'll kill more rabbits than the fox will, wouldn't you say?"

"I would say," says Jake Reuter.

"Sure," says Norman.

"Just as many anyway," says Jake.

"Just as many, yeah," Norman echoes.

"Some guys just love to trap," Jake observes.

"Just for the sport of it," Norman elaborates.

"For the enthusiasm," Jake interjects.

"Recreation, yeah," Norman avers.

Beneath the bridge the water tumbles out of Plains, Breeches, and Papoose Branches into the Oswego River and beyond, spilling into the navigable waters of the Wading and Mullica rivers, flowing past the ruins of Martha, past the hometowns of foxhunters from New Gretna and Port Republic, and finally leaving the banks that retain it, losing its form to the sea.

Hoping to get a look at the fox, the hunters relocate to positions on the far side of the cranberry bogs. Standing on a dam of sand and turf, we regard the deep green cedar spires across the sky-blue expanse of a flooded bog. We watch as the dense orb of sound pulses its way across the forest and rises to a fierce crescendo, arresting the ears, minds, and hearts of its listeners.

"Wow," says Caroline Taylor, breaking the human silence.

"It doesn't get any better than that," says Norman. "Does it Jake?"

"No," Jake says, "It doesn't."

In coarse squalls, rhythmic yelps, lilting ululations, and sonorous hollers, the hunters' story goes on. It is a story that never fails to tantalize, that never surrenders its secrets all at once. "Listen to 'em," Jack Davis once told me. "They're talkin' to you."

"What are they saying?" I asked.

"They're tellin' you the fox is ahead of 'em!" he said, and a sly smile lit up his face.

Appendix I: Glossary of Terms Used by Pine Barrens Foxhunters

The following list includes colloquial foxhunting vocabulary, landscape terminology, archaisms, and arcane usages.

Awful: adj. Tremendous, awesome, great. "That dog's got an awful note onto her" (Bobby Emmons, hound auction, November 2, 1986). "He'd give you an awful chase for three hours" (Freeman Taylor, foxchase, March 17, 1979).

Babble: v. (of hounds). To tongue when trailing or running without smelling the fox. "They yell where a fox ain't been" (Freeman Taylor, foxchase, March 17, 1979).

Back track, backfoot: n. The cold trail leading away from the fox. v. to backtrack: said of hounds following a backtrack. "Not *all* your dogs'll take a cold trail. Well, then you have to be careful, because they might take a backfoot . . . they might go backwards on that track. They don't know the difference. I've seen dogs run them right back to their bed" (Robly Champion, interview, September 1979).

Black and Tan: A strain of hound, popular among Pine Barrens foxhunters in the 1930s, 1940s, and 1950s, now more commonly used by coonhunters.

Blacktop: Any road with a macadam surface. Also the foxhunter's proper name for Mount Misery Road in Lebanon State Forest.

Blue tick: Mottled hound with black, blue-gray, and white markings.

Bog: Marshy area in which cranberries are cultivated.

Boo-hoo: v. (of hounds) To have the scent but fail to distinguish a trail. "They get a trail and they can't move it" (Norman Taylor, interview, January 22, 1986).

Bother: See "miss."

Bottom: A hound's endurance, often measured in hours. (See also "foot.") "A hound's gotta have at least eight hours worth [of bottom]" (John Earlin, foxchase, November 15, 1980).

Break: v. To remove the hounds from the trail of the fox; also to train a dog to ignore the scent of deer.

Bunch up: v. (of hounds) To run together in a tight group. Also called "packing up."

Burnt ground: Common landscape feature in late winter, produced by controlled burning prior to spring fire season to reduce brush and lessen the chance of wildfires. "Soon as they jump he'll go on that burnt ground—burnt black as the ace of spades" (Freeman Taylor, foxchase, March 17, 1979).

Cast: v. To set the hounds in search of a fox's trail.

Cheat: v. (of hounds) To gain an advantage over other hounds by following the fox's aerial scent rather than its terrestrial scent.

Check: v. See "miss."

Chop: n. Staccato utterance of a hound running a fox. "When they're trailin' they have a long yell. Soon's they jump it, then it's chop. It's faster" (Robly Champion, interview, September, 1979).

Cold trail: n. Old trail laid by fox that is not currently running. v. Said of hounds following the cold trail.

Crooked: adj. (of hounds) Dishonest. A hound with a tendency to run around the pack to get ahead from behind is said to be "crooked." "He gouges on dogs to get in front of 'em" (Norman Taylor, telephone conversation, March 1991).

Crossway: n. Slab road made by lumbermen for crossing marshy terrain. Mike's Crossway and Sandy Crossway, now roads through the woods, began as such structures.

Culls: n. Hounds that a hunter eliminates from his pack.

Cut: v. To take a short cut in order to get ahead of the pack and closer to the fox. "If they cut, that goes against 'em. Now if a dog is behind and cuts to get up, well, I mean, that's okay. But you don't want 'em to cut when they're ahead" (Robly Champion, interview, September, 1979).

Dam: n. Structure made of sand and turf for holding water in cranberry reservoirs, topped by sand roads and equipped with sluice gates.

Deer dog: A hound that chases deer despite efforts to "break" it of the habit.

Deerproof: (also "deerbroke") adj. Used to describe a dog that will not chase deer.

Do-gooders: Environmentalists and animal rights activists. "I seen a write-up in the paper where the do-gooders said, 'The hunters set the woods on fire so they can stand there with their guns and shoot the deer'" (Donald Pomeroy, foxchase, March 17, 1979).

Dogtalk: n. Conversation about dogs.

Double: v. (of foxes) To reverse direction temporarily along a trail in order to confuse the hounds. "He mighta never even crossed the road—maybe just went to the road and doubled back" (Donald Pomeroy, foxchase, March 17, 1979). n. The point at which the fox reversed its direction on the trail. "I know that it's my hound picked up the double" (Milton Collins, interview, December 18, 1980).

Drive: adj. (Of hounds) A hound's energy and ambition. v. (Of hounds) To push the fox hard.

Dry up: v. Become silent. "She used to dry up, you wouldn't hear nothin' out of her, and she would trail. I'd say, 'We'll jump that fox in another minute'" (Robly Champion, interview September 1979).

Dump in: See "throw in."

Firelines: Narrow swaths cut through woodlands for use in controlling forest fires.

Foot: n. A hound's endurance. See also "bottom."

Front track: The fox's trail forward, that is, toward the fox.

Game: adj. Used to describe an enthusiastic hound that is always ready to trail and run fox to the best of its ability. "They'll give you everything they've got. Like one of the family" (Don Cramer, telephone conversation, February 1991).

Ganderbrush: Springy vegetation in a Pitch Pine lowland area, predominantly covered with leatherleaf (*Chamaedaphne calyculata*).

Glass eye: A blue eye on a hound, said to have held special significance for old-timers. Also called a "watch eye" (Don Cramer, interview, February 1991).

Gravel road: Unimproved road topped with gravel.

Gyp: n. (1) Polite term for bitch. (2) Mildly deprecating term for dog dealer.

Hark: v. (of hounds) To attend to the fox's trail. Also "to hark in": to get in the chase.

Hassocks: Natural formations in cedar swamps comprised of cedar roots ("knees") protruding above ground and covered with sphagnum moss.

Honor: v. (of dogs) To respectfully acknowledge the hound that has the scent. "The dog has to honor the other dog and run right" (John Earlin, interview, November 21, 1980).

Hot track: n. The trail of a fox in flight

Hound: n. Dog bred for tracking game. Often specifies Maryland hound. "You can't run Walkers with hounds " (Robly Champion, interview September 1979).

Jump: v. To rouse a fox from its bed, inducing it to run and deposit fresh scent. "You can easily tell when they jump it. They get right close to it and jump it, jump it out of its bed" (Robly Champion, interview, September 1979).

Laps: n. Fallen trees overlapping one another, often slash from cedar harvest or "windthrow" from storms.

Lie: v. (of hounds) To deliberately misrepresent the trail; to speak to a line that is not there. "I've never heard him lie in his life. He never hollers unless he has the scent" (Norman Taylor, interview, January 25, 1986). n. Alternative term for "story."

Line: n. The trail of the fox.

Locate: v. (of hounds) To find the running pack or the honking truck by hearing. "He'll locate your pickup for you" (Norman Taylor, interview, August 12, 1982).

Long note: n. Legato utterance emitted by hound on the cold trail. "Most all of your dogs have a squallin' note when they're trailin'—a long note" (Robly Champion, interview, September 1979).

Loward: adj. Leeward, downwind. "Listening to the dogs it's important you keep to the loward of 'em" (Milton Collins, interview, December 18, 1980).

Maryland hound: A regional strain of foxhound used on the Middle Atlantic coastal plain.

Miss: v. (of hounds) To lose the fox's trail momentarily.

Mouth: A hound's capacity for speaking or singing.

Nose: A hound's capacity for scenting. "When a dog has a cold nose, they'll tongue the cold track" (Milton Collins, interview, December 18, 1980).

Oil road: Unimproved road treated with oil to control dust. Pack up, pack together: See "bunch."

Parti-colored: adj. (of hounds) A hound with black, brown, and white markings, also termed "pied."

Pennmarydel: Alternate term for Maryland hound.

Plowed lanes: See "firelines".

Potlicker: Hounds bred from whatever stock is available close to home, with little attention to lineage or form of breed. Also termed a "home-grown" variety.

Pushcover: Any heavy brush-covered area favored by gray fox, difficult for hounds to run in.

Reservoir: Man-made lake on cranberry plantation containing water supply for harvesting carnberries and protecting vines from frost.

Running: v. Hounds pursuing an actual fox. "Are they running or just trailing?" (Donald Pomeroy, foxchase, March 17, 1979).

Scouter: See "crooked."

Slate road: Alternative term for blacktop.

Speak: (of hounds) To vocalize when encountering fox scent.

Spong: Marshy, low-lying area at the edge of a hardwood swamp.

Start: v. (of hounds) To jump a fox. adj. Starter or starting dog: a hound good at jumping a fox. "We just used him for jumpin'. Startin' dog " (Freeman Taylor, foxchase, March 17, 1979).

Straight fox: adj. A hound that pursues nothing but fox is said to be "straight fox."

Strike: v. To hit the trail of a fox; to put hounds on the trail of a fox. "We strike 'em ahead of our pickups" (Robly Champion, interview, September 1979). See also "cast."

Swing: v. To veer from the trail; to loop back. "They [foxes] get to the end of their territory and then they swing" (Milton Collins, interview, December 18, 1980) Swinger: n. a dog that swings.

Tar road: Alternate term for blacktop.

Throw in: To place one's hounds in a chase in progress. "Go ahead and throw in with us, Charlie " (Norman Taylor, foxchase, January 25, 1986)

Throwed out: adj. Said of a hound that cannot keep up in a chase. "Lots of times you'll have dogs get throwed out of the chase " (Robly Champion, Interview, September 1979)

Tongue: v. See "speak."

Trader foxes: Foxes that, during breeding season, travel out of their territories, to which they return when pursued by hounds.

Trail: n. The terrestrial scent of the fox. v. To follow a cold track.

Trash: n. All quarry but fox. v. To trash: to pursue anything but fox.

Tree: v. (of hounds) To "tree" a fox, i.e., force a fox to climb a tree.

Tree-barking: (of hounds) Baying at a treed fox. "They were tree-barking a fox" (Norman Taylor, telephone conversation, June 1989).

Walker: Breed of hound developed in the eighteenth century by John W. Walker of Madison County, Kentucky, now widely used for hunting fox and racoon.

Watch eye: See "glass eye".

Wind: v. To catch scent transmitted through the air. "When the fox crosses, a good many times he'll come up and wind you and go back" (Milton Collins, interview, December 18, 1980). "If they're [the hounds] ahead and they cut, see they wind 'em and don't say nothin'. Boy, that'll bust your chase up" (Robly Champion, interview, September, 1979).

Wind splitter: A hound that "cheats" to get ahead of the other hounds. See also "wind" and "crooked."

Windwards: In the direction the wind is coming from; upwind. "A Walker'll run to the windwards, you know. They'll run so they can smell . . . it in the air" (Robly Champion, interview, September 1979).

Woods road: n. Narrow sand road, often made by lumberers or hunters to enhance access to timber or game.

Appendix II: John Earlin's Foxhunting Stories

The following is a transcription of a set of stories that John Earlin committed to tape sometime during the early to mid-1970s. For a discussion of why and how he came to create this record of his foxhunting experiences, see Chapter 7.

FIRST STORY

I'd like to tell you a story that I just remembered. Many years ago, Ben was runnin' a fox on the east side of 539 and I was trailin' a fox on the west side, and after a bit, our dogs got together.

And at that time I had an old Black and Tan dog that I had just got. I bought him off of Jake—and I hadn't ever seen him run before. And my dogs and Ben got in, and they were really doin' the job on this gray fox, and they were takin' him around and around.

And my old Black and Tan, he just stood there and listened. And they run him maybe for an hour, an hour and a half. And out he came, and he came right in the middle of the road. He run right up there and the Black and Tan stood right in the middle of the road, and the old fox went right between the legs of the Black and Tan, and he turned around and "Pow!"— caught him.

And I mean to tell you, you want to hear a man that really was mad, that was Ben. He said, "The worthless son-of-a-gun," he said. "Can you imagine a dog that wouldn't run nothin', catchin' that fox!?" Now he was very unhappy about the whole situation, and I couldn't hardly blame him. I think that the dog should have showed some sign of going in there.

SECOND STORY

I'm going to tell you another story about Ben and I. This has been many, many a year ago. I was runnin' the fox a long time at North Branch, and along come Benny, and of course he threw in with us, and they were runnin' this fox to catch. The dogs would go up, and they'd go back again. We seen him, I guess we seen him ten or fifteen times.

So, I made up my mind, I said, "Benny," I said, "I'm gonna catch that fox." So I went in there on the crossroad where he had run several times, and along he came, and I took after him, and I picked him right up.

And, man, I'm telling you, I didn't any more than have the fox in my arms and I had the dogs: they throwed me on the ground, and they were nabbin' at the fox, tryin' to get him away from me, and then they caught him and tore him up to pieces. But they certainly left me alone. I was really at the bottom of that bunch of dogs, and there must have been about thirty-five or forty, and, well, that was quite an experience, I'm telling you right now.

THIRD STORY

Well, Ben and I went foxhunting quite a few times, and lots of times got somewhere near one another. And I had a really good dog that I thought an awful lot of, but every time this dog heard Ben's dogs, he would run right over there and get right in his chase and really show Ben how to run a fox. So Ben contacted me, he said, "Listen," he said, "that dog isn't doin' you any good. He's runnin' with me all the time. Why don't you sell him to me?"

I said, "No, I'm not going to sell that dog. I like the dog, I like the dog's note, and I like the way he runs."

So Ben said, "Well, I'll tell you, if you don't sell him to me, the next time he comes to me fox huntin', you'll never see him again."

Only he didn't say it that way. He said, "Next time you go foxhunting you'll probably never see him again." And so the next time I went fox-huntin', I lost the dog. I've never seen or heard of the dog since.

FOURTH STORY

Now, Jack Davis and I, we went foxhuntin', oh, pretty near every time I went, he went, we went together, and we, really, at that time we had some really good dogs. And they were running so good that the first thing in the spring, we started twenty-three straight fox and caught twenty-one out of 'em.

So, one evening, Jack—of course, he has the saloon, and he has a pool table in there. We was playin' pool, and he got to the point where he had maybe a drink or two too many.

So, it wasn't a beautiful evening, but he said, "I have five dollars." He said, "I'll bet that we'll start a fox tomorrow morning and catch it. I don't care if it's rainin', snowin', the wind blowin' or what."

And there wasn't anybody paying any attention to him, but after a while he looked in his pocket again, he says, "I got ten dollars to five," he says, "that we will start a fox tomorrow morning and catch him." So, nobody paid a bit of attention to him.

So after a bit he looked at his pocket, and he said, "I got fifteen to five." And still no one paid any attention. So he emptied his pocket out, and he looked and he had seventeen dollars in his pocket, and he says, "I'll bet you seventeen to five." So Webby, as we called him, he lived right across from Jack and right next to me, he says, "Jackson," he says, "I'll take that!"

Of course, Webby used to have foxdogs, and they would go out and kill the fox, and so forth and so on, and he didn't think it was possible for a dog to catch a fox.

So the next morning I got up, I hollered over to Jack to see if he was runnin', and he says, "Go ahead on up." He says. "I'll be right on up." So I went on up. I went up to North Branch. I struck a fox. And I trailed him. We trailed him, trailed him, trailed him. Run right over into South Branch—right where the water, the hassocks—at that time there had been a fire through there and the cedar trees lapped over one another and everything else.

About, oh fifteen or twenty minutes, around come Jack, and he said, "What in the hell," he said, "are you doin' in here?" I said, "Jack, I can't control where the fox is gonna go."

And it wasn't very long after they got in the swamp they jumped him. And they started, they were runnin'. They were really pushin' it to him. Up and down that swamp, up and down that swamp. And after a bit, Webby, he was with me at the truck, and out come the fox. And I think the fox was, oh, maybe sixty, seventy yards ahead of the dogs when he went out in the oaks. And he took them roarin' out there in the oaks, and when he came back, they were about fifty yards from him. Webby says, "Get in there! Get in there! That's the place to be! In at the swamp!" So, the old fox, he went right back in there, and they run around and around and around.

And in the meantime, Jack and I, we pulled over where we thought he was goin' to go on out the opposite side. We went over there, and sure enough the dogs stopped right in the middle of the swamp. And I said to

Jack, "Jack, we gotta have our fox, if you're gonna collect your money!" So, we both jumped on out, and jumped right in the swamp, and we both of us got our ass wet. And when we went there, here the dogs were, there was laps of cedar, and the old fox had been walkin on top of it. And we were in there quite a while, and after a bit, the old fox made up his mind I guess to get out, so away the hell he went, he went out.

And I had an old female that we called Big May, and she struck this, and she had a beautiful note and she didn't take long, she called them to her, and up the swamp they went. And of course Jack and I, we got the hell out of there and were wet clear to our ears, and we got back in our cars and we started down South Branch and we go up the gravel road that crosses South Branch. So we went on up South Branch and I went across to the opposite side over there and started walkin' up the road.

And here they come, they come around there, and I had at that time an old Black and Tan, that, we called him Grandpop. He's a real good old dog, and he could really run a fox. Old Grandpop had him by sight comin' up the road. And the old fox seen me, and he run right up the tree next to me, got right up in the top of it.

And the dogs got there, and they were bayin', and raisin' hell. And I hollered to the rest and the rest of the boys came over and we stood there and looked at him. And Webby said, "Oh, they didn't catch him." So there was another fellow, Josie Anderson. Josie was quite a woodsman, and he never believed a dog could ever catch a fox, but that's altogether a different story, I'll tell you about that. That'll be later. Anyway, Josie said, "They will," and he climbed up the tree.

But in the meantime I tried to get the dogs away from the tree, so somebody could chase him out and we'd have a little more chase. And Jack, he says to me, "Man," he said, "man, that's my money you're playin with!" So, anyway, Josie went up the tree and dropped the fox down, and the dogs caught the fox and Webby paid his five dollars. Jack was happy, of course, I was happy, and Webby, he wasn't quite that happy.

Well, that's a real interesting story, and I believe you should like that.

FIFTH STORY

This is a story about a chase that a number of the boys and I had up on Petticoat Hill. We were up on Petticoat Hill, that's a place up on the Plains, on the Jersey Plains they call it.

So the dogs were runnin'. I was runnin' with Norman Taylor and

Freeman Taylor and Herb Anderson, and myself. We were running up there and we had a gray fox that was giving us a lot of runnin' and the first thing you know, they were tryin' to catch him. The fox. So Freeman said, "I'm going in there and I'm going to catch that fox."

So Freeman went in and run right along, and out comes Freeman with a fox in his hand, and the whole bunch of us were all satisfied, we saved the fox's life. So we got all of our dogs put in the box and we stood in the road, we were on this hill, and the road went down this hill, and Freeman turned the fox loose.

The old fox run down the road and kept on goin' right on down the road, and there was a mud puddle down there, and he stopped in there, got a drink, laid in water, and panted, and after a bit, he made up his mind he was goin' to move on into the bushes, and we let him go.

And I think that was showin' a lot of sportsmanship, and we owe everybody a hand.

SIXTH STORY

I'll tell you a story, and this one's about my brother-in-law and I, and we made a bet. My brother-in-law was in the linoleum business at that time, and he laid floors. And he lived up in the city. Of course, he liked the country very well, but he lived up in the city and he came down to build a new home. And he came down to lay the floors in the kitchen.

I was goin' foxhuntin' that morning. It was on a Sunday morning, and I said to him, I said, "Russ, the dogs has been workin' real well," I said, "we been catchin a lot of fox. I'll bet you just one dollar that I bring a fox home with me that the dogs have caught." So he opened up his wallet, and he brought the dollar out. I put the dollar up, and we made the bet.

So I went foxhunting. I went up on the Plains, on the Jersey Plains. And I wasn't gone long, and I had a trail and my dogs started the fox and they were runnin'. They were runnin' real sharp, real hard. They begin to make him take notice. And it wasn't very long, they caught the fox. But that wasn't all of this story. I listened and along there come a pack of dogs headin toward me just as straight as they could come, and that was Norman Taylor. And my dogs, of course, they broke, and they went to him, just as hard as they could go, after they had caught theirs, and it wasn't very long, they had caught that fox.

So after we had gathered our dogs and we got settled, I said to Norman, I said, "Do you think that you had enough?" Norman said, "No! I didn't get too much of that fox!" I says, "Okay." So I went up a swamp that's called Plain Branch. And I went on up there and the dogs struck a track. They trailed. They jumped. And then after a period of time they were really ridin'. And Norman come on over and throwed in and we were takin' them up and down Plain Branch, and I'm tellin' you, they were really tearin' in, and it wasn't—oh I don't believe they were runnin' over an hour and a half, maybe two hours, they caught him.

Now that is the first time that I ever in my life was in a three-fox catch in one day, and I think that shows some of the type of dogs that we had at that time.

SEVENTH STORY

I have another story, about—a story I would call "The Fox in the Bush." We had run this fox up on the Plains, and the dogs had run him back and forth across the road. He was a beautiful running fox. He always had enough lead that we wasn't too much concerned about him. Matter of fact, we'd seen that fox fourteen times before the chase ended.

But this is the part of the story that amazes me. This fox at one time had stopped. And the dogs, they were raisin' hell. And I didn't pay too much about it. You'd hear one yip and one howl. And after a while they got a line, and they came on over closer to us, and the same thing happened close to us. You'd hear one dog, you'd hear him "Yi-ip! Yi-ip!" as if something was biting him or something.

The big fox, we walked in there, and he was sittin' in a ground oak bush. Whenever a dog would stick his nose into that ground oak bush, that fox would have him right on the end of the nose. And he was protecting himself pretty well, and as we walked in there he made up his mind that he was going to take off.

But that was the sorrowful part of the fox chase. The fox took off and of course the dogs got down and just took advantage of him. But it was amazing to see a fox hold back a pack of dogs and have enough protection so the dogs couldn't get him in the right spot. I'm amazed about it.

EIGHTH STORY

A lot of these stories are told about foxhunting in New Jersey. But here's one about a Delaware foxhunt. I went down to Delaware, to a couple of friends of mine named Bert and Spence Willets, and Jack Davis and I, we went down and stayed overnight, and got up in the morning, and we went foxhunting.

Bert took us over where he had a fox that would run right around a field, and all you had to do was get up a tree, and every time he'd come across the field you could see him going, and see the dogs going. So we went on over there, and went in where the fox was supposed to be, and Bert said to me, "Maybe if I put sticks in this hole we'll have a chase a little bit longer."

So we went up over and it was in a marshy country and the dogs went out there along the marsh and the first thing you know they jumped this fox and they were running him. They were puttin' it to him. Round and around and around and around. In around an hour or so I said to Bert, I said, "Bert." I knew exactly how the dogs acted when they were ready to catch a fox. I said, "Bert," I said, "that fox is in trouble." I said, "They're going to catch him."

"Oh," he says, "we been runnin' this fox for a long time." He says, "That fox isn't in any more trouble than he can get out of." I said, "Okay, but you remember what I told you." So they went on and they run him another half an hour or so, and I said to Bert again, I said, "Bert, they're gonna catch that fox."

"No-o-o," he said, "what are you talkin about? Hell, they won't ever catch that fox. We been runnin' that fox for a couple of years."

I said, "Alright."

So in the meantime, the old fox was goin' around this marsh and goin' around and around and then after a bit he took off, and he headed for his hole. Course, when he got there he couldn't get in it. The dogs went right on and the fox went right on and the first thing you know the dogs had him.

And the dogs shut up, and I knew that something had happened, and I walked on out there, and some man was out there in the road, and he said, "Those dogs rushed that fox hole right there on the other side of the road." I said, "They did?"

So Bert and the others didn't come out and so I walked on back in there and I said, "The fox chase is over." I said, "They caught him."

"What the heck are you tellin' me?"

I said, "Yeah! They caught the fox."

So they went out there and they looked, and tears almost came down their eyes. They were just about to cry, because they had had a lot of pleasure out of that fox.

So we went up, because there had been a couple dogs that split and went on a different fox. And we went over and throwed our dogs on that one, and it wasn't very long that fox was right in. So our foxchase was over, and the boys were sittin' on the bank and I said to Bert, I said, "Bert, are we gonna have a funeral today, or do you think we oughta have it tomorrow?"

And man, I'm tellin' you, you wanna see a man that was mad, he was mad. He really thought that there wasn't a dog in the country that could ever catch that fox.

NINTH STORY

This is another story about the Delaware foxhunting. See, we were invited down for a couple days to Ed Passwater's which, Ed and I were very good friends. He used to come up here and I'd go down there quite often.

So we had a little trouble finding a fox. So he told me, he said, "You go over to a certain place"—and I had been there before—he says, "and you'll probably be able to strike that fox, and I'll go over to somewhere else." So we did. I went over and the dogs struck this fox, tracked him, and jumped him, and they were really a-runnin' and bringin' him out. Brought him out to a road.

In the meantime, there was some native foxhunters there, they had pulled up there with their pickups, there were three loads of 'em. And my dogs came out to the road, and from then on they couldn't find the fox anywhere. What happened, I have no idea. I thought maybe the fox had come there, seen the pickup, turned and went back the other way.

So I tried to get the dogs to go back in and go off the other way. And I tried and I tried and I spent maybe fifteen, twenty minutes and then I came on out, and I talked to the boys that were out there and they said, "Well," they said, "we haven't had any luck, but, well, I think we'll go on over to so-and-so." I don't know what the name of the place was.

And it wasn't very long I heard dogs really a-running across the road on the other side maybe a quarter, three-quarters of a mile, I would say, and I knew right then and there what had happened. They had seen that fox cross, and they knew where he had run, and they gave him time to get there, and then they had throwed their dogs on my fox. So, there wasn't anything for me to do but turn around, load my dogs—I went over there.

One of the boys said, "Go ahead and throw in if you want to." They invited me to throw in on my own fox! So I did. I started a-lettin' dogs out. I had about twenty-five in the crate right there at that time. And they started goin', one after the other, one after the other, gettin' out of the crate and gettin' into the fox chase. And I heard one of them sayin' to the other walkin' down the road, "Hell, we'll run him out after a while. We don't have to worry about those dogs."

But I think before the day was over, they were really surprised. Before it got dark, there wasn't any boys around there. They had all gone home. But I never heard any more about the dogs bein' run out.

TENTH STORY

My good friend Ed invited me down again to go foxhunting. So we came down in the morning, and when we did we stopped into a diner, and we got our breakfast. After our breakfast we went on over to Ed's house, and sure enough his wife had a pile of sausage, ham, potatoes, eggs, there for us to eat. Well, to make a long story short, we sit down. We started to eat. We ate. We had ham, potatoes, we had sausage and eggs. We had a pile of eggs on the plate there that, I don't know, would stuff an elephant, I believe.

But anyway, we started eating, and as we started eating, Ed would say, "Look, we don't want to throw these away. Come on! Eat some more." When I got done, I had eaten fourteen eggs, besides the ham, potatoes, and sausage. And, that isn't the end of the story because that morning a friend of Ed's came there, and he was told about what I had eaten, so the next time that I was invited down, he was invited over to go foxhunting with us, and when he did he arrived there before we did.

And the old chickens were on the nest a-cacklin', and they were really raisin' heck. So he says to 'em, "Chicken," he says, "you better get on that nest if that big son-of-a-gun from Jersey comes down here," he said. And we all got a real kick out of it, after he told us about what he had said to the chickens.

ELEVENTH STORY

Well, we're back in Jersey now, and in 1955 I seed some land for sale up in the northern forest and I bought it, and I built myself a cabin there. This cabin is just about a castle, I would say, for anybody that likes to hunt and be in the woods like I do. So I met a friend called Jim Fisher. Jim had a nickname the boys put on him: Snuffy.

So, how I met Snuffy was up on the Plains one day. I was up there and I was runnin' a fox, and the dogs started away from me. I jumped in the car, and I started up this woods road, and who in the heck should I meet on the corner but Snuffy. I never met him before. We run right into one another, bumper to bumper, and nothing was hurt, but that is the way that I met Snuffy.

So a little later, I was runnin' a fox over by 539, and the dogs had run and run and they caught this fox in the woods there, and I had my car parked out on 539, and when I come out, sure enough, there was Snuffy and his father. They had been over on the Plains a-runnin' and came there. And I had gathered the dogs and brought it out, but I had some trouble with a couple of dogs layin down in there after they had curled up in the box, I couldn't get them to come.

So I said to Snuffy, I said, "What are you doin'? You gonna do anything?" He says, "No!" I says, "Well I got a heck of a stew up to the cabin. How about if I go up there and get some and bring it back? And the cabin was maybe four or five miles from where we were. He says, "Okay." So him and his father stayed there to see if any of the dogs came out while I went to the cabin and we got their supper.

And when I come back, Lord bless us, Snuffy never enjoyed anything like he did that stew. They ate and ate and ate, and after a bit we wandered back in there, and I found the dogs in there layin' near where they had caught the fox.

So that is the second story about Snuffy. Of course I invited him down to the cabin. I told him come on down.

TWELFTH STORY

So, it wasn't very long, Snuffy and I, we made arrangements to eat. He came down every Friday night. I was usually down there before that and had the fire goin' and so forth, and you could almost depend on seven o'clock in the evening, Snuffy would walk in the door. And he would have a little bundle of something to eat and so forth and so on, and we would greet one another and talk, and it wasn't very long, he had his dogs down here in one of the pens that I had there, and he foxhunted there.

We foxhunted for years, matter of fact, I would say probably five, six, seven years we hunted here like that. You could depend on Snuffy walkin' in that door at 7 o'clock. Just about 7 o'clock that door would open. So Snuffy told me one day, he says, "Listen, John," he says, "I'm getting married. Thursday night." I said, "Well that'll break your record, won't it? You won't be in here at 7 o'clock Friday night."

"Oh," he said, "yes I will. I'll be here."

I said, "Well, if you're getting married, I don't know how you're goin' to do it."

But you can depend on it. At seven o'clock Friday night he walked in the door. And I was never so surprised in my life, to see Snuffy on the night after he got married.

THIRTEENTH STORY

One day Snuffy and I were runnin' fox up on the Plains, and they were doin' a real good job and it was getting late, and we wanted to catch the dogs. So, to get around old 539, Snuffy went around over there, figurin' he'd get closer to them, and when he got over 539 the dogs were in the swamp right close to the highway.

So he made it in that road alongside of the swamp and he caught the dogs. And of course, he with one pickup had enough for two pickups, and he pulled out on 539 and some car stopped there and said to him, he says, "How many dogs do you have in there?" And of course, Snuffy said, "Well, he's tendin' to somethin' that isn't his business, and I better give a good answer." And he did. He said, "All of 'em!"

He got in the pickup and drove on around where I was, and we reloaded 'em and then came on home.

FOURTEENTH STORY

The story that I'm about to tell you is a story about a dog that I used to have. His name was Blockhead. He was a real good running dog but he was a dog that would kind of slide along rather than jump. We were runnin' a fox over near the Jersey Central Railroad and they were doing what I call an excellent job.

After the railroad they stopped. And then I looked, I took those dogs, I tried to get those dogs to go on. I went up the railroad, down the railroad, on the tar road, on down back, and I couldn't find that fox anywhere. And old Blockhead he stood there in the road and looked at me, kind of silly lookin', and I didn't particularly know what he had in mind.

But after a bit he walked right on across the road right in the bushes and out he come. He had the old fox in his mouth, and laid it on the road. He wanted to show me that I have no reason to get excited about them not runnin' that fox anymore.

Bibliography

Ables, E. D. 1975. "The Ecology of the Red Fox in North America." In *The Wild Canids*, ed. Michael Fox, 216–35. New York: Van Nostrand.

Abrahams, Roger. n.d. "Men as Animals and Other Strange Stereotypic Notions." Unpublished manuscript.

———. 1977. "Toward an Enactment-Centered Approach to Folklore." In *Frontiers of Folklore*, ed. William R. Bascom. Boulder, Col.: Westview Press.

———. 1986. "Ordinary and Extraordinary Experience." In *The Anthropology of Experience*, ed. Victor W. Turner and Edward M. Bruner. Urbana: University of Illinois Press.

Abrams, David M. and Brian Sutton-Smith. 1977. "The Development of the Trickster in Children's Narratives." *Journal of American Folklore* 90:29–47.

Allen, Barbara. 1990. "The Genealogical Landscape and the Southern Sense of Place." In *Sense of Place: American Regional Cultures*, ed. Barbara Allen and Thomas J. Schlereth. Lexington: University Press of Kentucky.

American Kennel Club. 1985. *The Complete Dog Book*. New York: Howell Book House.

Babcock-Abrahams, Barbara. 1975. "'A Tolerated Margin of Mess': The Trickster and His Tales Reconsidered." *Journal of the Folklore Institute* XI:147–86.

———. 1977 [1976]. "The Story in the Story: Metanarration in Folk Narrative." *Studia Fennica* 20:177–84. Reprinted in *Verbal Art as Performance*, ed. Richard Bauman, 61–79. Project Park, Ill.: Waveland Press.

Badley, George W. 1979. "The Elder Hounds." *Hunter's Horn* 57 (11):57–58.

Basso, Keith. 1984. "'Stalking with Stories': Names, Places, and Moral Narratives Among the Western Apache." In Basso, *Text, Play, and Story: The Construction and Reconstruction of Self and Society*, 19–55. Washington, D.C.: American Ethnological Society.

Bateson, Gregory. 1972 [1955]. "A Theory of Play and Fantasy." *Psychiatric Research Reports* 2:39–51. Washington, D.C.: American Psychiatric Association. Reprinted in Bateson, *Steps to an Ecology of Mind*, 201–27. New York: Ballantine Books.

Bauman, Richard. 1986. *Story, Performance, and Event: Contextual Studies of Oral Narrative*. Cambridge: Cambridge University Press.

Beck, Henry Charlton. 1963 [1937]. *More Forgotten Towns of New Jersey*. New Brunswick, N.J.: Rutgers University Press.

Berger, John 1977. "Animals as Metaphor." *New Society* 39:504–05.

Berger, Jonathan and John W. Sinton. 1985. *Water, Earth, and Fire: Land Use and Environmental Planning in the New Jersey Pine Barrens*. Baltimore: Johns Hopkins University Press.

Berger, Peter and Thomas Luckmann. 1967. *The Social Construction of Reality*. New York: Anchor.

Bulmer, Ralph. 1967. "Why is the Cassowary Not a Bird? A Problem of Zoological Taxonomy Among the Karam of the New Guinea Highlands." *Man* 2:5–25.

Burke, Kenneth. 1968 [1931]. *Counter-Statement*. New York: Harcourt Brace. Reprint Berkeley: University of California Press.

Burton, Maurice. 1955. "Dog-Fox and Cats." *Illustrated London News*, April 2, p. 62.

Chatman, Seymour. 1978. *Story and Discourse: Narrative Structure in Fiction and Film*. Ithaca, N.Y.: Cornell University Press.

Coppinger, Lorna and Raymond Coppinger. 1982. "Dogs in Sheep's Clothing Guard Flocks." *Smithsonian* 13 (1):64–73.

Cramer, Donald. 1990. "In My Opinion." *Hunter's Horn*.

Csikszentmihalyi, Mihaly. 1975. "Play and Intrinsic Rewards." *Journal of Humanistic Psychology* 15 (3):41–63.

Csikszentmihalyi, Mihaly and Eugene Rochberg-Halton. 1981. *The Meaning of Things: Domestic Symbols and the Self*. Cambridge: Cambridge University Press.

Dale-Green, Patricia. 1967. *Lore of the Dog*. Boston: Houghton Mifflin.

Dannemann, Manuel. 1980. "Fox Hunting: A Form of Traditional Behaviour Providing Social Cohesiveness." In *Folklore Studies in the Twentieth Century: Proceedings of the Centenary Conference of the Folklore Society*. London: D. S. Brewer, Rowman and Littlefield.

Dorst, John. 1989. *The Written Suburb: An American Site, An Ethnographic Dilemma*. Philadelphia: University of Pennsylvania Press.

Douglas, Mary. 1966. *Purity and Danger: An Analysis of Concepts of Pollution and Taboo*. London: Routledge and Kegan Paul.

———. 1968. "The Social Control of Cognition: Some Factors in Joke Perception." *Man* 3:361–76.

———, ed. 1973. *Rules and Meanings: The Anthropology of Everyday Knowledge*. Middlesex, Eng.: Penguin.

Dundes, Alan 1980 [1964]. "Text, Texture, and Context." *Southern Folklore Quarterly* 18:251–65. Reprinted in Dundes, *Interpreting Folklore*, 20–32. Bloomington: Indiana University Press.

Emrich, Duncan. 1972. "Hound Dog Names." In *Folklore on the American Land*, 141–44. Boston: Little, Brown, and Co.

Fernandez, James. 1986. *Persuasions and Performances: The Play of Tropes in Culture*. Bloomington: Indiana University Press.

Forman, Richard T. T., ed. 1979. *Pine Barrens: Ecosystem and Landscape*. New York: Academic Press.

Fox, Michael W. 1971. *Behaviour of Wolves, Dogs and Related Canids*. London: Jonathan Cape.

———, ed. 1975. *The Wild Canids*. New York: Van Nostrand Reinhold.

Garfinkel, Harold. 1973. "Background Expectancies." In *Rules and Meanings*, ed. Mary Douglas, 21–23. Middlesex: Penguin.

Georges, Robert. 1969. "Toward an Understanding of Story-telling Events." *Journal of American Folklore* 82:313–28.

Geertz, Clifford. 1972. "Deep Play: Notes on the Balinese Cockfight." *Daedalus* 101(1):1–37.

———. 1983. "Blurred Genres: The Refiguration of Social Thought." *American Scholar* 49:165–79.

Goffman, Erving 1959. *The Presentation of Self in Everyday Life.* New York: Anchor.

———. 1967. *Interaction Ritual: Essays in Face-to-Face Behavior.* New York: Anchor.

———. 1974. *Frame Analysis.* New York: Harper Colophon Books.

Goldstein, Kenneth S. 1964. *A Guide for Fieldworkers in Folklore.* Hatboro, Pa.: Folklore Associates.

Goodman, Nelson 1978. *Ways of Worldmaking.* Sussex: Harvester Press.

Grekoski, Walt. 1986. "Donald Pomeroy." *Hunter's Horn* 65(1):48–49.

Gup, Ted. 1991. "The Fugitive." *Washington Post Magazine,* February 3.

Halpert, Herbert. 1947. "Folktales and Legends from the New Jersey Pines: A Collection and Study." Ph.D. Dissertation, Indiana University.

Halverson, John. 1977. "Animal Categories and Terms of Abuse." *Man* 11:505–16.

Harshberger, John W. 1916. *The Vegetation of the New Jersey Pine Barrens: An Ecologic Investigation.* Philadelphia: Christopher Sower Company.

Henry, J. David. 1980. "Fox Hunting." *Natural History Magazine,* December, 61–69.

Howe, James. 1981. "Fox Hunting as Ritual." *American Ethnologist* 8:278–300.

Hufford, Mary. 1987. "The Fox." In *American Wildlife in Symbol and Story,* ed. Angus K. Gillespie and Jay Mechling, 163–202 Knoxville: University of Tennessee Press.

Hufford, Mary, Marjorie Hunt, and Steven J. Zeitlin. 1987. *The Grand Generation: Memory, Mastery, Legacy.* Seattle and Washington D.C.: SITES and University of Washington Press.

Hymes, Dell. 1981 [1975]. "Breakthrough into Performance." In *Folklore: Performance and Communication,* ed. Dan Ben-Amos and Kenneth S. Goldstein. Reprinted in Hymes, *"In vain I tried to tell you": Essays in Native American Ethnopoetics,* 79–141. Philadelphia: University of Pennsylvania Press. 1981.

Ihde, Don. 1976. *Listening and Voice: A Phenomenology of Sound.* Athens: Ohio State University Press.

James, William. 1890. *The Principles of Psychology.* Vol. 2. New York: Henry Holt and Company.

Jason, Heda. 1972. "Jewish Near Eastern Numskull Tales: An Attempt at Interpretation." *Asian Folklore Studies* 31:1–39.

Kirshenblatt-Gimblett, Barbara. 1974. "The Concept and Varieties of Narrative Performance in East European Jewish Culture." In *Explorations in the Ethnography of Speaking,* ed. Richard Bauman and Joel Scherzer, 283–308. New York: Cambridge University Press.

———. 1975. "A Parable in Context: A Social Interactional Analysis of a Storytelling Performance." In *Folklore: Performance and Communication,* ed. Dan Ben-Amos and Kenneth S. Goldstein, 105–30. The Hague: Mouton.

———. 1987. "Authoring Lives." Paper presented at the American-Hungarian Folklore Conference on Life History as Cultural Construction and Performance, Budapest.

Kluckhohn, Clyde. 1972 [1942]. "Myths and Rituals: A General Theory." *Harvard Theological Review* 35:45–79.

Labov, William. 1972. "The Transformation of Experience in Narrative Syntax." In Labov, *Language in the Inner City: Studies in the Black English Vernacular*, 354–96. Philadelphia: University of Pennsylvania Press.

Langer, Susanne K. 1942. *Philosophy in a New Key*. Cambridge, Mass.: Harvard University Press.

Lansing, J. S. 1979. "In the World of the Sea Urchin: The Application of Husserlian Phenomenology to Cultural Symbols." In *The Imagination of Reality: Essays in Southeast Asian Coherence Systems*, ed. A. L. Becker and Aram Yengoyan, 75–83. Norwood, N.J.: Ablex Publishing Corp.

Leach, Edmund. 1964. "Anthropological Aspects of Language: Animal Categories and Verbal Abuse." In *New Directions in the Study of Language*, ed. Eric H. Lenneberg, 23–63. Cambridge, Mass.: MIT Press.

Lévi-Strauss, Claude. 1955. "The Structural Study of Myth." *Journal of American Folklore* 78:428–44.

———. 1966. *The Savage Mind*. Chicago: University of Chicago Press.

———. 1972. "The Bear and the Barber." In *Reader in Comparative Religion*, ed. William A. Lessa and Evon Z. Vogt, 181–88. New York: Harper and Row.

Licht, Michael. 1980. "Trailing the Fox Chase." Paper presented at the annual meeting of the Society for Ethnomusicology, Bloomington, Indiana.

Longrigg, Roger. 1975. *The History of Foxhunting*. New York: Clarkson N. Potter.

Lorenz, Konrad. 1952. *King Solomon's Ring*. New York: Thomas Y. Crowell.

———. 1955. *Man Meets Dog*. Boston: Houghton-Mifflin.

Lynch, Kevin. 1960. *The Image of the City*. Cambridge, Mass.: MIT Press.

Lyne, David C. 1976. "What Are They Saying? A Study of the Jargon of Hilltopping." Master's thesis, University of Kentucky, Bowling Green.

Marks, Stuart. 1991. *Southern Hunting in Black and White: An Interpretation of Hunting Roles and Rituals in a Southern Society*. Princeton, N.J.: Princeton University Press.

Moore, Sally F. and Barbara Myerhoff. 1977. *Secular Ritual*. Amsterdam: Van Gorcum, Assen.

Morgan, Jane, Christopher O'Neill, and Rom Harre. 1979. *Nicknames: Their Origins and Social Consequences*. London: Routledge and Kegan Paul.

Myerhoff, Barbara. 1978. *Number Our Days*. New York: E. P. Dutton.

Natanson, Maurice. 1962. *Literature, Philosophy and the Social Sciences*. The Hague: Mouton.

———. 1970. *The Journeying Self*. London: Addison-Wesley.

Newall, Venetia J. 1983. "The Unspeakable in Pursuit of the Uneatable: Some Comments on Fox-Hunting." *Folklore* 94:86–90.

Ortega y Gasset, José. 1972 [1942]. *Meditations on Hunting*. New York: Charles Scribner's Sons.

Ortner, Sherry. 1974. "Is Female to Male as Nature Is to Culture?" In *Woman, Culture, and Society*, ed. Michelle Zimbalist Rosaldo and Louise Lamphere, 67–87. Stanford, Ca.: Stanford University Press.

Perceval, W. Keith. 1982. "An Eighteenth-Century View of Animal Communication." *Semiotica* 39:55–73.

Radcliffe-Brown, A.R. 1929. "The Sociological Theory of Totemism." *Proceedings of the Fourth Pacific Science Congress* (Java, 1929). Batavia, 1930.

Radin, Paul. 1972. *The Trickster: A Study in American Indian Mythology*. New York: Schocken Books.

Rennick, Robert M. 1968. "Obscene Names and Naming in Folk Tradition." *Names* 16:207–29.

Ricoeur, Paul. 1967. *Husserl: An Analysis of His Phenomenology*. Evanston, Ill.: Northwestern University Press.

———. 1973. "The Model of the Text: Meaningful Action Considered as a Text." *New Literary History* 5:91–117.

Salter, James. 1888. [Names for Hounds]. *Roxburghe Ballads* 6:269–70.

Schafer, R. Murray. 1985. "Acoustic Space." In *Dwelling, Place and Environment: Towards a Phenomenology of Person and World*, ed. David Seamon and Robert Mugerauer. Dordrecht: Martinus Nijhoff.

Schutz, Alfred. 1970. *On Phenomenology and Social Relations*, ed. Helmut Wagner. Chicago: University of Chicago Press.

Sebeok, Thomas A. 1976. "Zoosemiotic Components of Human Communication," In Sebeok, *The Sign and Its Masters*, 35–60. Austin: University of Texas Press.

Sharlsono, Teddy. 1980. "A New Decade and a Catch." *Hunter's Horn* 58 (12):72–73.

Shuman, Amy. 1986. *Storytelling Rights*. Cambridge: Cambridge University Press.

Simmel, Georg. 1971. *On Individuality and Social Forms*, ed. Donald N. Levine. Chicago: University of Chicago Press.

Stahl, Sandra. 1983. "Personal Experience Stories." In *Handbook of American Folklore*, ed. Richard M. Dorson, 268–76. Bloomington: Indiana University Press.

Stewart, Susan. 1979. *Nonsense: Aspects of Intertextuality in Folklore and Literature*. Baltimore: Johns Hopkins University Press.

Streever, Fred 1948. *The American Trail Hound*. New York: A. S. Barnes and Company.

Tambiah, S. J. 1969. "Animals Are Good to Think and Good to Prohibit." *Ethnology* 8:424–59.

Thomas, Keith. 1983. *Man and the Natural World: A History of the Modern Sensibility*. New York: Pantheon Books.

Titon, Jeff Todd. 1980. "The Life Story." *Journal of American Folklore* 93:276–92.

Toelken, Barre. 1979. *The Dynamics of Folklore*. Boston: Houghton Mifflin.

Tuan, Yi Fu. 1977. *Space and Place: The Perspective of Experience*. St. Paul: University of Minnesota Press.

Turner, Victor. 1969. *The Ritual Process: Structure and Anti-Structure*. Chicago: Aldine.

———. 1977. "Variations on a Theme of Liminality," In *Secular Ritual*, ed. Sally Falk Moore and Barbara Myerhoff, 37–52. Amsterdam: Van Gorcum.

———. 1980. "Social Dramas and Stories About Them." *Critical Inquiry* 7:141–68.

———. 1986. "Dewey, Dilthey, and Drama: An Essay in the Anthropology of

Experience." In *The Anthropology of Experience*, ed. Victor W. Turner and Edward M. Bruner. Urbana: University of Illinois Press.

Uexküll, Jakob von. 1982 [1940]. *The Theory of Meaning*. Special issue of *Semiotica*, ed. Thure von Uexkull, 42:1–87.

———. 1957. "A Stroll Through the World of Animals and Men: A Picture Book of Invisible Worlds." In *Instinctive Behavior*, ed. Claire H. Schiller, 5–82. New York: International Universities Press.

Van Urk, John Blan. 1940. *The Story of American Foxhunting: From Challenge to Full Cry*. New York: Derrydale Press.

Walker, Ernest P. 1975. *Mammals of the World*. Baltimore: Johns Hopkins University Press.

Watson, J. N. P. 1977. *The Book of Foxhunting*. New York: Arco Publishing Company.

Wilson, David Scofield. 1978. *In the Presence of Nature*. Amherst: University of Massachusetts Press.

Wolfson, Nessa. 1982. *CHP: The Conversational Historical Present in American English Narrative*. Dordrecht: Foris Publications.

Young, Katharine Galloway. 1987. *Taleworlds and Storyrealms: The Phenomenology of Narrative*. Dordrecht: Martinus Nijhoff.

Index

Permission is acknowledged to reprint materials from published sources:

Barbara Myerhoff. *Number Our Days*. New York: E.P. Dutton, 1978. Copyright © 1978 by Barbara Myerhoff. Reprinted by permission of Lescher & Lescher Ltd. and Penguin USA.

Maurice Burton. "Dog-Fox and Cats." *Illustrated London News*, 2 April 1955. Reprinted by permission of The Illustrated London News Picture Library.

Patricia Dale-Green. *Lore of the Dog*. Boston: Houghton Mifflin, 1967. Copyright © 1966 by Patricia Dale-Green. Reprinted by permission of Houghton Mifflin Company.

Eddie Jones (words and music). "I Only Want a Buddy, Not a Sweetheart." Copyright © 1932 by Duchess Music Corporation; copyright renewed. Used by permission of MCA Music Publishing.

Katharine Galloway Young. *Taleworlds and Storyrealms: The Phenomenology of Narrative*. Dordrecht: Martinus Nijhoff, 1987. Copyright © 1987 by Martinus Nijhoff. Reprinted by permission of Martinus Nijhoff Publishers.

Hunter's Horn. Excerpts from articles by Teddy Sharlsono, George Badley, Walt Grekoski, Don Cramer. Reprinted by permission of The Hunter's Horn.

Lorna Coppinger and Raymond Coppinger. "Dogs in Sheep's Clothing Guard Flocks." *Smithsonian Magazine* 13(1) (1982): 64–73. Reprinted by permission of the Smithsonian Institution.

J. S. Lansing. "In the World of the Sea Urchin: The Application of Husserlian Phenomenology to Cultural Symbols." In *The Imagination of Reality*, ed. A. L. Becker and Aram Yengoyan. Norwood, NJ: Ablex, 1979. Copyright © 1979 by Ablex Publishing Co. Reprinted by permission of Ablex Publishing Co.

Michael Fox. *Behaviour of Wolves, Dogs and Related Canids*. London: Jonathan Cape, 1971. Copyright © 1971 by Jonathan Capte Ltd. Reprinted by permission of Jonathan Cape Ltd.

Ted Gup. "The Fugitive." *Washington Post Magazine*, 3 February 1991. Copyright © 1991 by The Washington Post Magazine. Reprinted by permission of The Washington Post Magazine.

José Ortega y Gasset. *Meditations on Hunting*. New York: Charles Scribner's Sons/Macmillan, 1972, 1985. Reprinted by permission of Charles Scribner's Sons/Macmillan Publishing Company.

Herbert Halpert. "Folktales and Legends from the New Jersey Pines: A Collection and Study." Dissertation, Indiana University, 1947. Used by permission of Herbert Halpert.

Konrad Lorenz. *King Solomon's Ring*. New York: Thomas Y. Crowell, 1952. Reprinted by permission of Deutscher Taschenbuch Verlag.

This book has been set in Linotron Galliard. Galliard was designed for Mergenthaler in 1978 by Matthew Carter. Galliard retains many of the features of a sixteenth century typeface cut by Robert Granjon but has some modifications that give it a more contemporary look.

Printed on acid-free paper.